MORE

MICROSOFT®
OFFICE 2000
FOR WINDOWS®
FOR
DUMMIES®

D1710320

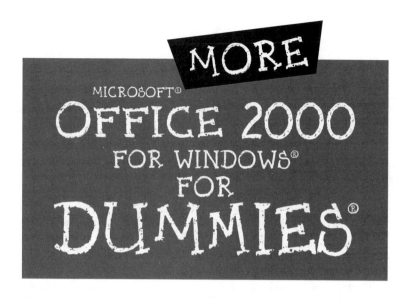

MORE
MICROSOFT®
OFFICE 2000
FOR WINDOWS®
FOR
DUMMIES®

by Wallace Wang

IDG Books Worldwide, Inc.
An International Data Group Company

Foster City, CA ◆ Chicago, IL ◆ Indianapolis, IN ◆ New York, NY

MORE Microsoft® Office 2000 For Windows® For Dummies®

Published by
IDG Books Worldwide, Inc.
An International Data Group Company
919 E. Hillsdale Blvd.
Suite 400
Foster City, CA 94404
www.idgbooks.com (IDG Books Worldwide Web site)
www.dummies.com (Dummies Press Web site)

Library of Congress Catalog Card No.: 99-66443

ISBN: 0-7645-0605-6

Printed in the United States of America

10 9 8 7 6 5 4 3 2 1

1B/QR/RR/ZZ/IN

Distributed in the United States by IDG Books Worldwide, Inc.

Distributed by CDG Books Canada Inc. for Canada; by Transworld Publishers Limited in the United Kingdom; by IDG Norge Books for Norway; by IDG Sweden Books for Sweden; by IDG Books Australia Publishing Corporation Pty. Ltd. for Australia and New Zealand; by TransQuest Publishers Pte Ltd. for Singapore, Malaysia, Thailand, Indonesia, and Hong Kong; by Gotop Information Inc. for Taiwan; by ICG Muse, Inc. for Japan; by Intersoft for South Africa; by Eyrolles for France; by International Thomson Publishing for Germany, Austria and Switzerland; by Distribuidora Cuspide for Argentina; by LR International for Brazil; by Galileo Libros for Chile; by Ediciones ZETA S.C.R. Ltda. for Peru; by WS Computer Publishing Corporation, Inc., for the Philippines; by Contemporanea de Ediciones for Venezuela; by Express Computer Distributors for the Caribbean and West Indies; by Micronesia Media Distributor, Inc. for Micronesia; by Chips Computadoras S.A. de C.V. for Mexico; by Editorial Norma de Panama S.A. for Panama; by American Bookshops for Finland.

For general information on IDG Books Worldwide's books in the U.S., please call our Consumer Customer Service department at 800-762-2974. For reseller information, including discounts and premium sales, please call our Reseller Customer Service department at 800-434-3422.

For information on where to purchase IDG Books Worldwide's books outside the U.S., please contact our International Sales department at 317-596-5530 or fax 317-596-5692.

For consumer information on foreign language translations, please contact our Customer Service department at 1-800-434-3422, fax 317-596-5692, or e-mail rights@idgbooks.com.

For information on licensing foreign or domestic rights, please phone +1-650-655-3109.

For sales inquiries and special prices for bulk quantities, please contact our Sales department at 650-655-3200 or write to the address above.

For information on using IDG Books Worldwide's books in the classroom or for ordering examination copies, please contact our Educational Sales department at 800-434-2086 or fax 317-596-5499.

For press review copies, author interviews, or other publicity information, please contact our Public Relations department at 650-655-3000 or fax 650-655-3299.

For authorization to photocopy items for corporate, personal, or educational use, please contact Copyright Clearance Center, 222 Rosewood Drive, Danvers, MA 01923, or fax 978-750-4470.

is a registered trademark under exclusive license to IDG Books Worldwide, Inc. from International Data Group, Inc.

About the Author

Not only does **Wallace Wang** write computer books and perform stand-up comedy, but he's an actor as well. For his latest performance on the Internet, Wallace managed to convince thousands of men all over the world that he's actually a 23-year old blonde. Besides performing stand-up comedy, Wallace has written *Visual Basic For Dummies, Beginning Programming For Dummies,* and *Microsoft Office For Dummies,* as well as writing a monthly computer humor column for *Boardwatch Magazine* (www.boardwatch.com) and contributing jokes to the Laugh Lines humor column in the *Los Angeles Times.* Here's an example:

America Online has signed an alliance with the Internet health care Web site drkoop.com. The two companies hope that drkoop.com's health care information combined with AOL's lack of customer service could help create the world's first Internet-based HMO.

Wallace has appeared on *A & E's Evening at the Improv* and performs regularly at the Riviera Hotel Comedy Club in Las Vegas (www.theriviera.com). During a business convention for martial artists, held one recent July 4th weekend at the Alexis Park Hotel in Las Vegas, Wallace had this to say: "I admire karate instructors since they have the best job in the world. Because in what other job can you take out your frustration by hitting all of your customers?"

Wallace probably holds the dubious distinction of being the only person in the world to have taped an interview for National Public Radio on the same day that he appeared (and got gonged) on *The Extreme Gong Show,* a remake of the old *Gong Show.* He says of this experience: "Talking to intelligent and literate people on National Public Radio and then trying to entertain morons and idiots on *The Extreme Gong Show* later that same day was like watching the de-evolution of the human intellect occur before my eyes. After seeing the type of people who attend tapings of *The Extreme Gong Show,* I came away with the feeling that not all human lives are worth saving after all."

Currently Wallace divides his time between computer book writing, stand-up comedy, and dabbling in computer animation. He can be reached at bothecat@home.com.

ABOUT IDG BOOKS WORLDWIDE

Welcome to the world of IDG Books Worldwide.

IDG Books Worldwide, Inc., is a subsidiary of International Data Group, the world's largest publisher of computer-related information and the leading global provider of information services on information technology. IDG was founded more than 30 years ago by Patrick J. McGovern and now employs more than 9,000 people worldwide. IDG publishes more than 290 computer publications in over 75 countries. More than 90 million people read one or more IDG publications each month.

Launched in 1990, IDG Books Worldwide is today the #1 publisher of best-selling computer books in the United States. We are proud to have received eight awards from the Computer Press Association in recognition of editorial excellence and three from Computer Currents' First Annual Readers' Choice Awards. Our best-selling *...For Dummies®* series has more than 50 million copies in print with translations in 31 languages. IDG Books Worldwide, through a joint venture with IDG's Hi-Tech Beijing, became the first U.S. publisher to publish a computer book in the People's Republic of China. In record time, IDG Books Worldwide has become the first choice for millions of readers around the world who want to learn how to better manage their businesses.

Our mission is simple: Every one of our books is designed to bring extra value and skill-building instructions to the reader. Our books are written by experts who understand and care about our readers. The knowledge base of our editorial staff comes from years of experience in publishing, education, and journalism — experience we use to produce books to carry us into the new millennium. In short, we care about books, so we attract the best people. We devote special attention to details such as audience, interior design, use of icons, and illustrations. And because we use an efficient process of authoring, editing, and desktop publishing our books electronically, we can spend more time ensuring superior content and less time on the technicalities of making books.

You can count on our commitment to deliver high-quality books at competitive prices on topics you want to read about. At IDG Books Worldwide, we continue in the IDG tradition of delivering quality for more than 30 years. You'll find no better book on a subject than one from IDG Books Worldwide.

John Kilcullen
Chairman and CEO
IDG Books Worldwide, Inc.

Steven Berkowitz
President and Publisher
IDG Books Worldwide, Inc.

Eighth Annual Computer Press Awards 1992

Ninth Annual Computer Press Awards 1993

Tenth Annual Computer Press Awards 1994

Eleventh Annual Computer Press Awards 1995

IDG is the world's leading IT media, research and exposition company. Founded in 1964, IDG had 1997 revenues of $2.05 billion and has more than 9,000 employees worldwide. IDG offers the widest range of media options that reach IT buyers in 75 countries representing 95% of worldwide IT spending. IDG's diverse product and services portfolio spans six key areas including print publishing, online publishing, expositions and conferences, market research, education and training, and global marketing services. More than 90 million people read one or more of IDG's 290 magazines and newspapers, including IDG's leading global brands — Computerworld, PC World, Network World, Macworld and the Channel World family of publications. IDG Books Worldwide is one of the fastest-growing computer book publishers in the world, with more than 700 titles in 36 languages. The "...For Dummies®" series alone has more than 50 million copies in print. IDG offers online users the largest network of technology-specific Web sites around the world through IDG.net (http://www.idg.net), which comprises more than 225 targeted Web sites in 55 countries worldwide. International Data Corporation (IDC) is the world's largest provider of information technology data, analysis and consulting, with research centers in over 41 countries and more than 400 research analysts worldwide. IDG World Expo is a leading producer of more than 168 globally branded conferences and expositions in 35 countries including E3 (Electronic Entertainment Expo), Macworld Expo, ComNet, Windows World Expo, ICE (Internet Commerce Expo), Agenda, DEMO, and Spotlight. IDG's training subsidiary, ExecuTrain, is the world's largest computer training company, with more than 230 locations worldwide and 785 training courses. IDG Marketing Services helps industry-leading IT companies build international brand recognition by developing global integrated marketing programs via IDG's print, online and exposition products worldwide. Further information about the company can be found at www.idg.com.
1/24/99

TM

References for the Rest of Us! ®

BESTSELLING BOOK SERIES

Are you intimidated and confused by computers? Do you find that traditional manuals are overloaded with technical details you'll never use? Do your friends and family always call you to fix simple problems on their PCs? Then the *...For Dummies®* computer book series from IDG Books Worldwide is for you.

...For Dummies books are written for those frustrated computer users who know they aren't really dumb but find that PC hardware, software, and indeed the unique vocabulary of computing make them feel helpless. *...For Dummies* books use a lighthearted approach, a down-to-earth style, and even cartoons and humorous icons to dispel computer novices' fears and build their confidence. Lighthearted but not lightweight, these books are a perfect survival guide for anyone forced to use a computer.

> *"I like my copy so much I told friends; now they bought copies."*
>
> — Irene C., Orwell, Ohio

> *"Quick, concise, nontechnical, and humorous."*
>
> — Jay A., Elburn, Illinois

> *"Thanks, I needed this book. Now I can sleep at night."*
>
> — Robin F., British Columbia, Canada

Already, millions of satisfied readers agree. They have made *...For Dummies* books the #1 introductory level computer book series and have written asking for more. So, if you're looking for the most fun and easy way to learn about computers, look to *...For Dummies* books to give you a helping hand.

IDG BOOKS WORLDWIDE

Dedication

This book is dedicated to all the wonderful people who have helped me down the rocky road of stand-up comedy:

Cassandra (my wife) and all four of our cats (Bo, Scraps, Tasha, and Nuit).

Patrick DeGuire for his invaluable help in running our comedy booking company, Top Bananas Entertainment (www.topbananas.com).

Budd Friedman for putting me on his show *"A&E's Evening at the Improv."*

Pat Buckles for putting me on the show *"The Extreme Gong Show."*

Steve Schirripa and Don Learned for putting me on stage at the Riviera Comedy Club, located in the Riviera Hotel & Casino in Las Vegas (www.theriviera.com).

Gene Perret (and his whole wonderfully wacky family) for offering his comedy wisdom and advice through his comedy books and annual Round Table comedy conventions.

And of course, to all the wonderful stand-up comedians I've met throughout the years including Dobie "Mr. Lucky" Maxwell (catch his comedy act or his comedy classes in the Chicago area), Chris "The Zooman" Clobber, and Leo "The Man, the Myth, the Legend" Fontaine.

Author's Acknowledgments

A hearty round of thanks goes to Bill Gates and the Microsoft Corporation for creating the monstrosity known as Microsoft Office 2000 and peppering it with so many features that nobody can figure out how to use it without extensive documentation, such as this book. Thanks Bill! Keep up the good work, and next time try to make Windows a little more stable as an operating system while you're at it.

Also a large round of thanks goes to Matt Wagner, Bill Gladstone, and all the other happy people cheerfully working away at the seaside resort offices of Waterside Productions. Waterside Productions is the best book agent in the world, so be sure to send them your thanks along with 15 percent of your profits, just like I do with every book.

Naturally, this book would still be an out-of-print title if the friendly folks at IDG Books didn't think it was worth updating once more to provide the public with still more information about Microsoft Office 2000. So thanks go to Nicole Haims, Pam Wilson-Wykes, and technical editor Kevin McCarter for the fine work they did on this book. Without their judicious editing talent, this book may have been heavier and thicker, so their work has kept you and thousands of bookshelf stockers all over the world from hurting your backs, trying to lift a copy of this book.

Final thanks go to Robert Cherewick for his slightly bizarre PG-rated Web site (dubbed "Babes on Bob" www.babesonbob.com) that showed me all sorts of neat Microsoft FrontPage 2000 tricks for spicing up a Web page.

Publisher's Acknowledgments

We're proud of this book; please register your comments through our IDG Books Worldwide Online Registration Form located at http://my2cents.dummies.com.

Some of the people who helped bring this book to market include the following:

Acquisitions, Editorial, and Media Development

Project Editor: Nicole Haims

    (Previous Edition: Nancy DelFavero)

Acquisitions Editor: Steven Hayes

Copy Editor: Pam Wilson-Wykes

Technical Editor: Kevin McCarter

Editorial Manager: Rev Mengle

Editorial Assistants: Jamila Pree, Beth Parlon

Production

Project Coordinator: Maridee V. Ennis

Layout and Graphics: Amy M. Adrian, Kate Jenkins, Barry Offringa, Doug Rollison, Brent Savage, Brian Torwelle, Maggie Ubertini, Dan Whetstine, Erin Zeltner

Proofreaders: Laura Albert, John Greenough, Henry Lazarek, Marianne Santy, Rebecca Senninger, Charles Spencer

Indexer: C2 Editorial Services

General and Administrative

IDG Books Worldwide, Inc.: John Kilcullen, CEO; Steven Berkowitz, President and Publisher

IDG Books Technology Publishing Group: Richard Swadley, Senior Vice President and Publisher; Walter Bruce III, Vice President and Associate Publisher; Joseph Wikert, Associate Publisher; Mary Bednarek, Branded Product Development Director; Mary Corder, Editorial Director; Barry Pruett, Publishing Manager; Michelle Baxter, Publishing Manager

IDG Books Consumer Publishing Group: Roland Elgey, Senior Vice President and Publisher; Kathleen A. Welton, Vice President and Publisher; Kevin Thornton, Acquisitions Manager; Kristin A. Cocks, Editorial Director

IDG Books Internet Publishing Group: Brenda McLaughlin, Senior Vice President and Publisher; Diane Graves Steele, Vice President and Associate Publisher; Sofia Marchant, Online Marketing Manager

IDG Books Production for Dummies Press: Debbie Stailey, Associate Director of Production; Cindy L. Phipps, Manager of Project Coordination, Production Proofreading, and Indexing; Tony Augsburger, Manager of Prepress, Reprints, and Systems; Laura Carpenter, Production Control Manager; Shelley Lea, Supervisor of Graphics and Design; Debbie J. Gates, Production Systems Specialist; Robert Springer, Supervisor of Proofreading; Kathie Schutte, Production Supervisor

Dummies Packaging and Book Design: Patty Page, Manager, Promotions Marketing

♦

The publisher would like to give special thanks to Patrick J. McGovern, without whom this book would not have been possible.

♦

Contents at a Glance

Cartoons at a Glance

By Rich Tennant

page 323

page 161

page 195

page 251

page 271

page 9

page 213

page 87

Fax: 978-546-7747 • E-mail: the5wave@tiac.net

Table of Contents

Introduction

• •

Despite several decades of continuous improvements that make computer equipment obsolete as soon as they're introduced, most computers and their accompanying programs are still too hard to understand and use. Even worse, many software publishers are simply throwing up their hands and releasing programs without any manuals at all — as if telling the general public, "Yes, we know our computer manuals are worthless, so we won't even bother giving you the illusion that you may actually find them useful."

Naturally, a monstrous program like Microsoft Office 2000 is no exception. Although Microsoft has added a bundle of new features in a desperate attempt to make Office 2000 easier to use, you may still find Office 2000 confusing, complicated, and downright frustrating. So that's what this book is about, to help relieve and reduce your mental anguish so that you can actually use Microsoft Office 2000 to get something useful done with your computer.

This book won't make you into a Microsoft Office 2000 expert overnight, but it will show you how to use the various Office 2000 programs to accomplish specific tasks. Just browse through the tips and tricks that interest you, and you'll gradually understand more about the programs and features that you find most useful. Within a short time, you'll know enough about Microsoft Office 2000 to work faster, more efficiently, and more productively than ever before (unless, of course, you don't want to).

Who Should Buy This Book

Bill Gates and Microsoft should buy this book and bundle it with every copy of Microsoft Office 2000, so that you wouldn't have to go out and buy the book on your own. But, because Microsoft isn't likely to go along with that idea any time soon, you should buy this book if you already have — or are planning to get — Microsoft Office 2000. Then you can use this book to guide you through the mental land mines of frustration that accompany the task of learning any new computer program.

If you're not already familiar with the basics of Microsoft Office 2000, first grab a copy of *Microsoft Office 2000 For Dummies* by none other than yours truly and Roger C. Parker (IDG Books Worldwide, Inc.). Make sure that you get that particular book, easily spotted by its bright yellow and black cover. Accept no substitutions or cheap imitations!

After you're familiar with the basics, such as starting Microsoft Office 2000 and saving data, you can make maximum use of this book, which shows you the more advanced techniques buried inside Microsoft Office 2000. You soon discover how to harness the power of Microsoft Office 2000 to get done fast and easy whatever you have to do using your computer, regardless of your previous experience with computers.

How This Book Is Organized

This book is organized by using paper, glue, and ink. The text itself is organized into several parts, where each part covers a specific program in Microsoft Office 2000. Whenever you need help (or just want to look as if you're doing something at work while you're really flipping through the cartoons), browse through this book, find the part that covers the topic you're looking for, and then toss the book aside and get back to work before your boss catches you goofing off.

Part I: Power Writing with Microsoft Word 2000

Whether you write letters, memos, newsletters, novels, or ransom notes, you find that Microsoft Word 2000 provides a feature to make your task easier. This part of the book reveals various time-saving shortcuts so that you can spend your time being creative instead of wrestling with the program's limitations (known in the advertising brochures as "features").

Part II: Number Crunching with Microsoft Excel 2000

Besides calculating results from a bunch of numbers and formulas that you type into a spreadsheet, Microsoft Excel 2000 can create maps from your data, automate your spreadsheets with macros, and even help you check your formulas to make sure that the answers you're getting actually make sense.

Part III: The Microsoft PowerPoint 2000 Dog-and-Pony Show

Sure, looks aren't *everything*, but they are somewhat important — they can help you win a million-dollar role in a bad TV show that people will joke about years from now. Also, pretty presentations with Microsoft PowerPoint 2000 can help you dazzle the competition and pacify your supervisors when you should really be working and doing something productive.

Part IV: Getting Organized with Microsoft Outlook 2000

Like everyone else, you would probably love to be more organized so you can accomplish the tasks that really mean something to you. Unfortunately, most of us have to work, which gobbles up most of our precious time. To help you plan your time more effectively, use Microsoft Outlook 2000 to turn your $2,000 computer into a $49.95 electronic organizer.

By using Microsoft Outlook 2000 daily, you can plan dreams for the future, set goals for turning your dreams into reality, schedule tasks for reaching your goals, and eventually live the type of life that you really want to live rather than settle for endless days of mediocrity that provide the main source of revenue for psychiatrists all over the world.

Part V: Storing Stuff in Microsoft Access 2000

If you're using the Professional, Premium, or Developer edition of Microsoft Office 2000, you get to play around with a bonus program called Microsoft Access 2000, which is a special database program that lets you store names, addresses, phone numbers, part numbers, invoices, or any other type of information that you think you may need at a future date. (Storing the names of valuable business contacts is wise. Storing your report cards from third grade probably is not.)

By letting you decide how you want to store, organize, and display information, Microsoft Access 2000 gives you the power to create your own custom programs to track inventory, print reports, or store customer names and addresses.

Part VI: Printing Stuff with Microsoft Publisher 2000

If you need to create brochures, flyers, signs, — or even origami and paper airplanes, Microsoft Publisher 2000 can make this task easy for you. This part of the book explains how to use Microsoft Publisher 2000's features to design and lay out text and graphics so that you can print the best-looking publications possible.

(Microsoft Publisher 2000 comes with every version of Microsoft Office except for the Standard edition of Microsoft Office 2000. If you buy the Standard edition, you have to buy Microsoft Publisher 2000 separately or just ignore this part of the book instead.)

Part VII: Playing with Microsoft FrontPage and PhotoDraw 2000

If you're fortunate enough (or rich enough) to own the Premium edition of Microsoft Office 2000, you get two bonus programs — Microsoft FrontPage 2000 and Microsoft PhotoDraw 2000. With Microsoft FrontPage 2000 you can design your own Web pages, and with Microsoft PhotoDraw 2000 you can create or modify graphics or digitized photographs.

Despite their power and sophistication, both FrontPage and PhotoDraw are actually easy to use. Even if you have little or no experience designing Web pages or drawing, both FrontPage and PhotoDraw can help you design and create quality Web pages and graphics in no time.

Part VIII: Using Microsoft Office 2000's Small Business Tools

The Small Business Tools come with every version of Microsoft Office 2000, except for the Standard edition. The Small Business Tools are Microsoft's way of helping you create and manage a company or business. After all, if the business principles embedded in these programs can work for Microsoft, they can probably work for you, too.

These tools can guide you into starting a business, running a direct mail advertising campaign, managing your customer relations, and organizing your cash flow so that you can tell whether your business is actually making money or not. Although using these Small Business Tools may not help your company grow to the size of Microsoft, they can help you wipe out your competition — just as Microsoft has.

How to Use This Book

You can use this book as a reference, a tutorial, a weapon, or a shield (it's thick enough). Don't feel the need to read every page of this book. Instead, just browse through the parts that interest you and ignore the rest.

Although you aren't likely to use *every* program in Microsoft Office 2000, take some time to browse through the parts of the book that describe the programs you don't use often. Fooling around with spreadsheets may seem dull if you're not an accountant or an engineer, but by playing around with spreadsheets, you just may find a way to make them useful in your personal life or business. You paid for Microsoft Office 2000, so you may as well try all the programs Microsoft gives you. At the very least, you can always erase the programs that you don't want and never bother with them again.

How much do you need to know?

As long as you know how to turn on a computer and use a mouse, you should be able to follow the instructions in this book with no major, trauma-inducing problems. If you find Windows to be somewhat of a strange beast to master, you may want to get a copy of *Windows 95 For Dummies,* 2nd Edition or *Windows 98 For Dummies* by Andy Rathbone (published by IDG Books Worldwide, Inc.).

Conventions

To avoid later confusion (because computers do such a good job of creating confusion on their own), be sure that you understand the following terms:

- When you look at the screen, you may see two items: a *cursor* (which appears as a vertical, blinking line) and an *I-beam pointer* (which sometimes appears as a white arrow when you move it over certain parts of the screen).

  The blinking cursor moves whenever you use the keyboard to type a letter or number, or to press one of the four (up, down, left, right) arrow keys. The I-beam pointer moves whenever you move the mouse.

- *Clicking* means pressing the left mouse button once and letting go. Clicking is how you activate icons in the toolbar, for example.

- *Double-clicking* means pressing the left mouse button twice in rapid succession. Double-clicking typically activates a command.

✔ *Dragging* selects items that you want to move, delete, or format. To drag, place the I-beam pointer to the left of the item that you want to select, hold down the left mouse button, and move the mouse in the desired direction. When you release the mouse button, Windows selects that item. You can tell when an item is selected because it appears in white against a black background.

✔ *Right-clicking* means clicking the mouse button on the right. (Some mice have three buttons, so ignore the middle button for now.) Right-clicking usually displays a shortcut menu on the screen.

Icons used in this book

This icon highlights information that can be helpful (as long as you don't forget it, of course).

This icon marks certain steps or procedures that can save you time when you use Microsoft Office 2000.

Watch out! This icon warns you of potential trouble that you may run into while using Microsoft Office 2000.

This icon highlights detailed information that's nice to know but not essential for using Microsoft Office 2000.

Choosing commands in Microsoft Office 2000

Microsoft Office 2000 gives you two ways to choose commands:

✔ Clicking the mouse on an icon or menu command

✔ Pressing a keystroke combination, such as Ctrl+S (which means hold down the Ctrl key, press the S key, and then release both keys simultaneously)

Most keyboard shortcuts involve holding down the Ctrl or Alt key (typically located to the left and right of the spacebar on your keyboard) in combination with one of the function keys (the keys labeled F1, F2, F3, and so on) or a letter key (A, B, C, and so on).

Use the method that you like best. Some people use the mouse, some use the keyboard, some use both, and some just hire another person to do all their hard work for them, instead.

Your first tip

Don't be afraid to experiment, fool around, or play with any of the multitude of commands available in Microsoft Office. Anytime you choose a command by mistake, tell Microsoft Office 2000 to take it back by pressing Ctrl+Z (hold down the Ctrl key, press the Z key, and let go of both keys at the same time).

Now that you know how to undo commands, feel free to pick a command at random, just to see what happens. Then press Ctrl+Z to return your data to normal. By freely experimenting with Microsoft Office 2000 and keeping the handy Ctrl+Z keystroke ready at all times, you can teach yourself how to use many features of Microsoft Office 2000 practically all by yourself, using the same method by which most people learn best, anyway: trial and error.

Getting Started

Now that you have a copy of Microsoft Office 2000 on your computer (you did pay for it, didn't you?), you're ready to start using the advanced features that Microsoft buried in the most obscure places. But don't worry. As you pick up various tips and tricks from this book, you soon see that Microsoft Office 2000 really can make you more productive with your computer in ways that you may never have dreamed about until now. So what are you waiting for? Stop reading this paragraph and turn the page.

Part I

Power Writing with Microsoft Word 2000

Yes, macros do save time, but only if they're CORRECT! Right now, we're efficiently producing cards that wish people a "Happy Hollidog," "Seasons Creepings," and "Joy to the Whirled."

Bob's Card Co.

In this part . . .

Besides playing games, most people use a computer to write with a word processor (provided they can get their computer to work in the first place). Fortunately, Microsoft Word 2000 provides plenty of time-saving short-cuts, such as macros (which can automate your writing), templates (so you don't have to waste time formatting your documents yourself), and automatic index– and table-of-contents–generating features.

As usual, Microsoft tried (emphasis on *tried*) to make these advanced features of Word 2000 easy to use, but if you need more help than what Microsoft's cartoon Office Assistants and help screens can provide, dig through this part of the book to master the secrets of Word 2000.

Chapter 1

Making Menu and Keystroke Shortcuts

• •

In This Chapter

▶ Customizing your menus

▶ Renaming menu titles

▶ Making keystroke shortcuts

• •

*T*he pull-down menus in Microsoft Word 2000 contain every command you could possibly want to use. Unfortunately, digging through menus crowded with commands that you don't understand can make any program seem harder to use. So, in an effort to please everyone, Microsoft Word 2000 gives you the ability to add, delete, rename, or even create your own pull-down menus.

In another gesture of benevolence, Microsoft Word 2000 also lets you assign keystroke shortcuts to your most commonly used commands. Instead of digging through a pull-down menu every time you want to choose a command, you can press a strange keystroke combination, such as Ctrl+F11. By assigning your own keystroke shortcuts to specific commands, you can make Microsoft Word 2000 even easier to use.

Customizing Pull-Down Menus

You can customize all of Microsoft Word 2000's pull-down menus by adding, deleting, or rearranging menu commands. That way you can display only those commands that you use most often and keep other commands completely off the pull-down menu to avoid confusing you any more than necessary.

If you modify the pull-down menus in your version of Microsoft Word 2000, other people may have trouble using your copy of Microsoft Word 2000. Depending on your situation, this can be extremely troublesome or just highly amusing.

Rearranging commands on a pulldown menu

If you don't like the way Microsoft Word 2000 displays commands on your pull-down menus, then move the commands around. To move a command to a new location or to a different pull-down menu altogether, follow these steps:

1. **Choose Tools⇨Customize.**

   The Customize dialog box appears.

2. **Click on a pull-down menu title.**

   A black border appears around the menu title.

3. **Click on the menu command that you want to move.**

   A black border appears around your chosen menu command, as shown in Figure 1-1.

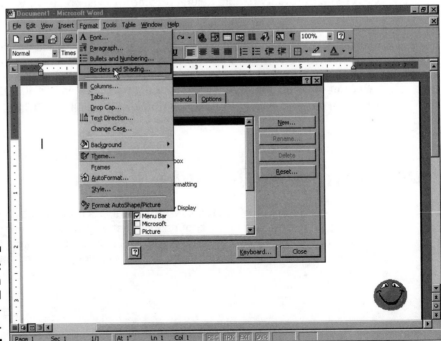

Figure 1-1:
Moving a command on a pull-down menu.

4. **Hold down the left mouse button and drag the mouse to a new location.**

   A black line appears to show the new location of the command if you release the left mouse button.

5. **Release the left mouse button when you're happy with the position of the command.**

6. **Click on the Close button in the Customize dialog box.**

   All done!

Copying a pull-down menu command

If you use a particular command often, you can have the command appear in two or more pull-down menus. To copy a menu command, follow these steps:

1. **Choose Tools⇨Customize.**

   The Customize dialog box appears.

2. **Click on a pull-down menu title and then move the mouse pointer over the menu command that you want to copy.**

3. **Hold down the Ctrl key and then hold down the left mouse button while dragging the mouse to another pull-down menu title.**

   A black line appears to indicate where the copy of the command will appear if you let go of the left mouse button.

4. **Release both the Ctrl key and the left mouse button when you're happy with the position of the command.**

5. **Click on the Close button in the Customize dialog box.**

   From this point on, the command you copied appears both in its original and its new locations.

Deleting commands from a pull-down menu

Chances are you won't use every command that appears on a pull-down menu. To avoid cluttering up your menus, take a few moments and yank off those commands that you probably won't use in a million years.

To delete a command from a pull-down menu, follow these steps:

1. **Choose Tools⇨Customize.**

   The Customize dialog box appears.

2. **Click on a pull-down menu title and then click on the menu command that you want to delete.**

   A black border appears around your chosen menu command.

3. **Hold down the left mouse button and drag the mouse anywhere off the pull-down menu.**

4. **Release the left mouse button.**

   Your chosen menu command no longer appears on the pull-down menu.

5. **Click on the Close button in the Customize dialog box.**

   The command you've removed no longer appears in its original pull-down menu.

Changing your menu command icons

To provide a visual relationship between specific menu commands and those cryptic little icons that appear on the toolbars, Microsoft Word 2000 displays icons within the pull-down menus themselves. For example, if you click on the File menu, you can see that the icons that appear next to the Open and New commands also appear on the Standard toolbar.

Removing menu icons

In case you don't like icons cluttering up your pull-down menus, you can get rid of them by following these steps:

1. **Choose Tools⇨Customize.**

   The Customize dialog box appears.

2. **Click on a pull-down menu title and then click on the menu command that displays the icon that you want to delete.**

3. **Click the right mouse button.**

   A pop-up menu appears, as shown in Figure 1-2.

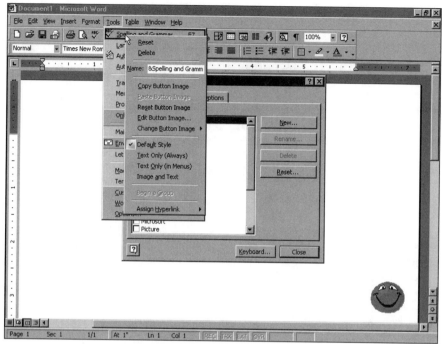

Figure 1-2:
Deleting an
icon on a
pull-down
menu.

4. **Click on Text Only (in Menus).**

5. **Click on Close in the Customize dialog box.**

The pesky icon no longer appears in the pull-down menu.

Choosing a new menu icon

If you don't like the icons that currently represent your menu commands, go ahead and pick your own icons instead. To choose a new icon for a menu command, follow these steps:

1. **Choose Tools⇔Customize.**

The Customize dialog box appears.

2. **Click on a pull-down menu title and then click on a menu command to which you want to add a new icon.**

3. **Click the right mouse button.**

A pop-up menu appears (refer to Figure 1-2).

4. **Click on Change Button Image.**

Another pop-up menu appears, as shown in Figure 1-3.

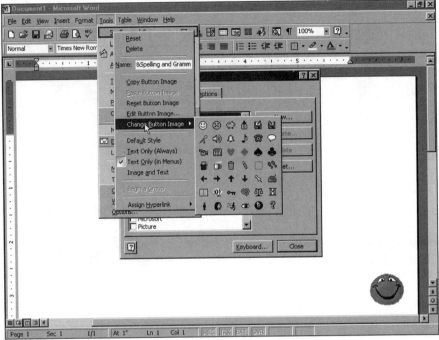

5. Click on a new icon that you want to represent your menu command.

6. Click on Close in the Customize dialog box.

> The new icon appears in the pull-down menu, and the old icon is gone forever.

Changing an icon in a pull-down menu doesn't change that same icon in a toolbar.

You can also use the preceding steps to add an icon to a menu command that doesn't have an icon next to it.

Editing a menu icon

For those with an artistic bent, Microsoft Word 2000 gives you the power to edit an icon and draw a new one if you like. To edit or draw an icon for a menu, follow these steps:

1. Choose Tools⇨Customize.

> The Customize dialog box appears.

2. Click on a pull-down menu title and then click on the menu command displaying the icon that you want to edit.

3. **Click the right mouse button.**

   A pop-up menu appears (refer to Figure 1-2).

4. **Click on Edit Button Image.**

   A Button Editor window appears, as shown in Figure 1-4.

5. **Click on a color in the Colors group.**

6. **Move the mouse pointer over the icon in the Picture box and click (or hold down) the left mouse button when you want to paint in your chosen color.**

   Click on the Erase box to draw the default background color of your icon. (This erases whatever color is already there.)

7. **Click on OK when you're done drawing or modifying your icon.**

8. **Click on Close in the Customize dialog box.**

   Now sit back and congratulate yourself for your artistic skills.

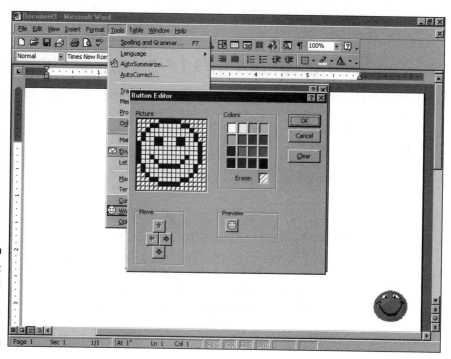

Figure 1-4:
Editing an
icon on a
pull-down
menu.

Resetting a menu icon

Naturally, if you mess up the icons that appear in your pull-down menus, you may want to restore them to their appearance before you got too creative (or too careless). To reset your menu icons to their original appearance, follow these steps:

1. **Choose Tools⇨Customize.**

   The Customize dialog box appears.

2. **Click on a pull-down menu title and then click on the menu command displaying the icon that you want to reset.**

3. **Click the right mouse button.**

   A pop-up menu appears (refer to Figure 1-2).

4. **Click on Reset Button Image.**

5. **Click on Close in the Customize dialog box.**

   Wonder at your ability to recognize your artistic limitations and thank Bill Gates for not forcing you to look at a mutated icon for ever after.

Adding commands to a pull-down menu

In case a pull-down menu doesn't display a particular command that you need, you can add that command to a menu yourself. To add a command to a pull-down menu, follow these steps:

1. **Choose Tools⇨Customize.**

   A Customize dialog box appears.

2. **Click on the Commands tab.**

3. **Click on the pull-down menu title where you want to add your new command (such as the File or Window menu).**

   You may have to move the Customize dialog box to see both the dialog box and your chosen pull-down menu.

4. **In the Categories list box of the Customize dialog box, click on a category for the command that you want to add to a pull-down menu.**

   For example, if you want to add a command that appears in the Edit category, click on Edit in the Categories list box.

5. **Move the mouse pointer over the command that you want to put on the menu (such as the Find or Open command, or as shown in Figure 1-5, a Search the Web command).**

6. **Hold down the left mouse button and drag the mouse to the pull-down menu where you want to add the command, as shown in Figure 1-5.**

   A black I-beam icon appears to show you where the command will appear on the menu.

7. **Release the left mouse button.**

8. **Click on Close to remove the Customize dialog box.**

   The command you've added is now in the pull-down menu.

Renaming a pull-down menu title or command

Although Microsoft Word 2000 uses standard pull-down menu titles, such as File, View, and Window, you can choose more descriptive titles instead. For maximum flexibility, you can rename both your menu titles (the ones that appear at the top of the screen) and your menu commands (the ones that appear within a pull-down menu).

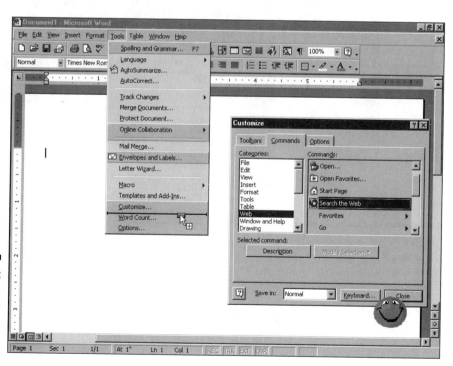

Figure 1-5:
Adding a command to a pull-down menu.

Renaming pull-down menu titles

To rename a pull-down menu title, follow these steps:

1. **Choose <u>T</u>ools⇨<u>C</u>ustomize.**

   The Customize dialog box appears.

2. **Move the mouse pointer over the pull-down menu title that you want to rename and then click the right mouse button.**

   A pop-up menu appears, as shown in Figure 1-6.

3. **Click on the <u>N</u>ame text box and type a new name for your pull-down menu.**

   To underline a letter in your menu title, put an ampersand character (&) in front of the letter. For example, &Stuff appears on the pull-down menu as <u>S</u>tuff.

4. **Click on Close to make the Customize dialog box go away.**

   You've successfully changed the pull-down menu's name.

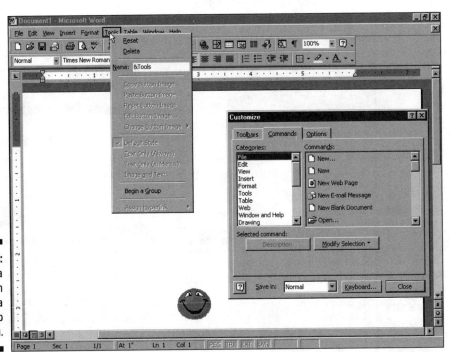

Figure 1-6:
Renaming a pull-down menu with a pop-up menu.

Renaming commands on a pull-down menu

To rename a command on a pull-down menu, follow these steps:

1. **Choose Tools⇨Customize.**

   The Customize dialog box appears.

2. **Click on the pull-down menu title containing the command that you want to rename; then, move the mouse pointer over the command that you want to rename.**

3. **Click on the right mouse button.**

   A pop-up menu appears.

4. **Click on the Name text box and type a new name for your pull-down command.**

   To underline a letter in your menu command, put an ampersand character (&) in front of the letter. For example, &Kill File appears on the pull-down menu as Kill File.

5. **Click on Close to make the Customize dialog box go away.**

   You've successfully changed the command's name.

Resetting a pull-down menu

Rearranging your pull-down menus can be fun and mind-expanding, but you may want to restore your pull-down menus to their original appearance in case you want your copy of Microsoft Word 2000 to look like it did before you started messing around with your menus.

Resetting a pull-down menu wipes out any modifications that you may have made. Therefore, choose this command only if you really want to delete any of your modifications.

To reset a menu, follow these steps:

1. **Choose Tools⇨Customize.**

   The Customize dialog box appears.

2. **Move the mouse pointer over the pull-down menu title that you want to reset and click on the right mouse button.**

   A pop-up menu appears (refer to Figure 1-6).

3. **Click on Reset.**

4. **Click on Close to remove the Customize dialog box.**

   Your original menu is now restored.

Making Keystroke Shortcuts

If you use a particular command often enough, you may want a faster way of choosing it than taking your hands off the keyboard and reaching for the mouse each time. To give touch-typists an additional edge over their counterparts who rely on the mouse to do everything, Microsoft Word 2000 lets you assign your own keystroke shortcuts to any Microsoft Word 2000 command.

For example, if you don't like the idea of choosing the Print Preview command by clicking on the Print Preview icon on the toolbar or choosing Print Preview from the File menu, create a keystroke shortcut, such as F12 instead. Then, just press F12 every time you want to choose the Print Preview command.

Assigning keystroke shortcuts

To assign your own keystrokes to a command, follow these steps:

1. **Choose Tools⇨Customize.**

   The Customize dialog box appears.

2. **Click on the Toolbars tab.**

3. **Click on the Keyboard button.**

   A Customize Keyboard dialog box appears, as shown in Figure 1-7.

4. **Click on the Categories list box and choose a category, such as File or Edit.**

5. **Click on the Commands list box and choose a command to which you want to assign a keystroke shortcut.**

6. **Click on the Press new shortcut key box.**

7. **Press the key combination that you want to assign as your shortcut, such as Ctrl+F11.**

8. **Click on Assign.**

9. **Click on Close to make the Customize Keyboard dialog box go away.**

10. **Click on Close to make the Customize dialog box disappear.**

    Your new personalized keystroke shortcut is set.

You should choose keystroke shortcuts that are both easy to remember and to press. For example, Ctrl+E is much easier to press and remember than Alt+Shift+F2. Just remember that most of the simpler keystrokes have already been assigned to commonly used commands, such as Save (Ctrl+S) or Print (Ctrl+P).

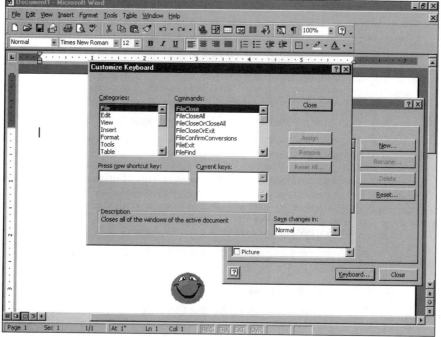

Figure 1-7:
The
Customize
Keyboard
dialog box
for assign-
ing your
own key-
stroke
shortcuts.

Microsoft Word 2000 allows you to assign your keystroke shortcuts in two
ways:

- Sort of permanent: The shortcuts are in place whenever anyone tries to
  use your copy of Microsoft Word 2000.

- Sort of temporary: The shortcuts exist only in the current document
  that you're editing.

Unless you specify otherwise, Microsoft Word 2000 blindly assumes that you
want to use your keystroke shortcuts every time you use Microsoft Word
2000. To tell Microsoft Word 2000 to save your keystroke shortcuts only in
the current document, click on the Save changes in list box after Step 8 and
then click on the name of the current document you're editing. Then proceed
with Steps 9 and 10.

Deleting keystroke shortcuts

You can get rid of keystroke shortcuts that you never use, and you can also
remove a keystroke shortcut from one command and use it for another one.

To delete a keystroke shortcut, follow these steps:

1. **Choose Tools⇨Customize.**

   The Customize dialog box appears.

2. **Click on the Toolbars tab.**

3. **Click on the Keyboard button.**

   A Customize Keyboard dialog box appears (refer to Figure 1-7).

4. **Click on the Categories list box and choose a category, such as File or Edit.**

5. **Click on the Commands list box and choose a command that you want to remove a keystroke shortcut from.**

6. **Click on the keystroke shortcut that you want to delete in the Current keys box.**

   Note: Not all commands may have keystroke shortcuts assigned to them.

7. **Click on Remove.**

8. **Click on Close to make the Customize Keyboard dialog box go away.**

9. **Click on Close to make the Customize dialog box disappear.**

   The keystroke shortcut is now free to assign to another command.

Resetting your keystroke shortcuts

Reassigning keystroke shortcuts can be fun and amusing, but it can confuse other people who may want to use your copy of Microsoft Word 2000. In case you need to return your keystroke shortcuts to their original, pristine, unblemished-by-human-hands state of innocence, you can.

To reset your keystroke shortcuts, follow these steps:

1. **Choose Tools⇨Customize.**

   The Customize dialog box appears.

2. **Click on the Toolbars tab.**

3. **Click on the Keyboard button.**

   A Customize Keyboard dialog box appears (refer to Figure 1-7).

4. **Click on Reset All.**

   A dialog box appears, warning you that Microsoft Word 2000 will wipe out all your custom keystroke shortcuts, as shown in Figure 1-8.

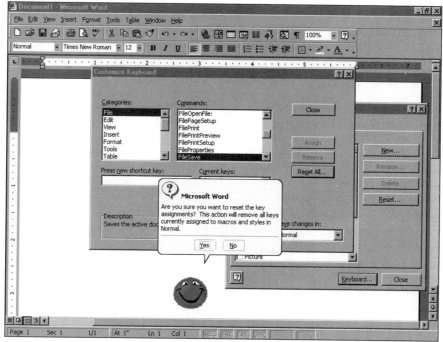

Figure 1-8:
A dialog box
warning that
you may
wipe out all
your custom
keystroke
shortcuts in
one click of
the mouse.

5. **Click on Yes (if that's what you really want to do).**

6. **Click on Close to make the Customize Keyboard dialog box go away.**

7. **Click on Close to make the Customize dialog box disappear.**

   Your preset keyboard shortcuts are now restored.

Chapter 2

Fooling Around with Macros

. . . .

In This Chapter

▶ Recording macros as toolbar buttons, menu items, and keystroke combinations

▶ Renaming macros

▶ Deleting macros

▶ Protecting against macro viruses

. . . .

To help you work faster, Microsoft Word 2000 lets you create *macros* filled with one or more of your specific instructions. When you want to repeat a task, you don't have to type a bunch of words or click on a dozen menu commands all over again. Just tell Microsoft Word 2000 to follow the instructions stored in your macro and move on with your work.

Suppose that you have to type a long-winded phrase, such as *Acme's Super Acne Medication Cream,* or choose multiple commands to create a three-column document repeatedly. You can type all those words (or choose all those commands) multiple times and risk making a mistake, or you can use a macro.

If you use a macro, you have to type the words or choose the commands only once. You can use Microsoft Word 2000's macro feature to "capture" words or commands (like bugs in amber) and then "replay" them (like a recording) at the touch of a button. In this way, a macro lets you perform complicated tasks without thinking, which is the way most people act when they're working for somebody else anyway.

Recording Your Own Macros

When you record a macro, you can store the macro in one of three ways:

✔ **As a toolbar button:** If you store a macro on a toolbar, you choose the macro by simply clicking on its button.

✔ **As a menu command:** If you store a macro on a menu, you choose the macro by pulling down the menu and then clicking on the macro's name.

✔ **As a unique keystroke combination, such as Ctrl+W:** If you store a macro as a keystroke combination, you can quickly choose the macro by pressing the proper keystrokes. (The only hard part is remembering the macro's particular keystroke combination.)

Which method you should use depends on how you like to use Microsoft Word 2000. If you want simple point-and-click access to your macros, store your macros as toolbar buttons. If you don't want macros cluttering your screen as buttons, store them as menu commands. If you want to access your macros faster than you can by clicking on either toolbar buttons or menu commands, store the macros as keystroke combinations. If you don't like macros at all, skip this chapter altogether.

Microsoft Word 2000 gives you the option of saving your macros in a template or in your current document. If you save your macro to a template, then you can use your macro in any document created from that template. (Check out Chapter 3 for more information about templates.) If you save your macro in the current document, then you can use your macro only in that particular document.

Macros as toolbar buttons

When you record a macro as a toolbar button, you need to choose two items:

✔ A button to represent the macro

✔ A toolbar (such as the Standard or Formatting toolbar) on which to store the button that represents your macro

If you want to display a macro button on a specific toolbar — such as the Formatting or Web toolbar — make sure that the toolbar appears on the screen before performing the following steps. To make a specific toolbar visible, choose View➪Toolbars and then click on the toolbar you want to make visible.

To record a macro and store it as a toolbar button, follow these steps:

1. **Choose Tools➪Macro➪Record New Macro.**

   A Macro dialog box appears, as shown in Figure 2-1.

2. **Type a descriptive name for your macro (one word only, no spaces allowed) in the Macro name box.**

3. **Click on the Store macro in list box and click on the template or document in which you want to save your macro.**

4. **Type a description for your macro in the Description text box.**

   This step is optional but can be helpful when trying to remember what a particular macro actually does.

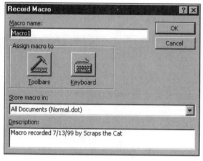

Figure 2-1:
Recording a
new macro
with the
Macro
dialog box.

5. **Click on the Toolbars button in the Assign macro to group.**

   The Customize dialog box appears.

6. **Click on the Commands tab.**

   The Customize dialog box displays the name of your newly created macro, as shown in Figure 2-2.

Figure 2-2:
The
Customize
dialog box
that appears
when you
create a
macro.

7. **Move the mouse pointer over the macro name displayed in the Commands list box, and simultaneously hold down the left mouse button while you drag the mouse to the toolbar on which you want to store your macro — such as the Standard toolbar displayed at the top of the screen.**

   Microsoft Word 2000 displays a dark vertical line on the toolbar to show you where your macro button will appear when you release the left mouse button.

8. **When you're happy with the location of your macro button on a toolbar, release the left mouse button.**

9. **Click on the Modify Selection button.**

   A pop-up menu appears, as shown in Figure 2-3.

Macro button on the toolbar

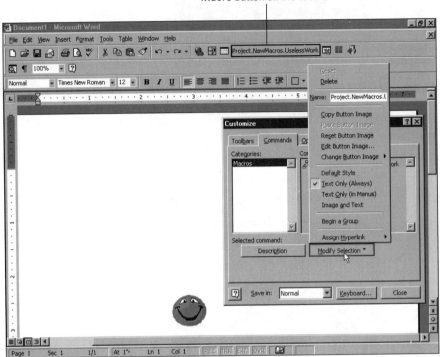

Figure 2-3:
The Modify
Selection
pop-up
menu.

10. **Click on the Name text box and then type the descriptive text that you want to appear on your macro button.**

11. **Click on Change Button Image and then click on an image that you want to appear on your macro button.**

12. **Click on Close.**

    The Macro Recording toolbar, shown in Figure 2-4, appears, floating in the middle of the screen. The mouse pointer displays a cassette tape icon to let you know that Microsoft Word 2000 is recording your macro.

13. **Press any keys or choose any commands that you want to store in your macro.**

    When you're recording a macro but don't want to record certain keystrokes or commands, you can temporarily turn off the macro recorder by clicking on the Pause button (refer to Figure 2-4). To turn the macro recorder back on, just click on the Pause Recording button again.

14. **Click on the Stop Recording button on the Macro Recording toolbar when you're done recording your macro.**

    Congratulations! You've just recorded a macro. To use this macro at any time, click on its toolbar button.

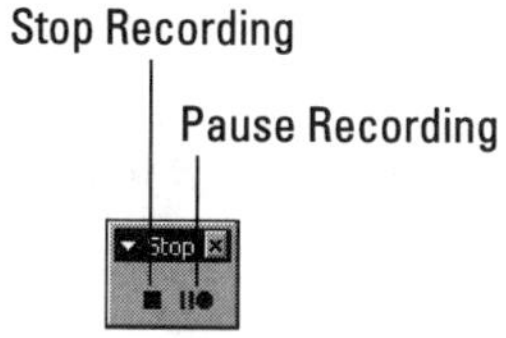

Figure 2-4:
The Macro
Recording
toolbar
appears like
a floating,
disembod-
ied spirit on
the screen.

Stop Recording

Pause Recording

Don't worry. If you don't like macro buttons cluttering up your toolbars, you can always remove them later. To remove a single macro button from your toolbar, follow these steps:

1. **Choose Tools⇨Customize.**

   The Customize dialog box appears.

2. **Move the mouse pointer over the macro button that you want to remove and simultaneously hold down the left mouse button and drag the macro button off the toolbar.**

3. **Release the left mouse button.**

   Microsoft Word 2000 deletes your macro button from the toolbar.

4. **Click on Close.**

REMEMBER

When you remove a macro button from a toolbar, you just remove the icon; the macro still exists on your hard disk. To delete macros, go to the "Wiping out macros" section later in this chapter.

Macros as menu commands

When you record a macro as a menu command, you need to choose two things:

✔ A descriptive name for the macro

✔ A pull-down menu — such as the Tools or View menu — in which to store the macro

To record a macro and store it as a command on a pull-down menu, follow these steps:

1. **Choose Tools⇨Macro⇨Record New Macro.**

   A Macro dialog box appears (refer to Figure 2-1).

2. **Type a descriptive name for your macro (one word only, no spaces are allowed) in the <u>M</u>acro name box.**

3. **Click on the <u>S</u>tore macro in list box and click on the template or document in which you want to save your macro.**

4. **Type a description for your macro in the <u>D</u>escription text box.**

   This step is optional but can be helpful when trying to remember what a particular macro actually does.

5. **Click on the <u>T</u>oolbars button in the Assign macro to group.**

   The Customize dialog box appears (refer to Figure 2-2).

6. **Click on the <u>C</u>ommands tab.**

7. **Move the mouse pointer over the macro name displayed in the Comman<u>d</u>s list box, hold down the left mouse button, and drag the mouse to the pull-down menu on which you want to store your macro.**

   Microsoft Word 2000 displays a dark horizontal line on the pull-down menu to show you where your macro button will appear when you release the left mouse button.

8. **When you're happy with the location of your macro button on a pull-down menu, release the left mouse button.**

9. **Click on the <u>M</u>odify Selection button.**

   A pop-up menu appears (refer to Figure 2-3).

10. **Click on <u>N</u>ame and then type the descriptive text that you want to appear for your macro.**

11. **Click on Change <u>B</u>utton Image and then click on an image that you want to appear next to your macro name on the pull-down menu.**

12. **Click on Close.**

    The Macro Recording toolbar appears, floating in the middle of the screen (refer to Figure 2-4). The mouse pointer displays a cassette tape icon to let you know that Microsoft Word 2000 is recording your macro.

13. **Press any keys or choose any commands that you want to store in your macro.**

    When you're recording a macro but don't want to record certain keystrokes or commands, you can temporarily turn off the macro recorder by clicking on the Pause button (refer to Figure 2-4). To turn the macro recorder back on, just click on the Pause Recording button again.

14. **Click on the Stop Recording button on the Macro Recording toolbar when you're done recording your macro.**

    To use this macro at any time, just display the pull-down menu in which you stored the macro name (in Step 8) and then click on the macro name displayed on the menu.

To remove the macro from a pull-down menu, follow these steps:

1. **Choose Tools⇨Customize.**

   The Customize dialog box appears.

2. **Click on the pull-down menu containing your macro, point to the macro that you want to remove, hold down the left mouse button, and drag the macro button off the pull-down menu.**

3. **Release the left mouse button.**

   Microsoft Word 2000 deletes your macro button from the pull-down menu.

4. **Click on Close.**

When you remove a macro from a pull-down menu, that macro still exists on your hard disk — it's just hiding. To delete macros, go to the "Wiping out macros" section later in this chapter.

Macros as keystroke combinations

When you record a macro as a keystroke combination, you need to choose two things:

- ✔ A descriptive name for your macro
- ✔ A unique two- or three-keystroke combination to represent your macro

To record a macro and store it as a keystroke combination, follow these steps:

1. **Choose Tools⇨Macro⇨Record New Macro.**

   A Macro dialog box appears (refer to Figure 2-1).

2. **Type a descriptive name for your macro (one word only, no spaces allowed) in the Macro name box.**

3. **Click on the Store macro in list box and then click on the template or document in which you want to save your macro.**

4. **Type a description for your macro in the Description text box.**

   This step is optional but can be helpful when trying to remember what a particular macro actually does.

5. **Click on the Keyboard button in the Assign macro to area of the Record New Macro dialog box.**

   The Customize Keyboard dialog box appears, as shown in Figure 2-5.

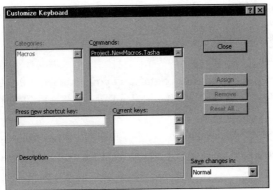

Figure 2-5:
The
Customize
Keyboard
dialog box.

6. **Click on the Press new shortcut key text box and then press the keystroke that you want to represent your macro, such as Ctrl+F11.**

7. **Click on Assign.**

   Repeat Steps 6 and 7 for each additional keystroke combination that you want to assign to your macro.

8. **Click on Close.**

   The Macro Recording toolbar appears, floating in the middle of the screen (refer to Figure 2-4). The mouse pointer displays a cassette tape icon to let you know that Microsoft Word 2000 is recording your macro.

9. **Press any keys or choose any commands that you want to store in your macro.**

   When you're recording a macro but don't want to record certain keystrokes or commands, you can temporarily turn off the macro recorder by clicking on the Pause button (refer to Figure 2-4). To turn the macro recorder back on, just click on the Pause Recording button again.

10. **Click on the Stop Recording button on the Macro Recording toolbar when you're done recording your macro.**

To use this macro at any time, press the keystroke combination that you assigned in Step 6.

Modifying Macros

After you've created a macro, you can rename or delete it at any time by using the steps in the following sections:

Editing a macro

In case you create a macro and later find out that you misspelled a word or recorded too many extra commands, you can edit your macro and modify its commands.

To edit a macro, you should understand the Visual Basic for Applications (VBA) programming language. To learn more about the language, pick up a copy of *VBA For Dummies* by Steve Cummings (IDG Books Worldwide, Inc.).

To edit an existing macro, follow these steps:

1. **Choose Tools⇨Macro⇨Macros, or press Alt+F8.**

   The Macro dialog box appears.

2. **Click on the macro name that you want to edit.**

3. **Click on Edit.**

   The Visual Basic Editor appears, as shown in Figure 2-6.

4. **Make any changes to your macro.**

5. **Choose File⇨Close and then return to Microsoft Word, or press Alt+Q.**

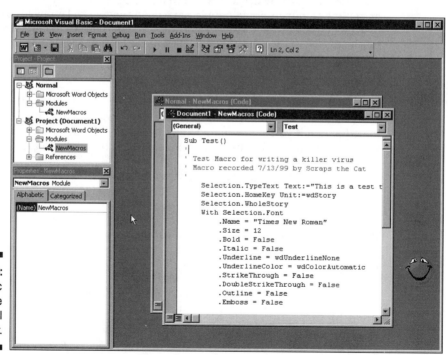

Figure 2-6: The cryptic appearance of the Visual Basic Editor.

Wiping out macros

If you decide that you'll never need a certain macro again, you can delete it for good. To delete a macro, follow these steps:

1. **Choose Tools⇨Macro⇨Macros, or press Alt+F8.**

   The Macro dialog box appears.

2. **Click on the macro name that you want to delete and then click on Delete.**

   A dialog box appears, asking whether you really want to delete your macro.

3. **Click on Yes.**

   Your macro is gone for good!

4. **Click on Close.**

Protecting against Macro Viruses

Because Microsoft Word 2000's macro language is basically a miniature programming language, some people have used the macro language to create a new breed of computer viruses, known as macro viruses. Macro viruses can infect all types of Microsoft Office 2000 files but are especially common in infecting Word documents (and to a lesser extent, Excel and PowerPoint files).

Macro viruses work by infecting a template. Every time you create a new document based on an infected template file, your new document files become infected. And if you share an infected document file with someone else, the macro virus infects that person's document and template files, too.

The best protection against macro viruses are antivirus programs, such as the Norton Antivirus (www.symantec.com) or McAfee's VirusScan (www.mcafee.com).

People create new macro viruses almost daily, so make sure you keep your antivirus program up to date so that it can catch the newest macro viruses attacking computers all over the world.

As a first line of defense against macro viruses, follow these steps:

1. **Choose Tools⇨Macro⇨Security.**

   The Security dialog box appears, as shown in Figure 2-7.

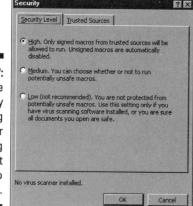

Figure 2-7:
The
Security
dialog
box for
protecting
against
macro
viruses.

2. **Click on the Security Level tab.**

3. **Click on the High option button.**

   The High security level only allows macros from trusted sources — such as those created by you on your own computer — to run under your copy of Microsoft Word 2000. By default, Word 2000 automatically chooses the High security level, unless you specifically choose a different security level.

4. **Click on OK.**

If you click the Medium option button in Step 3, Microsoft Word 2000 displays a dialog box warning you when it's about to run a macro. If you click the Low option button in Step 3, Microsoft Word 2000 will cheerfully run any and all macros stored in any document, which can run a macro virus that can infect your computer. Unless you know what you're doing with macros coming from unknown sources, stick with the High or Medium security level for Step 3.

Chapter 3

Fast Formatting with Styles and Templates

*T*wo of Microsoft Word 2000's most useful features are styles and templates. A *style* lets you define a specific way to format text. A *template* is a file that stores multiple styles so that you can use them over and over again.

If most of your writing requires unusual formatting — such as writing screenplays, typing financial reports, or pasting together ransom notes — styles and templates can spare you the headache of manually formatting individual paragraphs all by yourself.

Formatting Text with Styles

A *style* defines a specific way to format text, such as the font, font size, alignment, color, boldface, italic, underline, or anything else that keeps your documents from looking as dull as if you typed them on an antique typewriter. (Remember those ancient machines?)

By creating a predefined style, you don't have to keep highlighting text and changing all these formatting options yourself. Instead, you can just click on the text that you want to format and choose a style. Then, Microsoft Word 2000 formats your text for you automatically.

Styles are not the same as macros. A *style* defines the formatting of text but not the text itself. A *macro* can type text for you automatically but does nothing to define the formatting of that text. For more information about macros, see Chapter 2.

Using a style

If you create a Word document by choosing the File⇔New (or Ctrl+N) command, guess what? Word creates a blank document that includes several built-in styles, as shown in Figure 3-1.

To use a style, follow these steps:

1. **Move the cursor (or click the mouse pointer) in the paragraph or word that you want to format using a style.**

2. **Click on the Style list box and choose a style you want to use.**

   Word automatically formats your text according to your chosen style.

If you have hidden the Formatting toolbar, you won't be able to see the Style list box. To display a hidden Formatting toolbar, choose View⇔Toolbars⇔ Formatting to put a check mark in front of the Formatting toolbar.

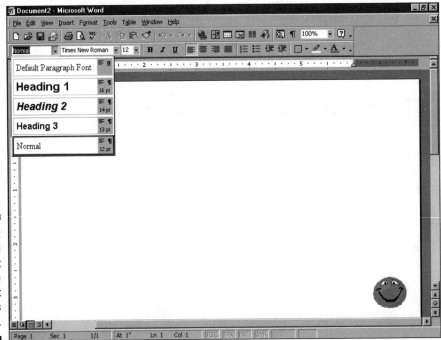

Figure 3-1:
A typical document showing the different styles available.

If you choose a style and then suddenly realize that it looks ugly, you can remove the style by pressing Ctrl+Z.

Creating a style

If you want to format text in a specific way, you need to create a new style. When you create a style, you must define the following items:

- The style name
- Whether the style is based on an existing style
- Whether the style affects an entire paragraph or just a single word
- The style of the paragraph that follows the one you're formatting

Although you can name your styles anything you want (including four-letter words), using memorable style names (such as Hanging Indent, Dialogue, or Eye-Catching Headline) is a good idea.

To save time when you create new styles, you can use an existing style as a starting point. That way, you don't have to waste time creating styles from scratch when you only need to slightly modify an existing style. This technique is similar to copying someone else's term paper and then rewriting it a little, instead of writing your own term paper from scratch.

When you create a style, you must decide whether you want to create a character style or a paragraph style. A *character style* changes the formatting for one or more characters. A *paragraph style* changes the format for an entire paragraph. Most of the time, styles affect the format for an entire paragraph because changing the format of a single character (or group of characters) by yourself is usually easy to do without creating a style.

After you create a style, you can define the style for the paragraph that appears after the one you're formatting. That way, if two styles normally appear one after the other, Word can choose the second style for you automatically.

To create your own style, follow these steps:

1. **Choose Format➪Style.**

   The Style dialog box appears, as shown in Figure 3-2.

Character styles versus paragraph styles

A character style can format a single character, word, or group of words; a paragraph style can format an entire paragraph. What happens, however, if you use a character style to format words and then later use a paragraph style to format the entire paragraph?

Fortunately, Microsoft Word 2000 isn't as dim-witted as you may expect. Any characters formatted by using a character style retain their formatting. The paragraph style simply formats all text within a paragraph, except for text formatted by character styles. Isn't that comforting?

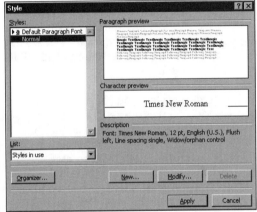

Figure 3-2:
The Style dialog box.

2. Click on New.

The New Style dialog box appears, as shown in Figure 3-3.

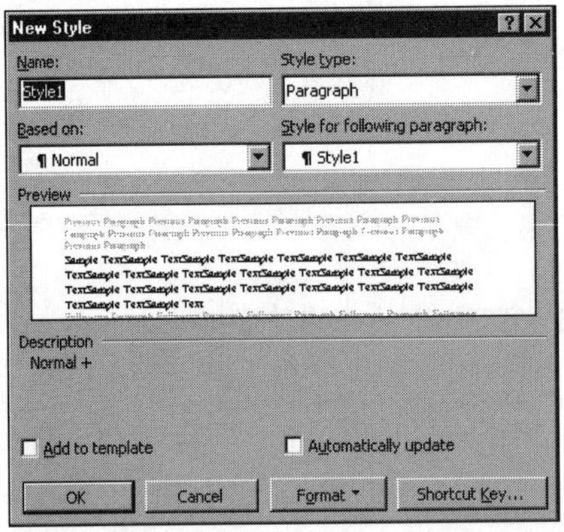

Figure 3-3:
The New Style dialog box.

3. **Type a name for your style in the <u>N</u>ame box.**

4. **Click on the arrow in the Style <u>t</u>ype list box and then choose one of the following:**

   - Paragraph (format an entire paragraph)

   - Character (format a single word)

5. **Click on the arrow in the <u>B</u>ased on list box and then choose an existing style, if you want to create your new style based on another style.**

6. **Click on the arrow in the <u>S</u>tyle for following paragraph list box and then choose a style that you want Word to use in the paragraph immediately following your new style.**

   Congratulations! You have created your very own style. Of course, your style right now won't do anything, so you need to define how you want your style to format text.

7. **Click on OK to save your style, or skip ahead to Step 3 in "Modifying a style" in the following section to define how your style formats your text.**

Modifying a style

After you create a style, you can always modify it later. The first time that you create a style, however, you need to modify that style so that it actually does something useful. A style can define the following items:

- ✔ **Border:** Any borders around text

- ✔ **Font:** The font, type size, color, and other text effects, such as shadows, superscript, or strikethrough of text

- ✔ **Frame:** A frame around your chosen text

- ✔ **Language:** The text to be treated for grammar and spell checking in different languages

- ✔ **Numbering:** Numbering or bulleting for text

- ✔ **Paragraph:** The alignment, indentation, and spacing of text

- ✔ **Tabs:** The alignment and tab locations of text

Be careful when you modify a style. If you've used a specific style to format text and then later change that style, guess what? Microsoft Word 2000 automatically reformats all your text according to the newly modified style. Modify a style only if you're absolutely sure that you want all the text formatted with that style to change as well. Otherwise, create a new style.

To modify a style, follow these steps:

1. **Choose Format⇨Style.**

   The Style dialog box appears (refer to Figure 3-2).

2. **Click on the style name that you want to modify.**

3. **Click on Modify.**

   The Modify Style dialog box appears (refer to Figure 3-3).

4. **Click on Format and then click on Font.**

   The Font dialog box appears, as shown in Figure 3-4.

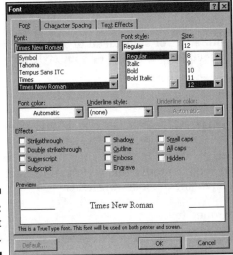

Figure 3-4:
The Font
dialog box.

5. **Choose the font, font style, size, color, and effects that you want to use and then click on OK.**

6. **Click on Format and then click on Paragraph.**

   The Paragraph dialog box appears, as shown in Figure 3-5.

7. **Choose the desired Left or Right indentation and Line spacing and then click on OK.**

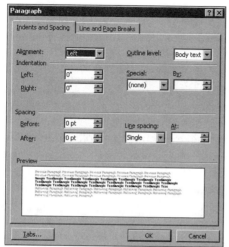

Figure 3-5:
The
Paragraph
dialog box.

8. **Click on Format and then click on Tabs.**

   The Tabs dialog box appears, as shown in Figure 3-6.

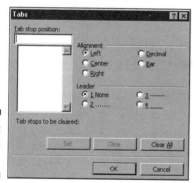

Figure 3-6:
The Tabs
dialog box.

9. **Choose a Tab stop position, Alignment, and Leader and then click on OK.**

10. **Click on Format in the New Style dialog box; choose Border, Language, Frame, or Numbering; and then define any options that you want to save in your style.**

11. **Click on Close.**

Choosing a style with a keystroke

Normally you can choose a style to format your text by choosing that style from the Style list box. But if you want a faster way to choose a style, you can assign a specific keystroke to a style. That way you can just move the cursor or mouse pointer in the text you want to format, press a special keystroke combination (such as Alt+F11), and apply your style to the text right away.

To choose a style using a keystroke combination, follow these steps:

1. **Choose Format⇨Style.**

   The Style dialog box appears (refer to Figure 3-2).

2. **Click on the style name that you want to assign to a keystroke combination.**

3. **Click on Modify.**

   A Modify Style dialog box appears (refer to Figure 3-3).

4. **Click on Shortcut Key.**

   The Customize Keyboard dialog box appears, as shown in Figure 3-7.

5. **Click on the Press new shortcut key box and then press the keystroke combination that you want to assign to your style, such as Ctrl+F9 or something equally unusual.**

6. **Click on Assign and then click on Close.**

7. **Click on OK.**

   The Style dialog box appears again.

8. **Click on Close.**

   Now the next time you want to choose the style you chose in Step 2, just press the keystroke combination you chose in Step 5.

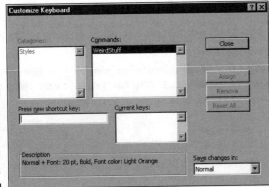

Figure 3-7:
The
Customize
Keyboard
dialog box.

Deleting a style

You may occasionally create a style and then later decide that you don't need it after all. To wipe a style off the face of the earth, follow these steps:

1. **Choose Format⇨Style.**

   The Style dialog box appears (refer to Figure 3-2).

2. **Click on the style that you want to delete, destroy, obliterate, or otherwise eliminate.**

3. **Click on Delete.**

   A dialog box appears and asks whether you're sure that you want to delete your chosen style.

4. **Click on Yes.**

   Kiss your style good-bye.

5. **Click on Close.**

The moment that you delete a style, any text formatted in that style reverts to the Normal style.

If you delete a style by mistake, you can recover it by pressing Ctrl+Z right away.

Creating Document Templates

A document template acts like a cookie cutter for text. Just modify a document once and save all the formatting in the document as a template. Then, the next time you want a document with all the fancy formatting, spacing, and indentations already designed for you, just create a new document based on your template.

For example, suppose that you need to create a newsletter that has a bold-face headline in large print and two columns that divide the page in half. Setting up the column spacing, width, and headline formatting every time that you want to create another newsletter can be a tiresome task, which makes this the perfect job to give to someone who makes less money per hour than you do.

But in case you can't afford to delegate work to someone else, you can still save time by creating your newsletter once and then saving its various formatting in a separate file called a template. The next time you create a newsletter, you can create a new document based on your newsletter template. Then you can just focus on typing the text, because the template sets up all the formatting for you.

Document templates end with the .DOT file extension. Documents end with the .DOC file extension.

Document templates can contain the following items:

✔ Text, such as your company name, that must appear in every document based on your template

✔ Graphics, such as a company logo, that must appear in every document based on your template

✔ Any formatting or ruler settings

✔ Any styles that you may create

✔ Any macros that you may create

Using a template

To show you the power of templates, Microsoft Word 2000 contains several templates that some poor Microsoft employee had to create for you. To give you twice as many ways to accomplish the same task and to provide maximum possibility for confusion, Microsoft provides two ways to view and use a Microsoft Word 2000 template:

✔ From within a new document
✔ From the Windows desktop

If you don't choose a template, Microsoft Word 2000 assumes that you just want to use a blank template called Normal.dot.

Choosing a template from within a document

If you've already created and opened a document, you can tell Microsoft Word 2000, "Hey, I want my document to use a different template instead."

To choose a template for your Word document, follow these steps:

1. **Choose Format⇨Style Gallery.**

   The Style Gallery dialog box appears.

2. **Click on a template that you want to view, such as Elegant Fax or Professional Report.**

   You may need to insert your Microsoft Office 2000 CD in your computer to install some of the available templates.

3. **Click on the <u>E</u>xample or <u>S</u>tyle samples option button in the Preview group.**

   Click on the Example option button, shown in Figure 3-8, to see how attractive your document can look if you know what your doing. Click on the Style Samples option button to see the type of formatting that the template can create, as shown in Figure 3-9. (Not all templates can show examples or style samples.)

4. **Click on OK when you find a template that you want to use.**

   Your chosen template is ready to use. Just choose a style from the Style list box on the Formatting toolbar to start using a style stored in your template.

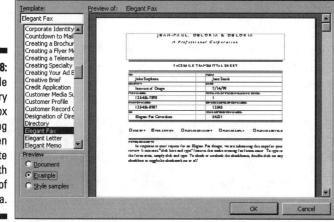

Figure 3-8:
The Style
Gallery
dialog box
showing
your chosen
template
filled with
examples of
data.

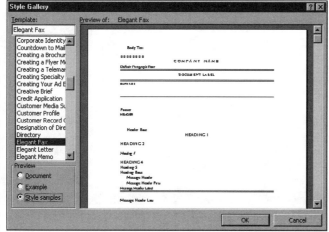

Figure 3-9:
The Style
Gallery
dialog box
showing
your chosen
template
with the dif-
ferent styles
used.

Choosing a template from the Windows desktop

If you know that you want to use a template to create a new Microsoft Word 2000 document, choosing a template directly from the Windows desktop is easier than opening a blank document and then changing the template.

To view and choose a template from the Windows desktop, follow these steps:

1. **Click on the Start button on the Windows taskbar and then click on New Office Document.**

   The New Office Document dialog box appears.

2. **Click on a tab (such as Publications or Reports).**

3. **Click on a template icon.**

   Microsoft Word 2000 displays a preview of your chosen template, as shown in Figure 3-10.

4. **Click on OK to start using your chosen template.**

   Microsoft Word 2000 displays a new document based on your chosen template.

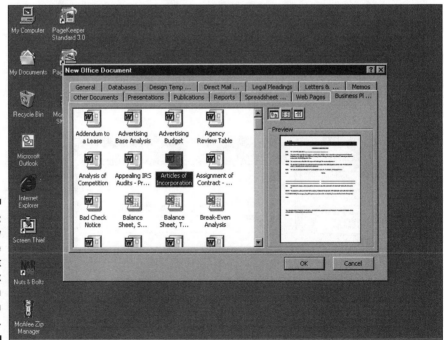

Figure 3-10: The New Office Document dialog box showing a preview of a template.

The preceding steps can be used to create Excel, Access, and PowerPoint files based on templates as well.

Creating a template by modifying an existing one

If someone creates a template for you or if you don't really like the templates that come with Microsoft Word 2000, feel free to change them. Modifying an existing template is much easier than creating a new template because copying someone else's work is always easier than doing the work yourself.

To modify an existing template, follow these steps:

1. **Choose File⇨Open.**

   The Open dialog box appears.

2. **Click on the arrow in the Files of type list box and then choose Document Templates, as shown in Figure 3-11.**

Figure 3-11: The Open dialog box displaying document templates.

3. **Click on the template that you want to modify and then click on Open.**

   You may have to search in different folders for the template files. Word displays your chosen document template.

4. **Choose Format⇨Style and click on the style that you want to modify and then change any settings (such as paragraph indentation, font, or font size) that follow the steps outlined in the previous section, "Modifying a style."**

5. **Choose File⇨Save to save your changes in the document template.**

If you choose File⇨Save As in Step 5, you can create a new template, based on the original one, without changing the original template.

Deleting a template

If you find that you never use a particular document template, you can wipe it out and save a minuscule amount of hard disk space in the process.

To delete a template, load Microsoft Word 2000 and then follow these steps:

1. **Choose File⇨Open.**

   The Open dialog box appears (refer to Figure 3-11).

2. **Click on the Files of type list box and choose Document Templates.**

3. **Click on the template that you want to delete and click on the right mouse button.**

   A pop-up menu appears. You may have to search in different folders for the templates.

4. **Choose Delete.**

   A Confirm File Delete dialog box appears.

5. **Click on Yes.**

6. **Click on Cancel to remove the Open dialog box.**

You can also use the preceding steps to delete Microsoft Word 2000 documents (or any other type of file) from within the Open dialog box as well.

Changing the Default Folder for Your Templates

You can create templates and store them in any folder on your hard disk. However, whenever you tell Microsoft Office 2000 to look for a template, it always looks for templates in a special default folder. Because you may have created and stored templates in a different folder, you may want to redefine the default folder where Office 2000 looks for templates.

In Microsoft Office 2000 to find which folder to look for templates in first, follow these steps:

1. **Choose Tools⇨Options.**

   The Options dialog box appears, as shown in Figure 3-12.

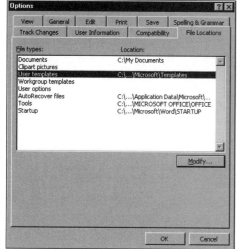

Figure 3-12: The Options dialog box where you can define the location of your templates.

2. **Click on the File Locations tab and then click on User Templates.**

3. **Click on Modify.**

   The Modify Location dialog box appears.

4. **Click on the folder you want to use as your default template folder and then click on OK.**

5. **Click on OK in the Options dialog box.**

If you change the folder where you store your Word 2000 document templates, you also change the folder where Microsoft Office 2000 looks for templates for other Office 2000 templates (such as Excel or Access) as well.

Chapter 4

Creating an Index and a Table of Contents

In This Chapter

▶ Organizing multiple documents with a master document

▶ Helping readers find topics by creating a table of contents

▶ Organizing your ideas in an index

*I*f you need to write long papers or books, you may get stuck creating an index and table of contents. You can create an index and a table of contents yourself, or you can take the easy way out and let Microsoft Word 2000 automatically create the table of contents and index as you write.

If you prefer to let Word 2000 do the difficult work for you, keep reading. If you prefer to do everything yourself, why did you bother getting a computer?

Working with Master Documents

Most people write with Microsoft Word 2000 in one of two ways:

✔ Cram everything into a single document

✔ Store chapters or logical sections in separate documents

If you cram everything into a single huge document consisting of several hundred pages, editing that document is a real nuisance. If you break your document into separate files, keeping track of page numbers to create an index or a table of contents is troublesome because the page numbers may change as you edit your separate documents. So if you plan on writing a large document that needs an index and a table of contents, Word 2000 offers the mysterious master document.

A *master document* is an outline where every heading links to another file, called a *subdocument,* as shown in Figure 4-1.

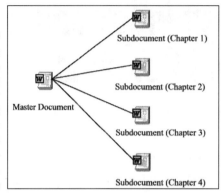

Figure 4-1: The headings in a master document link to separate subdocuments.

Headings represent a separate chunk of your total document. For example, each heading can represent a chapter title.

By dividing a master document into headings, you can organize a large chunk of text (such as a novel or a report) into separate but linked files. This organization feature allows Microsoft Word 2000 to take care of page numbering automatically and to create an accurate index and table of contents while storing your text in separate files for easy editing and viewing.

When working with master documents, choose View⇨Document Map to display your master document's headings in a panel (the document map) that appears on the left side of the screen, as shown in Figure 4-2. Now you can click on a heading in the document map to jump to that heading in your master document.

Creating a master document from scratch

The best time to create a master document is when you want to write a large document (such as a novel or a business report) and you want to store parts of your document (such as chapters) in separate files.

To create a master document, follow these steps:

1. **Choose View⇨Outline.**

   The Outline toolbar appears, as shown in Figure 4-3.

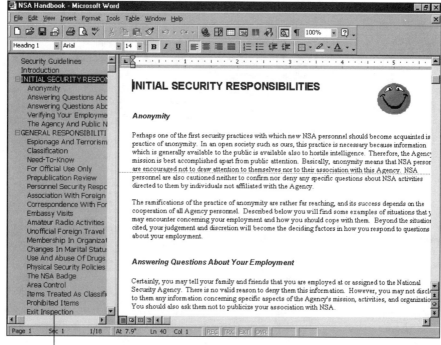

Figure 4-2:
The
document
map
helps you
navigate
through
your master
document.

Document map

2. **Type one or more headings using the Heading 1 style for each heading that represents a separate part of your complete document, such as a chapter.**

   Choose the Heading 1 style from the Style list box on the Formatting toolbar.

3. **Move the cursor to the heading that represents the subdocument you want to create.**

4. **Click on the Create Subdocument icon on the toolbar.**

   Microsoft Word 2000 draws a gray box around your heading and a new subdocument icon appears in your document, as shown in Figure 4-4.

5. **Double-click on the subdocument icon that appears in the upper-left corner of the gray box around your chosen heading.**

   Microsoft Word 2000 displays your subdocument in a window all by itself.

6. **Type any text that you want to store in your subdocument.**

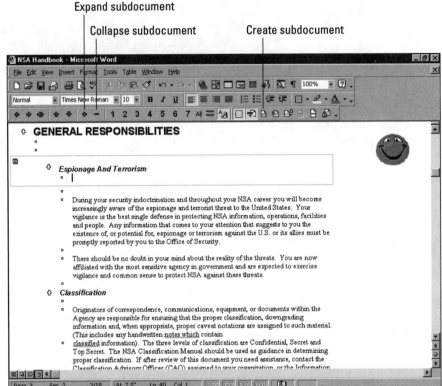

Expand subdocument

Collapse subdocument

Create subdocument

Figure 4-3:
The Outline toolbar automatically appears on your screen when you use Outline View.

7. **Choose File⇨Close when you finish typing your text.**

   Microsoft Word 2000 displays a dialog box, asking you whether you want to save your document.

8. **Click on Yes.**

   A Save As dialog box appears, using the heading of your subdocument as the file name.

9. **Type a name for your subdocument in the File name box (if you don't want to use the heading title as your file name) and then click on Save.**

   Microsoft Word 2000 displays your subdocument's text in the master document.

10. **Repeat Steps 3 through 9 for every heading that you want to convert into a subdocument.**

The new Create subdocument icon

The Outline toolbar Create
subdocument icon

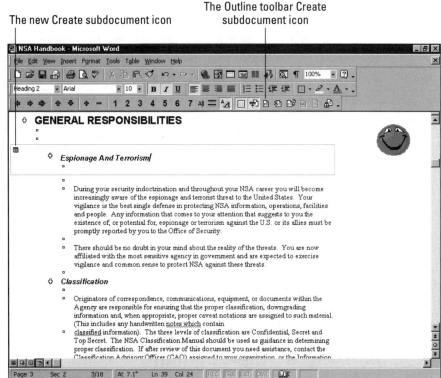

Figure 4-4:
Creating a
subdocu-
ment from a
heading.

Creating a master document from an existing document

Rather than create a master document from scratch, you can also convert an existing document into a master document. Converting a document can be handy if you've already created a huge document and then suddenly decide that it's getting too bulky to edit and read easily.

To convert an existing document into a master document, follow these steps:

1. **Open the document that you want to convert into a master document.**

2. **Click on a heading in your document and format it by using the Heading 1, Heading 2, Heading 3, or Heading 4 style.**

3. **Choose View⇨Outline.**

4. **Highlight the heading and the text that you want to convert into a subdocument.**

5. **Click on the Create Subdocument icon on the Outline toolbar.**

   Microsoft Word 2000 draws a gray box around your heading and displays a subdocument icon (refer to Figure 4-4).

6. **Double-click on the subdocument icon that appears in the upper-left corner of the gray box around your chosen heading.**

   Microsoft Word 2000 displays in a separate window the text and the heading that you chose in Step 4.

7. **Choose File⇨Save.**

   A Save dialog box appears, using the heading for the file name of your subdocument.

8. **Type a name for your subdocument in the File name box (if you don't want to use the heading title as your file name) and then click on Save.**

9. **Choose File⇨Close.**

   Microsoft Word 2000 displays your master document with a gray box around your newly created subdocument.

Editing a subdocument

After you create a master document and one or more subdocuments, you may want to edit the text stored in a subdocument. You can edit a subdocument in three ways:

✔ Open the subdocument by itself in a separate window.

✔ Open the master document and then open the subdocument in a separate window.

✔ Open the master document and then edit the subdocument within the master document.

No matter which method you choose, any changes that you make to the subdocument appear automatically in the master document.

Editing a subdocument by itself

If you just want to edit the text of a subdocument but don't necessarily care to see the rest of your master document, then save yourself some time and edit the subdocument by itself.

To edit a subdocument by itself, follow these steps:

1. **Choose File⇨Open.**

   An Open dialog box appears.

2. **Click on the subdocument that you want to edit and then click on Open.**

3. **Edit your subdocument.**

4. **Choose File⇨Save.**

5. **Choose File⇨Close.**

Editing a subdocument within a master document

Sometimes you may want to view your subdocument within the context of your master document. That way, you can see how the text in your subdocument fits in with the organization of the rest of your master document.

To edit a subdocument from within a master document, follow these steps:

1. **Choose File⇨Open.**

   An Open dialog box appears.

2. **Click on the master document containing the subdocument that you want to edit and then click on Open.**

   Microsoft Word 2000 displays your subdocument text as a hyperlink, showing the file name and folder where the subdocument is stored, as shown in Figure 4-5.

3. **Click on the hyperlink representing the subdocument that you want to edit.**

   Microsoft Word 2000 displays your subdocument text.

4. **Edit the subdocument text that you want to change.**

5. **Choose File⇨Save.**

6. **Choose File⇨Close.**

Viewing and editing all your subdocument text at once

When you have multiple subdocuments crammed within a master document, you can view them all as one continuous string of text, which can be as long as several hundred pages.

To view (and edit) all your subdocuments within a master document, follow these steps:

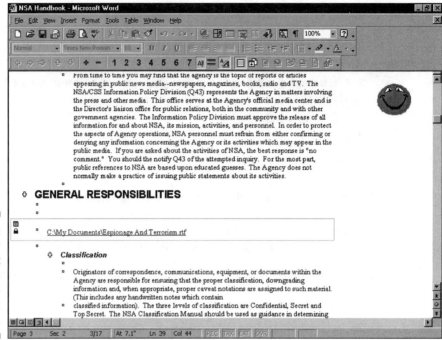

From time to time you may find that the agency is the topic of reports or articles appearing in public news media--newspapers, magazines, books, radio and TV. The NSA/CSS Information Policy Division (Q43) represents the Agency in matters involving the press and other media. This office serves at the Agency's official media center and is the Director's liaison office for public relations, both in the community and with other government agencies. The Information Policy Division must approve the release of all information for and about NSA, its mission, activities, and personnel. In order to protect the aspects of Agency operations, NSA personnel must refrain from either confirming or denying any information concerning the Agency or its activities which may appear in the public media. If you are asked about the activities of NSA, the best response is "no comment." You should the notify Q43 of the attempted inquiry. For the most part, public references to NSA are based upon educated guesses. The Agency does not normally make a practice of issuing public statements about its activities.

GENERAL RESPONSIBILITIES

C:\My Documents\Espionage And Terrorism.rtf

Classification

Originators of correspondence, communications, equipment, or documents within the Agency are responsible for ensuring that the proper classification, downgrading information and, when appropriate, proper caveat notations are assigned to such material. (This includes any handwritten notes which contain classified information). The three levels of classification are Confidential, Secret and Top Secret. The NSA Classification Manual should be used as guidance in determining

Figure 4-5:
A master document displaying a subdocument as a hyperlink.

1. **Choose File⇨Open.**

   An Open dialog box appears.

2. **Click on the master document containing the subdocument that you want to edit and then click on Open.**

3. **Click on the Expand Subdocuments icon in the Outline toolbar.**

   Microsoft Word 2000 displays all subdocuments as actual text, surrounded by a gray box.

4. **Edit any of your subdocument text.**

5. **Choose File⇨Save.**

Making Your Very Own Index

An *index* organizes your document's main ideas by page number. That way, people can quickly find what they're looking for without having to read your entire document. Because many people don't like reading anyway, indexes can be a great way to encourage people to at least browse through your text (and maybe even increase the national literacy rate in the process).

To create an index, you must decide

- ✔ The words or topics you want to include in your index
- ✔ The page numbers on which each word or topic appears
- ✔ Which visually pleasing format to use to display your index

Indexing a book or a document is an art in itself. Although Microsoft Word 2000 can make the task of indexing easier, it can't help you decide which words, topics, or synonyms to add to your index.

Selecting words and individual page numbers

Most indexes list topics and individual page numbers, such as:

Presidential affairs, 70

In this example, "Presidential affairs" is the index entry and "70" is the page number on which it appears. To mark words for an index, follow these steps:

1. **Highlight the word or words that you want to appear in your index.**

2. **Press Alt+Shift+X.**

   A Mark Index Entry dialog box appears, as shown in Figure 4-6. Your highlighted word (or words) appears in the Main entry box.

3. **Edit the word or words in the Main entry box so that they look the way you want them in your index.**

4. **In the Subentry box, type any index subentries that you want to include.**

   An example of a subentry, in which "projects" is the entry and "avoiding them," "examples of," and "stopping" are subentries, follows:

   projects, 49

   avoiding them, 78, 129

   examples of, 52

   stopping, 2

5. **Click on one of the following option buttons:**

   - **Cross-reference:** Directs readers to a related index entry
   - **Current Page:** Lists the current page for your index entry

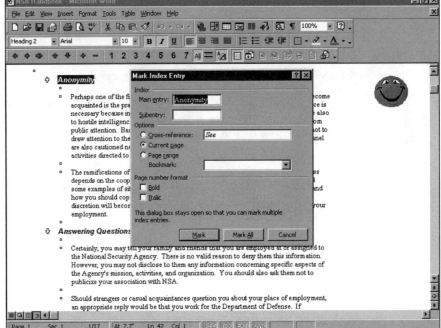

Figure 4-6:
The Mark
Index Entry
dialog box
for choosing
a word to
appear in an
index.

6. **Click on a check box to choose a page number format, such as Bold or Italic.**

7. **Click on Mark.**

   Microsoft Word 2000 marks your selected word or words by inserting an index entry next to them, as shown in Figure 4-7.

8. **Repeat Steps 1 through 7 until you've marked all the words that you want to appear in your index.**

9. **Click on Close.**

Marking words and page ranges for your index

Most of the time, the words that you select for your index appear only on a single page. But sometimes an index topic may span two or more pages, as shown in this example:

CIA, selling Stinger missiles illegally, 58–63

Marked index entries

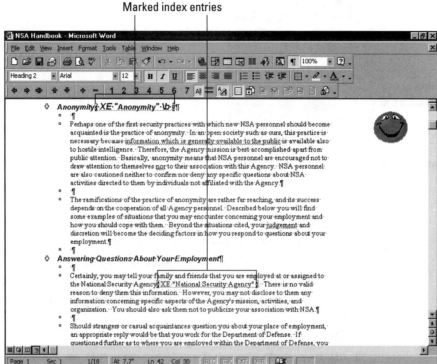

Figure 4-7:
What a
marked
index entry
looks like
within a
document.

In this example, "CIA, selling Stinger missiles illegally" is the index entry, and "58–63" represents the page range in which users can find the index entry.

When you want to index a page range, you must follow slightly different steps to include your chosen index topic and its page range in your index.

To mark words and page range for an index, follow these steps:

1. **Highlight the text (spanning one or more pages) that you want to include in your index.**

2. **Choose Insert⇨Bookmark.**

   A Bookmark dialog box appears, as shown in Figure 4-8.

3. **Type a name for your bookmark in the Bookmark name box.**

   Your bookmark name must be a single word, so be creative and make it descriptive, too.

4. **Click on Add.**

5. **Highlight the word or words that you want to appear in your index.**

Figure 4-8:
The
Bookmark
dialog box.

6. **Press Alt+Shift+X.**

   A Mark Index Entry dialog box appears (refer to Figure 4-6). Your high-lighted word or words appear in the Main entry box.

7. **Edit the word or words in the Main entry box so that they appear the way you want them in your index.**

8. **In the Subentry box, type any index subentries that you want to include.**

9. **Click on the Page range option button.**

10. **Click on the Bookmark list box and then click on the bookmark name that you created in Step 3.**

11. **Click on Mark.**

    Microsoft Word 2000 marks your selected word or words by inserting an index entry next to them.

12. **Repeat Steps 1 through 11 until you've marked all the words that you want to appear in your index.**

13. **Click on Close.**

Displaying your index in print

Every time you mark a word or words to appear in your index, Microsoft Word 2000 stores the words in its tiny electronic brain. When you finish choosing all your index entries, you're ready to print the index so that you can take a look at it.

Of course, Microsoft Word 2000 wouldn't seem like a real program if it didn't offer you a billion different options that most people never use. When you create an index, Word 2000 bombards you with multiple ways to make your index look nice.

Before you can create an index, you have to mark at least one word that you want to include in your index.

This list shows some of the available options that affect the look of your index:

- **Alignment of page numbers:** Determines how page numbers appear next to an index entry — such as separated by a comma like "Dog food, 4" or aligned on the far right side of the page

- **Index format:** Determines the overall look of your index, such as the fonts used for the letter headings

- **Number of columns used:** Determines the number of columns used to display your index

To choose the appearance of an index, follow these steps:

1. **Move the cursor to the spot where you want your index to appear (such as the end of your document).**

2. **Choose Insert➪Index and Tables.**

   An Index and Tables dialog box appears, as shown in Figure 4-9. (If you have any collapsed subdocuments, a dialog box appears asking if you want to expand them. Click on Yes to do so.)

3. **Click on the Index tab.**

4. **In the Formats list box, click on the format that you want (Modern or Bulleted, for example).**

   The Print Preview box shows you what your index will look like.

5. **Click on either the Indented or Run-in option button in the Type group.**

   You can see the differences between these two options in the Print Preview box.

Figure 4-9:
The Index and Tables dialog box.

6. **If you want to right-align your index page numbers, click on the <u>R</u>ight align page numbers check box.**

   If you click on the Run-in option button, you won't be able to choose the Right align page numbers check box.

7. **Click on the C<u>o</u>lumns list box and choose the number of columns that you want.**

8. **Click on the Ta<u>b</u> leader box and choose a tab leader.**

   Note: The Tab leader box is available only if you clicked on the Right align page numbers check box in Step 6.

9. **Click on OK.**

   Microsoft Word 2000 cheerfully displays your index on the screen for you to admire.

You can create an index only in the same document that contains the word or words that you select to appear in your index. After Microsoft Word 2000 creates your index and you're absolutely sure that none of the index entries will change, you can cut the index and paste it into a new document.

Creating an index (almost) automatically

Because computers are supposed to make our lives easier, you may be happy to know that Microsoft Word 2000 can create an index almost automatically, with just a little help from you. But before Microsoft Word 2000 can perform its automatic indexing magic for you, you must first create a separate document that contains two lists of words.

One list of words must contain the entries that you want to appear in your index. The second list of words must contain the actual words (or phrases) stored in your Microsoft Word 2000 document that you want to mark as an index entry.

You may have these two lists, for example:

CIA	Central Intelligence Agency
DIA	Defense Intelligence Agency
EIEIO	Farmer's Intelligence Agency
annoying people	Telemarketers
Copycat	A well-known rival computer-book publisher

Because the words that you type in both lists are case sensitive, if Microsoft Word 2000 finds the string typed as "Annoying people," then Word 2000 won't store the words in the index. Microsoft Word 2000 stores that string in your index only if the words are typed exactly as "annoying people" (in lowercase letters).

Using the preceding list as a guideline, Microsoft Word 2000 searches through your document for all occurrences of the words that appear in the list on the left. Whenever Microsoft Word 2000 finds the phrase "annoying people," for example, it looks in the list on the right to determine how to store this entry in your index.

Assuming that CIA appears on pages 59–65, DIA appears on page 90, EIEIO appears on page 493, "annoying people" appears on pages 78 and 90, and "Copycat" appears on page 746, Microsoft Word 2000 creates the following index for you:

> Central Intelligence Agency, 59–65
>
> Defense Intelligence Agency, 90
>
> Farmer's Intelligence Agency, 493
>
> Telemarketers, 78, 90
>
> A well-known rival computer-book publisher, 746

To create a list of words so that Microsoft Word 2000 knows what to look for in your document and how to store those words in your index, follow these steps:

1. **Choose File⇨New, or press Ctrl+N.**

   A new blank document appears.

2. **Choose Table⇨Insert⇨Table.**

   An Insert Table dialog box appears. Make sure that the dialog box displays the settings for creating a table composed of two (2) columns. (The number of rows should equal the number of entries that you want to type.)

3. **Click on OK.**

   Microsoft Word 2000 creates a table two columns wide.

4. **In the left column, type the word or words (CIA, for example) that you want Microsoft Word 2000 to search for in your document.**

5. **In the right column in the same row, type the way you want this word or words to appear in your index (Central Intelligence Agency, for example).**

6. **Repeat Steps 4 and 5 until you create a list that contains all the words that you want Microsoft Word 2000 to search for and store in your index.**

   You may need to add rows as necessary by choosing Table⇨Insert⇨Rows Above (or Below).

7. **Choose File⇨Save.**

   A Save As dialog box appears.

8. **Type a name for your document in the File name box and then click on Save.**

9. **Switch to the document that contains the words that you want to index.**

10. **Choose Insert⇨Index and Tables.**

    An Index and Tables dialog box appears (refer to Figure 4-9).

11. **Click on the Index tab.**

12. **Click on AutoMark.**

    An Open Index AutoMark File dialog box appears.

13. **Click on the Microsoft Word 2000 document that contains your two lists of words that you created in Steps 1 through 6, and then click on Open.**

    Microsoft Word 2000 silently marks all your selected words in your document.

14. **Move the cursor to the spot where you want the index to appear.**

15. **Choose Insert⇨Index and Tables.**

    The Index and Tables dialog box appears (refer to Figure 4-9).

16. **Make any changes to the format of your index and then click on OK when you're done.**

    Microsoft Word 2000 magically displays your automatically created index.

Updating your index

Ideally, you should create your index last, after you have already written your entire text. But because human beings don't always like being told what they can do and when they can do it, Microsoft Word 2000 can accommodate those people who insist on changing their text after they've already created an index. Whenever you create an index, you can always update your index if you need to add another word or two to it.

You only need to update your index if you want to add (or delete) words from your index. Microsoft Word 2000 automatically updates your index any time page numbers change.

To update an index, follow these steps:

1. **Highlight the word or words that you want to add to your index.**

2. **Press Alt+Shift+X.**

   A Mark Index Entry dialog box appears (refer to Figure 4-6).

3. **Click on Mark.**

4. **Repeat Steps 1 through 3 for every word that you want to add to your index.**

5. **Click on Close.**

6. **Choose Insert⊅Index and Tables.**

   The Index and Tables dialog box appears (refer to Figure 4-9).

7. **Click on the Index tab.**

8. **Click on OK.**

   A dialog box appears and asks whether you want to replace your selected index.

9. **Click on Yes.**

   Microsoft Word 2000 updates your index. Aren't computers wonderful?

Microsoft Word 2000 can create an index based on words stored in a single document. If you want to create an index that is based on words stored in separate documents, you must create a master document. To learn more about master documents, look in the "Working with Master Documents" section earlier in this chapter.

Creating a Table of Contents

An index enables readers to quickly find separate topics that may be scattered throughout a large document, such as a book or a magazine. A *table of contents,* however, enables your readers to see which topics your book or document discusses. Like an index, a table of contents also lists page numbers so that readers can quickly find what they're looking for without having to read the entire manuscript.

Before you can create a table of contents, you must first create headings within your document (such as the heading for this section, "Creating a Table of Contents") and format them by using Microsoft Word 2000's style feature.

Using Microsoft Word 2000's built-in styles to format headings

To quickly format headings to create a table of contents, use the built-in styles Heading 1, Heading 2, and Heading 3, as shown in Figure 4-10.

To create a table of contents, follow these steps:

1. **Format all the document headings that you want to include in your table of contents by using Heading 1, Heading 2, or Heading 3.**

2. **Move your cursor to the location where you want the table of contents to appear, such as at the beginning of your document.**

3. **Choose Insert⇔Index and Tables.**

4. **Click on the Table of Contents tab, as shown in Figure 4-11.**

5. **If you want to show page numbers, click on the Show page numbers check box.**

   Because you're working with the table of contents, this option really shouldn't be available, but Microsoft Word 2000 wants to give you a choice anyway. After all, what good is a table of contents without page numbers?

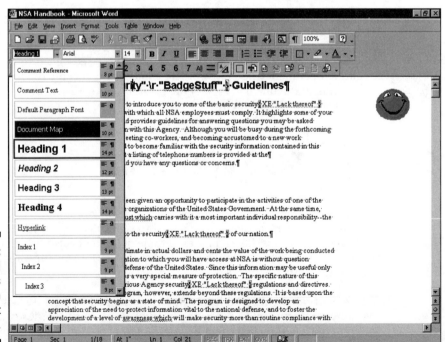

Figure 4-10: Heading styles appear in the Style list box.

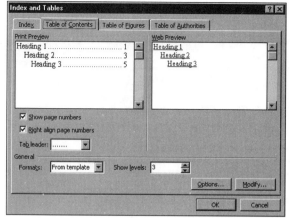

Figure 4-11:
The Table of
Contents
dialog box.

6. **Click on the <u>R</u>ight align page numbers check box if you want your index page numbers to be right-aligned on the page.**

7. **In the Forma<u>t</u>s list box in the General group, click on the format that you want, such as Modern or Fancy.**

   The Print Preview box shows you what your table of contents will look like.

8. **Click on the Show <u>l</u>evels list box and then choose how many levels you want to display.**

   Microsoft Word 2000 gives you the option of creating a detailed table of contents or a more general one. For example, you may want to create a detailed table of contents using the Heading 1, Heading 2, and Heading 3 styles. Or you may want a more general table of contents that uses only Heading 1 styles. If you want to include only Heading 1, Heading 2, and Heading 3 styles in your table of contents, choose 3.

9. **Click on the Ta<u>b</u> leader box and then choose a tab leader.**

   A tab leader consists of text or symbols that appear between a table of contents entry and its page number, as in this example:

   Euphemisms for Confusing the Public..............................23

   In this case, the tab leaders are the periods (dots) between the phrase "Euphemisms for Confusing the Public" and the page number 23.

   Note: If you don't choose to right-align page numbers in Step 6, the Tab leader box appears dimmed.

10. **Click on OK.**

    In the blink of an eye (or longer, depending on the speed of your computer), Microsoft Word 2000 creates your table of contents for you, as shown in Figure 4-12.

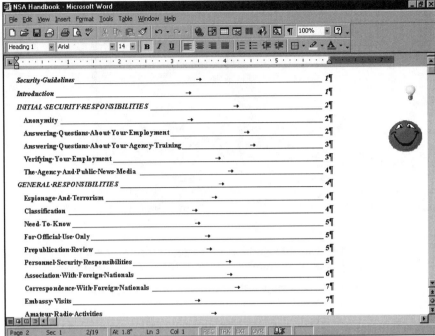

Figure 4-12:
A typical
Table of
Contents
created
automatically.

Using your own styles to format headings

For stubborn nonconformists (if you're a nonconformist, you probably shouldn't even be using any Microsoft programs in the first place), you can also create a table of contents based on your own styles rather than the Heading 1, Heading 2, and Heading 3 styles all the time. (To learn how to create your own styles, see Chapter 3.)

To create a table of contents based on your own styles, follow these steps:

1. **Format all the document headings by using your own particular styles.**

2. **Place the cursor in the document on the spot where you want the table of contents to be inserted (such as at the beginning of your document).**

3. **Choose Insert⇨Index and Tables.**

4. **Click on the Table of Contents tab to display the tab (refer to Figure 4-11).**

5. **If you want to show page numbers, click on the Show page numbers check box.**

6. **Click on the Right align page numbers check box if you want to right-align the page numbers in your table of contents.**

7. **Click on the Show levels list box and choose how many levels you want to display.**

8. **In the Formats list box, click on the format that you want, such as Modern or Fancy.**

   The Print Preview box shows what your table of contents will look like.

9. **First click on the Tab leader box and then choose a tab leader.**

   Note: If you don't choose to right-align page numbers, the Tab leader box appears dimmed.

10. **Click on Options.**

    A Table of Contents Options dialog box appears, as shown in Figure 4-13.

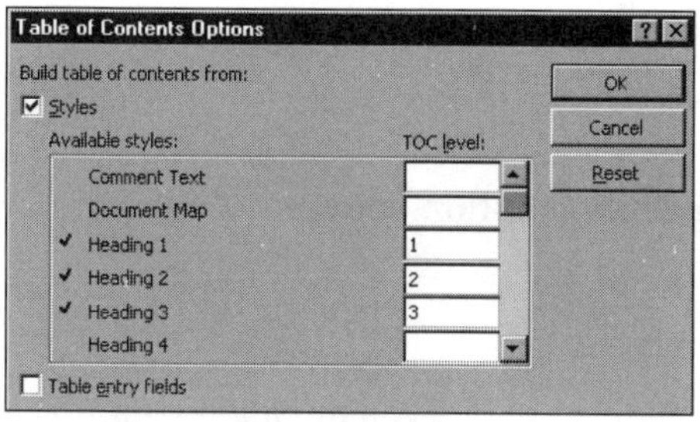

Figure 4-13:
The Table of
Contents
Options
dialog box
for choosing
the heading
levels to
use.

11. **Scroll through the styles displayed in the Available styles box and then type a number in the TOC level box to the right.**

    For example, type **1** to make that particular style (such as Normal) appear as a main heading in your table of contents, or type **2** to make the style appear as a subheading.

12. **Click on OK.**

    The Index and Tables dialog box appears again.

13. **Click on OK.**

    Microsoft Word 2000 creates your table of contents for you.

Updating your table of contents

Whenever you add or delete a heading or text that may change the page numbering, you must update your table of contents. To update a table of contents, follow these steps:

1. **Make any changes to your document or headings.**

2. **Move the cursor to anywhere inside the table of contents that you want to update.**

   Microsoft Word 2000 displays your table of contents in a shade of gray.

3. **Press F9.**

   An Update Table of Contents dialog box appears, as shown in Figure 4-14.

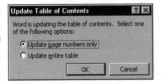

4. **Click on one of the following option buttons:**

   • Update page numbers only

   • Update entire table

   Choose Update page numbers only if you modified your text and thus altered the page numbering. Choose the Update entire table if you added, deleted, or modified any headings that appear in the table of contents.

5. **Click on OK.**

   Microsoft Word 2000 updates your entire table of contents.

Chapter 5

Sharing Your Microsoft Word 2000 Documents

• •

• •

*T*o help you write the best possible text, you may want to share your Microsoft Word 2000 documents with others so that they can edit, revise, and add any comments they feel are necessary.

Although you can print out your entire document so that somebody else can edit it by hand, many members of the computer generation consider printing anything on paper archaic. As a more futuristic alternative, just copy your Word 2000 documents onto a floppy disk or through a network and let somebody mark up your Word 2000 documents electronically.

By sharing Microsoft Word 2000 files on disk, on a network, or even through the Internet, you can view, edit, and comment on text without wasting paper printing it. Once your document looks perfect, then you can print it out for the world to see.

Adding Comments

When you print a letter or report, you can pass your document around to others and let them mark it up with comments about how to improve or alter your text. When you share Microsoft Word 2000 documents on a floppy disk or online over a modem or network, however, you don't have the convenience of scribbling comments in the side margins of a page.

At the simplest level, you could just shove your comments right into the middle of the text — something like "Hey, this last sentence doesn't make any sense!" Not only is interrupting the flow of text intrusive, but you also have to go through the trouble of deleting, one by one, all those comments from the text before you can print out the final, clean version. As a simpler solution, Microsoft Word 2000 offers you the chance to type comments directly into a Word 2000 document. These comments don't appear in the document itself but in a separate window that you can hide, display, or print at any time.

If you convert (export) a Microsoft Word 2000 document to another file format (such as WordPerfect or HTML format), you may lose all the comments that you or another person added.

Making a comment in a document

Rather than display your comments intrusively right in the middle of existing text, Microsoft Word 2000 puts a comment mark in the text so that other people can see it. To view the actual comment, you have to display the comment in a separate window at the bottom of your screen, as shown in Figure 5-1.

Comment mark

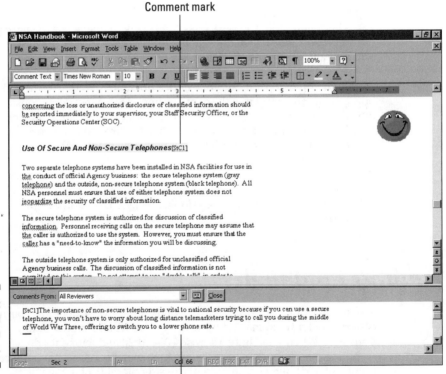

Figure 5-1:
A typical
comment in
a document.

Comment window

Each comment contains two parts:

✔ **The initials of the person who created the annotation.** Microsoft Word 2000 creates the comment abbreviation from the name you gave it when you installed Microsoft Office 2000 on your computer. If you entered your name in Microsoft Office 2000 as Bo the Cat, your initials may be BtC. To change your initials, choose Tools⇨Options, click on the User Information tab, and then type your new initials in the Initials box.

✔ **The sequential number of the annotation.** If you entered your name as Bo the Cat in Microsoft Office 2000, then your first comment appears as [BtC1], your second comment appears as [BtC2], and so on.

To create a comment in a Word document, follow these steps:

1. **Move the cursor where you want to add a comment.**

   If you want other people to see that the comment refers to two or more words, highlight the text that you want to comment on.

2. **Choose Insert⇨Comment.**

   Word highlights the word closest to the cursor (or highlights the text you chose in Step 1), places a comment mark in the document, and displays the comment window at the bottom of your screen (refer to Figure 5-1).

3. **Type your comments in the comment window.**

4. **Repeat Steps 1 through 3 for each comment that you want to add.**

5. **Click on Close when you finish.**

You may want to add comments to your own document to remind yourself to make a change later, or if you'd like to ask someone who will be reading the document a question.

Believe it or not, if you have a microphone attached to your computer, you can add a sound file as part of your comment. All you have to do is create a sound file (for example, your voice saying, "Bob, you're fired!") and then store it as a comment. If someone reads your comment and has a sound card on his or her computer, that person can hear your voice blaring through the speakers. Of course, not many people are likely to add sound to a comment, but it's nice to know that Microsoft is spending its time creating features that bring us closer to science fiction. To add a sound file to a comment, follow these steps:

1. **Record your sound file as a .WAV file.**

2. **Choose Insert⇨Comment.**

3. **Click on the Insert Sound Object icon (it looks like an audiocassette tape) in the comment window.**

   A Sound Object window appears.

4. **Choose Edit⇨Insert File.**

   An Insert File dialog box appears.

5. **Click on the .WAV sound file that you want to insert.**

To avoid seeing comment marks cluttering up your document, choose View⇨Comments. When you hide comment marks, yellow highlighted text is your only clue that comments exist in the document.

Viewing comments in a document

After you or your cowriters have inserted comments throughout a Microsoft Word 2000 document, you may want to read the comments. That way you can follow the advice or (more likely) ignore the comments altogether. To view comments buried within a document, follow these steps:

1. **Choose View⇨Comments.**

   Microsoft Word 2000 displays comment marks in the document and opens the comment window at the bottom of the screen.

2. **Click on the comment mark for the comment you want to view.**

   Microsoft Word 2000 politely displays the comment in the comment window. If you want to view comments from certain reviewers, click on the Comment From list box in the comment window and then choose that reviewer's initials.

3. **Click on Close when you finish viewing the comments.**

If a document has no comments buried in its text, the Comments command in the View menu appears dimmed.

Printing comments with your document

Occasionally you may want to print your document with comments so that you can see all the comments at one time. To print all the comments buried within a document, follow these steps:

1. **Choose Tools⇨Options.**

   The Options dialog box appears.

2. **Click on the Print tab.**

3. **Click on the Comments check box in the Include with document group.**

4. **Click on OK.**

The next time you print your document, Microsoft Word 2000 also prints your comments along with the rest of the text in your document.

Deleting a comment from a document

Comments are meant to be temporary, so you don't have to store a comment in a document after you've responded to it.

To delete a comment, follow these steps:

1. **Choose View⊃Comments.**

Microsoft Word 2000 displays any comment marks littered throughout the document and opens the comment window at the bottom of the screen.

2. **Right-click on the comment mark that contains the comment you want to wipe out.**

A pop-up menu appears.

3. **Click on Delete Comment.**

This action deletes the comment mark along with the comments in the comment window.

4. **Click on Close.**

If you delete a comment by mistake, press Ctrl+Z right away to retrieve it.

You can delete only one comment at a time, so if you have a lot of comments sprinkled throughout a document, you have to wipe each one out individually.

Tracking Changes in Your Text

Comments are great for jotting down ideas or suggestions, but what if you want to get right into the text and modify it yourself? With paper copies of a document, you can mark up the text with a red pen, indicating where to delete, add, or rearrange words or sections. With Microsoft Word 2000, you also can indicate where you deleted, added, or rearranged words in your document.

If you convert (export) a Microsoft Word 2000 document to another file format (WordPerfect, for example), Microsoft Word 2000 can't track any changes in the text.

Tracking your document changes

When you track changes in a document, the original text appears in one color and any modifications (deletions or additions) appear in a different color. That way you can see what someone added and deleted.

To tell Microsoft Word 2000 to track changes, follow these steps:

1. **Choose Tools⇨Track Changes⇨Highlight Changes.**

   The Highlight Changes dialog box appears, as shown in Figure 5-2.

Figure 5-2:
The
Highlight
Changes
dialog box.

2. **Click on the Track changes while editing check box so that a check mark appears.**

3. **Click on Options.**

   The Track Changes dialog box appears, as shown in Figure 5-3, with the following options available for customizing the appearance of your revised text:

   - **Inserted text:** Choose the color and appearance of any new text you add.

   - **Deleted text:** Choose the color and appearance of any text you delete.

   - **Changed formatting:** Choose the color and appearance of any text where you change the formatting.

   - **Changed lines:** Choose the color and appearance of the revision marks that appear in the margins of your document. Revision lines help you easily locate revised text.

4. **Customize the way Microsoft Word 2000 displays the color and appearance of inserted text, deleted text, and changed lines by clicking on the various list boxes and choosing a color or option.**

   For example, you can make inserted text appear red with an underline or make deleted text appear yellow with strikethrough.

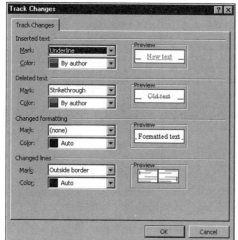

Figure 5-3:
The Track
Changes
dialog box.

5. Click on OK twice.

From now on, every time you add, delete, copy, or move text, Microsoft Word 2000 displays the original text and the new text in the colors and appearance you chose in Step 4. Figure 5-4 shows what a document with multiple revision marks looks like.

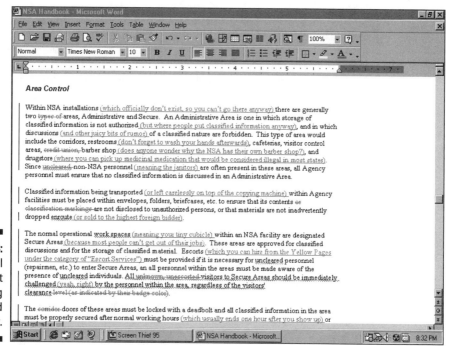

Figure 5-4:
A typical
document
displaying
changed
text.

To keep anyone from changing your document without your permission, you may want to protect it with a password. To require a password to modify a document, follow these steps:

1. **Choose File⇨Save As.**

   A Save As dialog box appears.

2. **Click on the Tools menu (inside the Save As dialog box) and choose General Options.**

   A Save dialog box appears.

3. **Click on the Password to modify box, type a password, and then click on OK.**

   A Confirm Password dialog box appears.

4. **Type your password a second time and then click on OK.**

5. **Click on Save.**

If you forget your password, you won't be able to modify your document either, so make sure you write down your password and store it in a safe place.

Reviewing your changes

After an editor, coworker, or critic has littered your document with changes, you can review the changes and selectively accept or reject each change. To review one by one the changes made to your document, follow these steps:

1. **Press Ctrl+Home to move the cursor to the top of your document.**

2. **Choose Tools⇨Track Changes⇨Accept or Reject Changes.**

   The Accept or Reject Changes dialog box appears, as shown in Figure 5-5. The View group displays three option buttons:

   - **Changes with highlighting:** Highlights changed text so that you can find the text easier.
   - **Changes without highlighting:** Displays modified text without highlighting so that the modified text appears as part of the original text.
   - **Original:** Does not display any changes made to the original text.

3. **Click on an option button for the View choice you want (such as Changes with highlighting).**

4. **Click on the Find button (that's the Find button with the arrow pointing to the right).**

   Microsoft Word 2000 highlights the first changed text that it finds.

5. **Click on Accept or Reject.**

   If you click on Accept, then Microsoft Word 2000 displays any added text as part of your document without color or underlining. If you click on Reject, then the changed text disappears as if someone had never typed it.

6. **Repeat Steps 4 and 5 for each changed text that you want to review.**

7. **Click on Close.**

Accepting (or rejecting) changed text all at once

In case you're feeling lazy or you have complete confidence (or no confidence) in the person who added or modified text within your document, you can accept (or reject) all changed text at one time.

To accept or reject all changed text in a document without reviewing the changes first, follow these steps:

1. **Choose Tools⊅Track Changes⊅Accept or Reject Changes.**

   The Accept or Reject Changes dialog box appears (refer to Figure 5-5).

2. **Click on Accept All or Reject All.**

   A dialog box appears, asking whether you're sure that you know what you're doing.

3. **Click on Yes.**

4. **Click on OK.**

If you accept or reject all revised text and then suddenly change your mind, press Ctrl+Z to immediately cancel the preceding four steps.

Comparing Documents

In an ideal world, people would share a single Microsoft Word 2000 document and type their comments or changes in that single file. However, in the real world, people often make two or more copies of the same document, and then wind up with separate comments and modified text stored in two or more copies of the same document.

To resolve the problem of having multiple copies of the (almost) same document, Microsoft Word 2000 can compare two documents and show you what differences may exist. Then you can save all your changes in a single document.

To compare (and combine) two documents, follow these steps:

1. **Open the first document that you want to compare.**

2. **Choose Tools⇨Track Changes⇨Compare Documents.**

   A Select File to Compare With Current Document dialog box appears.

3. **Click on the document that you want to compare with the currently displayed document and then click on Open.**

   Microsoft Word 2000 displays the changes between the two documents. When you see crossed-out text, that means the crossed-out text appears in the second document (the document you chose in Step 3) but does not appear in the first document (the document you chose in Step 1).

4. **Choose Tools⇨Track Changes⇨Accept or Reject Changes.**

   The Accept or Reject Changes dialog box appears (refer to Figure 5-5).

5. **Click on the Find button (that's the Find button with the arrow pointing to the right).**

   Microsoft Word 2000 highlights the first changed text that it finds.

6. **Click on Accept or Reject.**

   If you click on Accept, then Microsoft Word 2000 displays any added text as part of your document without color or underlining. If you click on Reject, then the changed text disappears as if someone had never typed it.

7. **Repeat Steps 5 and 6 for each changed text that you want to review.**

8. **Click on Close.**

9. **Choose File⇨Save to save your document.**

If you want to accept (or reject) all changes at once, right-click on any crossed out text and then click on Accept or Reject Changes. When an Accept or Reject Changes dialog box appears, click on either Accept All or Reject All.

Part II
Number Crunching with Microsoft Excel 2000

The 5th Wave
By Rich Tennant

"I told him we were looking for software that would give us greater productivity, so he sold me Microsoft's Excel 2000 and a bunch of these signs."

In this part . . .

*E*veryone loves money, yet most people hate math (which may explain why most people don't have much money). In case you need to use complicated formulas to calculate your profits (or losses), you'll be happy to know that Microsoft Excel 2000 includes hundreds of built-in functions to solve nearly any calculation you need.

Functions are simply formulas that someone already has written for you (and verified to make sure that they work correctly). By using built-in functions, you can save yourself time and trouble creating worksheets by yourself.

Because nobody (especially nobody using a computer) is perfect, Excel 2000 provides auditing features to help verify that your worksheets actually calculate numbers correctly. This part of the book shows you how to verify the accuracy of your worksheets (even if you don't have the slightest idea what you're doing otherwise).

Chapter 6

Customizing Microsoft Excel 2000

· ·

In This Chapter

▶ Saving your Excel 2000 worksheets

▶ Hiding rows and columns

▶ Freezing rows and columns

· ·

*N*obody likes being told what to do, which explains why many people don't like school or these so-called "user-friendly" programs that provide so little flexibility on how the application looks, works, or acts.

Fortunately, Microsoft Excel 2000 lets you customize its program features, so you can personalize your copy of Excel 2000 while confusing the living daylights out of someone who tries to use your computer and copy Excel 2000 without your permission.

Excel was originally written as a Macintosh spreadsheet program and quickly overtook its spreadsheet competition. Microsoft then wrote a version of Excel for Windows, which soon became even more popular than the mighty Lotus 1-2-3 spreadsheet application. This history lesson has nothing to do with customizing Excel 2000, but it's kind of neat to know anyway.

Saving Your Excel 2000 Worksheets

Because the way that Microsoft Excel 2000 works and looks can affect the way you use the program, take a little time to customize some of the more essential features in Excel 2000. That way you can make your copy of Excel 2000 more comfortable to use. After you've customized Excel 2000 to your liking, you can move on to more pressing matters.

Saving files automatically

To make saving your files easier, Microsoft Excel 2000 can periodically save your files without your having to even think about it. If you forget to save your file, Excel 2000 shrugs its shoulders, rolls its eyes, and saves the file for you — all on its own.

To make Excel 2000 save your files automatically, follow these steps:

1. **Choose Tools⇨Add-Ins.**

   The Add-Ins dialog box appears, as shown in Figure 6-1. (You may have to insert the installation CD that came in your Microsoft Office 2000 package to install the Add-Ins feature.)

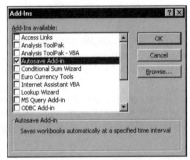

Figure 6-1:
The Add-Ins
dialog box.

2. **Click on the AutoSave Add-in check box so that a check mark appears and then click on OK.**

3. **Choose Tools⇨AutoSave.**

   An AutoSave dialog box appears, as shown in Figure 6-2.

Figure 6-2:
The
AutoSave
dialog box.

4. **Make sure that a check mark appears in the Automatic Save Every check box.**

5. **In the Minutes text box, type the time interval for Excel 2000 to automatically save your file (such as every 10 minutes).**

If you want Excel 2000 to save all open workbooks, then click on the Save All Open Workbooks option button. If you just want to save the workbook you're using at the time, then click on the Save Active Workbook Only option button.

6. **Click on OK.**

Where did I put that file?

Microsoft Office 2000 normally saves your files in the C:\Mydocuments directory. So, the next time you forget where you stored your file, look in that directory first. However, you may want to store your files in a different directory. Luckily for you, Microsoft graciously allows you this option.

To tell Microsoft Excel 2000 to store your files in a different directory, follow these steps:

1. **Choose Tools⇨Options.**

2. **Click on the General tab, as shown in Figure 6-3.**

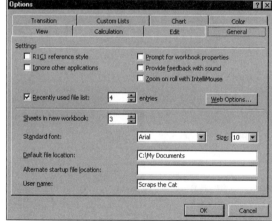

Figure 6-3:
The General tab in the Options dialog box.

3. **Click on the Default file location box and then type the name of the directory where you want Excel 2000 to store your files.**

   For example, type **c:\secret stuff** in the Default file location box.

4. **Click on OK.**

   From now on, Excel 2000 uses the new default file location you specified in Step 3.

Messing Around with the Appearance of Excel 2000

To help you adapt to Excel 2000 (and to encourage users of rival spread-sheets to defect to Excel 2000), Microsoft makes customizing Excel 2000 look easy. You can modify the font and text size to make your screens easier to read, and you can customize the way Excel labels its columns.

Playing with fonts

Unless you specify otherwise, Excel 2000 displays text in the Arial font at 10-point size. Although this font is fine for most people, you may want to choose a different font (for aesthetic reasons) or a different point size (to make your numbers easier to see, in case the tiny 10-point size is too small for you).

To change the font and point size of text displayed in Excel 2000, follow these steps:

1. **Choose Tools⇨Options.**

2. **Click on the General tab (refer to Figure 6-3).**

3. **Click on the Standard font list box and then select the font that you want to use.**

   For example, choose Courier in the Standard font list box.

4. **Click on the Size list box and then select the point size that you want to use.**

   For example, choose 15 in the Size list box.

5. **Click on OK.**

You may have to experiment to find the font and point size that looks best to you. Excel 2000 won't actually display your new font and point size until you click on OK and exit the Options dialog box.

Getting rid of gridlines

Excel displays gridlines to help you easily identify a particular cell in a row and column. Gridlines, however, can be as annoying as trying to view a beautiful sunset through a screen door. So, if you want to remove gridlines from sight, follow these steps:

1. **Choose Tools⇨Options.**

2. **Click on the View Tab.**

   The View tab appears in the Options dialog box, as shown in Figure 6-4.

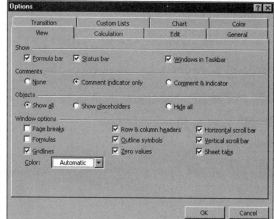

3. **Click on the Gridlines check box in the Windows options group.**

   To remove gridlines, make sure that a check mark does not appear in the Gridlines check box. To display gridlines, make sure that a check mark does appear in the Gridlines check box.

4. **Click on OK.**

Changing Your Point of View

If you stare at a long list of numbers, your eyes and mind are likely to numb over before you can understand everything that you see. That's why Microsoft Excel 2000 provides little features to help limit or alter the way you view your worksheets, so you can see what your numbers mean without being bombarded by too much information.

Hiding rows and columns on a worksheet

Unless you create simple worksheets that can fit onto a single computer screen, you normally won't be able to see an entire worksheet at one time. Rather than force you to tediously scroll up, down, right, or left (and risk missing some important connections among your numbers), Microsoft Excel 2000 can selectively hide and display rows and columns. Figure 6-5 shows a worksheet with no hidden rows, and Figure 6-6 shows how hiding rows can help you evaluate the data on your worksheet more easily.

The whole purpose of hiding rows or columns is to display only those numbers that are most important at the moment. For example, you don't want to wade through endless rows of numbers when you just need to look at the bottom line to find out whether your company is making a profit.

To hide a row or a column on a worksheet, follow these steps:

1. **Highlight the rows or columns that you want to hide.**

2. **Choose Format⇨Row (or Column)⇨Hide.**

    Excel 2000 hides the selected rows or columns.

When you hide a row or a column, you're not deleting it. You've simply tucked the row or column conveniently out of sight.

Figure 6-5:
A hideous worksheet with lots of confusing numbers.

	A	B	C	D	E
1	Monthly Expenses for the CIA				
2					
3		January	February	March	April
4	New maps	$7,936.11	$2,451.24	$6,358.92	$2,751.66
5	Computer hacker salaries	$6,358.72	$3,375.16	$6,473.24	$7,635.10
6	Illegal funding	$8,896.30	$9,635.26	$8,754.30	$3,241.08
7	Bay of Pigs explanations	$4,658.21	$9,685.36	$4,789.58	$2,587.79
8	Bribes to politicians	$3,785.24	$1,147.25	$1,547.36	$7,856.32
9	Gifts to other countries	$8,678.11	$9,713.55	$4,125.20	$2,689.57
10	Propaganda	$5,698.67	$7,414.25	$7,459.99	$4,879.56
11	Total =	$46,011.36	$43,422.07	$39,508.59	$31,641.08
12					
13					
14	Monthly Expenses for the NSA				
15					
16		January	February	March	April
17	Computers that don't crash	$7,796.14	$8,769.95	$7,977.45	$2,751.66
18	Backdoor encryption	$4,583.60	$4,931.25	$5,006.70	$4,608.57
19	PR for Clipper chip	$1,257.84	$3,578.01	$8,310.24	$3,241.08
20	Mysterious-looking logo	$8,763.20	$9,685.36	$4,789.58	$7,879.21
21	Bribes to Congressmen	$3,785.24	$1,147.25	$9,547.85	$7,856.32
22	Translation services	$4,789.25	$3,214.56	$4,125.20	$6,007.80
23	Misinformation	$1,504.67	$4,769.55	$6,009.44	$7,786.32
24	Total =	$32,479.94	$36,095.93	$45,766.46	$40,130.96
25					
26					
27					

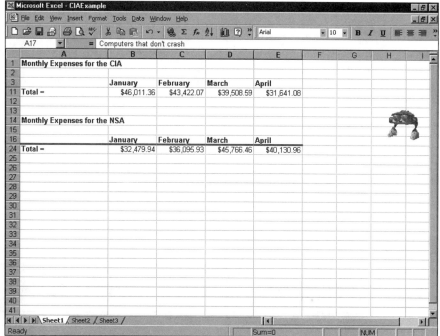

You may wonder, "How can I find a hidden row or column after it's hidden?" Fortunately, when you use Excel 2000 to hide rows or columns, Excel marks the rows or columns by skipping the numbering in the row or column labels. That way, you can see right away how many rows or columns are hidden. (Refer to Figure 6-6.)

To unhide a row or a column on a worksheet, follow these steps:

1. **Highlight the rows or columns labels that you want to unhide.**

   For example, if you want to unhide rows 3 through 6, highlight row labels 2 through 7.

2. **Choose Format⇨Row (or Column)⇨Unhide.**

   Excel 2000 displays your previously hidden rows or columns.

Freezing labels on a worksheet

If you clutter up a worksheet with endless rows and columns filled with numbers, your worksheet can look utterly confusing. To help identify what certain numbers mean, you can write descriptive labels next to your rows or columns of numbers so that anyone can see what those numbers represent.

Some examples of descriptive labels are *Total amount, January sales,* or *Profits lost due to Joe's incompetence.*

Unfortunately, if you scroll too far up/down or right/left, your descriptive labels also scroll up/down or right/left, which means they disappear out of sight altogether. Before you know it, you are staring at unlabeled rows and columns of numbers that once again don't make any sense.

Figure 6-7 shows a worksheet with labels that identify your numbers. The moment you start scrolling, however, the labels scroll out of sight, as shown in Figure 6-8.

To avoid having your descriptive labels scroll out of sight, Excel can *freeze,* or anchor, labels in specific rows or columns. When you freeze a row or column containing a label, as shown in Figure 6-9, that particular row or column never moves — no matter how much you scroll through your worksheet.

Figure 6-7:
A worksheet with easy-to-see labels.

	A	B	C	D	E	F	G	H	I
1	Monthly Expenses for every Major University in the Country								
2									
3		January	February	March	April				
4	Athletic scholarships	$4,835.01	$8,769.95	$6,358.92	$2,751.66				
5	Recruitment brochures	$6,358.72	$3,375.16	$6,473.24	$9,986.35				
6	Landscaping	$1,257.84	$9,635.26	$8,754.30	$3,241.08				
7	President's salary	$8,763.20	$9,685.36	$4,789.58	$2,587.79				
8	Unnecessary travel	$3,785.24	$1,147.25	$9,547.85	$7,856.32				
9	Alcohol	$8,678.11	$9,713.55	$4,125.20	$2,689.57				
10	Expensive gifts	$5,863.24	$7,414.25	$7,459.99	$7,786.32				
11	Maid service	$9,974.35	$1,221.07	$6,989.21	$8,862.14				
12	Limousine service	$5,587.14	$3,125.02	$9,785.25	$7,879.69				
13	Personal chef salary	$6,174.21	$9,658.33	$4,321.55	$8,571.07				
14	Clothing allowance	$7,789.21	$2,263.56	$4,635.28	$9,356.01				
15	Spending money	$7,889.30	$4,459.35	$4,587.21	$4,875.21				
16	Classroom supplies	$0.02	$0.50	$0.32	$0.07				
17	Professor salaries	$0.08	$0.01	$0.30	$0.45				
18	Dormitory maintenance	$0.91	$0.18	$0.23	$0.81				
19	Janitorial services	$0.39	$0.64	$0.38	$0.16				
20	Laboratory equipment	$0.48	$0.45	$0.06	$0.27				
21	Coaches salaries	$4,698.25	$4,526.35	$7,485.24	$7,884.24				
22	Football equipment	$4,125.01	$7,564.33	$1,458.25	$7,569.31				
23	Stadium improvements	$4,201.22	$4,587.36	$1,245.11	$9,478.55				
24	Campus safety	$0.24	$0.36	$0.18	$0.96				
25	Health services	$0.57	$0.90	$0.43	$0.64				
26	Student activities	$0.12	$0.79	$0.25	$0.35				
27	Campus computers	$0.65	$0.88	$0.36	$0.47				

Microsoft Excel - CollegeExample

File Edit View Insert Format Tools Data Window Help

Arial · 10 ·

F1

	A	B	C	D	E	F	G	H	I
4	Athletic scholarships	$4,835.01	$8,769.95	$6,358.92	$2,751.66				
5	Recruitment brochures	$6,358.72	$3,375.16	$6,473.24	$9,986.35				
6	Landscaping	$1,257.84	$9,635.26	$8,754.30	$3,241.08				
7	President's salary	$8,763.20	$9,685.36	$4,789.58	$2,587.79				
8	Unnecessary travel	$3,785.24	$1,147.25	$9,547.85	$7,856.32				
9	Alcohol	$8,678.11	$9,713.55	$4,125.20	$2,689.57				
10	Expensive gifts	$5,863.24	$7,414.25	$7,459.99	$7,786.32				
11	Maid service	$9,974.35	$1,221.07	$6,989.21	$8,862.14				
12	Limousine service	$5,587.14	$3,125.02	$9,785.25	$7,879.69				
13	Personal chef salary	$6,174.21	$9,658.33	$4,321.55	$8,571.07				
14	Clothing allowance	$7,789.21	$2,263.56	$4,635.28	$9,356.01				
15	Spending money	$7,889.30	$4,459.35	$4,587.21	$4,875.21				
16	Classroom supplies	$0.02	$0.50	$0.32	$0.07				
17	Professor salaries	$0.08	$0.01	$0.30	$0.45				
18	Dormitory maintenance	$0.91	$0.18	$0.23	$0.81				
19	Janitorial services	$0.39	$0.64	$0.38	$0.16				
20	Laboratory equipment	$0.48	$0.45	$0.06	$0.27				
21	Coaches salaries	$4,698.25	$4,526.35	$7,485.24	$7,884.24				
22	Football equipment	$4,125.01	$7,564.33	$1,458.25	$7,569.31				
23	Stadium improvements	$4,201.22	$4,587.36	$1,245.11	$9,478.55				
24	Campus safety	$0.24	$0.36	$0.18	$0.96				
25	Health services	$0.57	$0.90	$0.43	$0.64				
26	Student activities	$0.12	$0.79	$0.25	$0.35				
27	Campus computers	$0.65	$0.88	$0.36	$0.47				
28	Student counseling	$0.40	$0.75	$0.67	$0.28				
29	Donations to sororities	$9,751.34	$7,846.14	$7,589.24	$3,641.04				
30	Total =	$99,735.25	$94,997.75	$95,608.60	$105,020.81				

Sheet1 / Sheet2 / Sheet3 /

Ready NUM

Figure 6-8: A worksheet after the descriptive labels have been scrolled out of sight.

Microsoft Excel - CollegeExample

File Edit View Insert Format Tools Data Window Help

Arial · 10 ·

G6

	A	B	C	D	E	F	G	H	I
1	Monthly Expenses for every Major University in the Country								
2									
3		January	February	March	April				
22	Football equipment	$4,125.01	$7,564.33	$1,458.25	$7,569.31				
23	Stadium improvements	$4,201.22	$4,587.36	$1,245.11	$9,478.55				
24	Campus safety	$0.24	$0.36	$0.18	$0.96				
25	Health services	$0.57	$0.90	$0.43	$0.64				
26	Student activities	$0.12	$0.79	$0.25	$0.35				
27	Campus computers	$0.65	$0.88	$0.36	$0.47				
28	Student counseling	$0.40	$0.75	$0.67	$0.28				
29	Donations to sororities	$9,751.34	$7,846.14	$7,589.24	$3,641.04				
30	Total =	$99,735.25	$94,997.75	$95,608.60	$105,020.81				
31									
32									
33									
34									
35									
36									
37									
38									
39									
40									
41									
42									
43									
44									
45									

Sheet1 / Sheet2 / Sheet3 /

Ready NUM

Figure 6-9: A worksheet with descriptive labels frozen in place.

To freeze a single row or column, follow these steps:

1. **Click on the row number directly below the row that you want to freeze. (Or click on the column letter to the right of the column that you want to freeze.)**

   If you want to freeze row 2, for example, click the row 3 label to select the entire row. Or if you want to freeze column C, click the column D label to select the entire column.

2. **Choose <u>W</u>indows⇨<u>F</u>reeze Panes.**

   Excel displays a dark gray line to show where you froze your row or column (refer to Figure 6-9).

Sometimes you may not want labels on both a row and a column to scroll out of sight. In that case, you may want to freeze both a row and a column by following these steps:

1. **Click on the cell directly to the right of the column and below the row that you want to freeze.**

   If you want to freeze column A and row 2, for example, click on the cell in column B and row 3.

2. **Choose <u>W</u>indow⇨<u>F</u>reeze Panes.**

   Excel 2000 displays a dark gray line to show where you froze your row and column.

To unfreeze any rows and columns that you have frozen, choose <u>W</u>indow⇨<u>U</u>nfreeze Panes.

Splitting screens on a worksheet

If you want to see two or more parts of your worksheet at one time, you can split your screen into miniature views of your worksheet, known as *panes*. Each pane acts as an independent window that you can scroll separately from the rest of your worksheet. To show you where one pane begins and another pane ends, Excel displays thick pane lines, as shown in Figure 6-10.

To split a screen in half horizontally, follow these steps:

1. **Select the row directly below the row where you want to split your worksheet.**

For example, if you want to split your worksheet between rows 8 and 9, then click on the row 9 label.

2. Choose Windows⇨Split.

Excel displays a horizontal pane line to show you where you split your worksheet (refer to Figure 6-10).

To split a screen in half vertically, follow these steps:

1. Select the column directly to the right of where you want to split your worksheet.

For example, if you want to split your worksheet between columns B and C, click on the gray label named C to select column C.

2. Choose Windows⇨Split.

Excel displays a vertical pane line to show you where you split your columns.

	A	B	C	D	E	F	G	H	I
1	Monthly Expenses for every Major University in the Country								
2									
3		January	February	March	April				
4	Athletic scholarships	$4,835.01	$8,769.95	$6,358.92	$2,751.66				
5	Recruitment brochures	$6,358.72	$3,375.16	$6,473.24	$9,986.35				
6	Landscaping	$1,257.84	$9,635.26	$8,754.30	$3,241.08				
7	President's salary	$8,763.20	$9,685.36	$4,789.58	$2,587.79				
8	Unnecessary travel	$3,785.24	$1,147.25	$9,547.85	$7,856.32				
9	Alcohol	$8,678.11	$9,713.55	$4,125.20	$2,689.57				
10	Expensive gifts	$5,863.24	$7,414.25	$7,459.99	$7,786.32				
11	Maid service	$9,974.35	$1,221.07	$6,989.21	$8,862.14				
12	Limousine service	$5,587.14	$3,125.02	$9,785.25	$7,879.69				
13	Personal chef salary	$6,174.21	$9,658.33	$4,321.55	$8,571.07				
14	Clothing allowance	$7,789.21	$2,263.56	$4,635.28	$9,356.01				
15	Spending money	$7,889.30	$4,459.35	$4,587.21	$4,875.21				
16	Classroom supplies	$0.02	$0.50	$0.32	$0.07				
21	Coaches salaries	$4,698.25	$4,526.35	$7,485.24	$7,884.24				
22	Football equipment	$4,125.01	$7,564.33	$1,458.25	$7,569.31				
23	Stadium improvements	$4,201.22	$4,587.36	$1,245.11	$9,478.55				
24	Campus safety	$0.24	$0.36	$0.18	$0.96				
25	Health services	$0.57	$0.90	$0.43	$0.64				
26	Student activities	$0.12	$0.79	$0.25	$0.35				
27	Campus computers	$0.65	$0.88	$0.36	$0.47				
28	Student counseling	$0.40	$0.75	$0.67	$0.28				
29	Donations to sororities	$9,751.34	$7,846.14	$7,589.24	$3,641.04				
30	**Total =**	$99,735.25	$94,997.75	$95,608.60	$105,020.81				

Figure 6-10: Splitting a worksheet into two separate panes.

You can also split your worksheet into four different panes to give you yet another view of your numbers.

To split your worksheet into four panes, follow these steps:

1. **Click on the cell directly to the right of the column and below the row where you want the split.**

   For example, if you want to split your worksheet between columns B and C, and between rows 9 and 10, click on the cell in column C and row 10.

2. **Choose Windows⇨Split.**

   Excel splits your worksheet into four panes, as shown in Figure 6-11.

To remove your split screen and go back to a single-screen view, choose Windows⇨Remove Split. The worksheet window returns to its normal appearance.

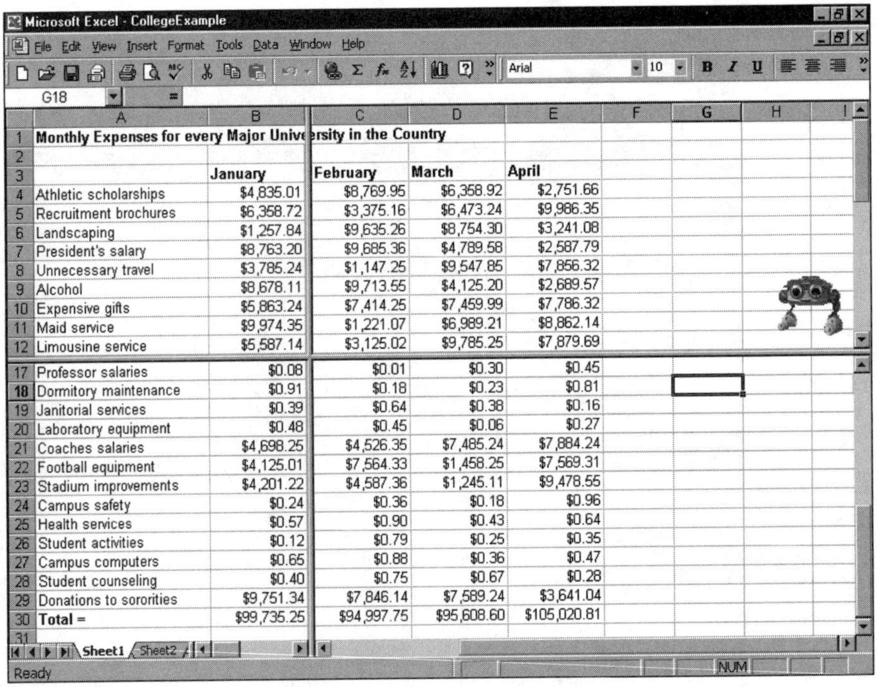

Figure 6-11:
A worksheet split into four separate panes.

Microsoft Excel - CollegeExample

File Edit View Insert Format Tools Data Window Help

G18

	A	B	C	D	E	F	G	H	I
1	Monthly Expenses for every Major University in the Country								
2									
3		January	February	March	April				
4	Athletic scholarships	$4,835.01	$8,769.95	$6,358.92	$2,751.66				
5	Recruitment brochures	$6,358.72	$3,375.16	$6,473.24	$9,986.35				
6	Landscaping	$1,257.84	$9,635.26	$8,754.30	$3,241.08				
7	President's salary	$8,763.20	$9,685.36	$4,789.58	$2,587.79				
8	Unnecessary travel	$3,785.24	$1,147.25	$9,547.85	$7,856.32				
9	Alcohol	$8,678.11	$9,713.55	$4,125.20	$2,689.57				
10	Expensive gifts	$5,863.24	$7,414.25	$7,459.99	$7,786.32				
11	Maid service	$9,974.35	$1,221.07	$6,989.21	$8,862.14				
12	Limousine service	$5,587.14	$3,125.02	$9,785.25	$7,879.69				
17	Professor salaries	$0.08	$0.01	$0.30	$0.45				
18	Dormitory maintenance	$0.91	$0.18	$0.23	$0.81				
19	Janitorial services	$0.39	$0.64	$0.38	$0.16				
20	Laboratory equipment	$0.48	$0.45	$0.06	$0.27				
21	Coaches salaries	$4,698.25	$4,526.35	$7,485.24	$7,884.24				
22	Football equipment	$4,125.01	$7,564.33	$1,458.25	$7,569.31				
23	Stadium improvements	$4,201.22	$4,587.36	$1,245.11	$9,478.55				
24	Campus safety	$0.24	$0.36	$0.18	$0.96				
25	Health services	$0.57	$0.90	$0.43	$0.64				
26	Student activities	$0.12	$0.79	$0.25	$0.35				
27	Campus computers	$0.65	$0.88	$0.36	$0.47				
28	Student counseling	$0.40	$0.75	$0.67	$0.28				
29	Donations to sororities	$9,751.34	$7,846.14	$7,589.24	$3,641.04				
30	Total =	$99,735.25	$94,997.75	$95,608.60	$105,020.81				
31									

Sheet1 / Sheet2

Ready

NUM

Zooming in for a closer look

In case your eyesight is poor or you like looking at your entire worksheet at one time, you can make the numbers on your worksheet appear larger (called *zooming* in) or smaller (called *zooming* out).

To make your worksheet numbers appear bigger, select a higher magnification, such as 200 percent. To make your worksheet numbers appear smaller, select a lower magnification, such as 50 percent. To make your worksheet appear normal size again, select 100 percent.

To change the zoom magnification on your worksheet, follow these steps:

1. **Choose View⇨Zoom.**

   A Zoom dialog box appears, as shown in Figure 6-12.

2. **Click on a magnification (such as 200%) and then click on OK.**

   Excel displays your worksheet in your chosen magnification, as shown in Figure 6-13. You also can enter a specific magnification, such as 145%. Excel displays your worksheet using the magnification that you entered.

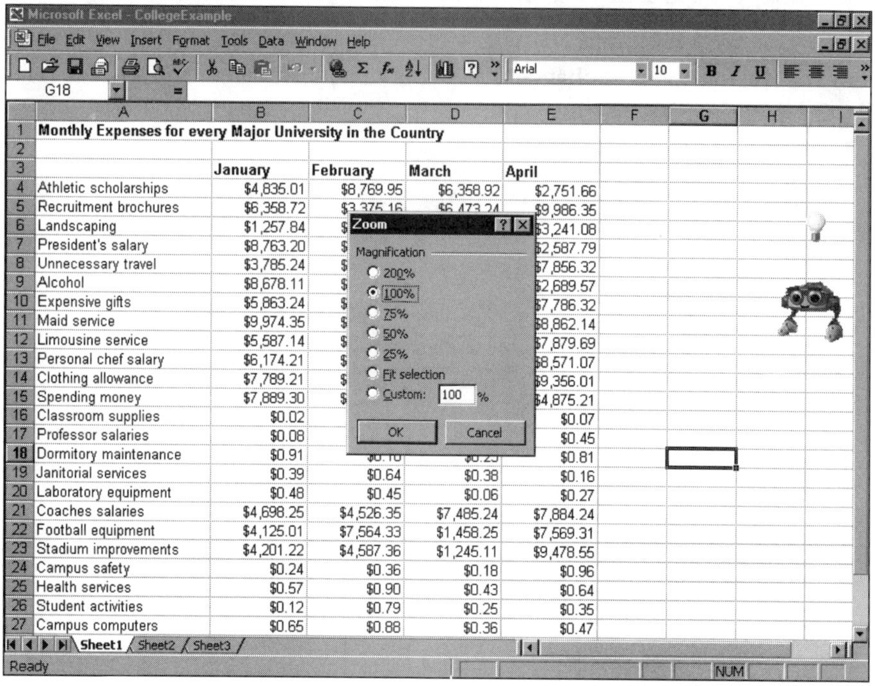

Figure 6-12: The Zoom dialog box.

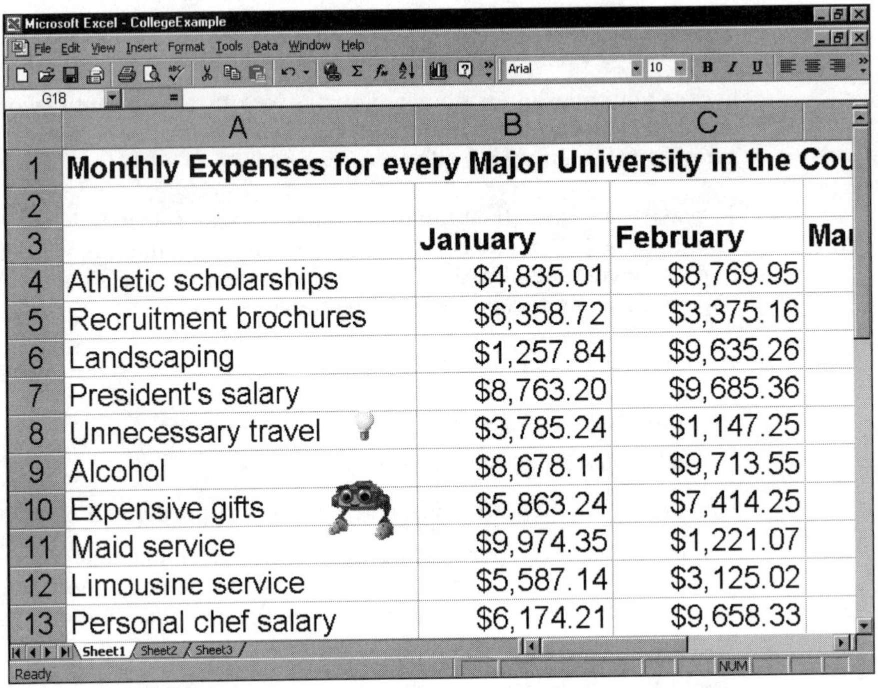

Microsoft Excel - CollegeExample

File Edit View Insert Format Tools Data Window Help

G18 =

	A	B	C	Mai
1	**Monthly Expenses for every Major University in the Cou**			
2				
3		**January**	**February**	**Mai**
4	Athletic scholarships	$4,835.01	$8,769.95	
5	Recruitment brochures	$6,358.72	$3,375.16	
6	Landscaping	$1,257.84	$9,635.26	
7	President's salary	$8,763.20	$9,685.36	
8	Unnecessary travel	$3,785.24	$1,147.25	
9	Alcohol	$8,678.11	$9,713.55	
10	Expensive gifts	$5,863.24	$7,414.25	
11	Maid service	$9,974.35	$1,221.07	
12	Limousine service	$5,587.14	$3,125.02	
13	Personal chef salary	$6,174.21	$9,658.33	

Sheet1 / Sheet2 / Sheet3 /

Ready

NUM

Figure 6-13:
Displaying
your work-
sheet at a
higher mag-
nification.

You can also change the magnification by clicking on the Zoom list box on the Standard toolbar.

Chapter 7

Goal Seeking and PivotTables

. . . .

In This Chapter

▶ Finding answers with Goal Seek

▶ Sorting tables and other cool database stuff

▶ Analyzing data with PivotTables

▶ Adding cell notes

. . . .

Microsoft Excel 2000 is more than a simple spreadsheet. By using Excel's Goal Seek and PivotTables features, you can use your computer to store data and to calculate the type of data you need to achieve certain results. If that sounds weird, you can find out how these features can help you by reading the rest of this chapter.

Seeking Your Goals

The typical worksheet works something like this: Enter data, create a formula, and get an answer. When you change any of your data, Microsoft Excel 2000 automatically uses your formula to calculate a new result.

Excel 2000, however, offers a unique feature called *goal seeking*. Goal seeking lets you specify the answer you want, so that Excel can figure out what data you need to input and then calculate your desired answer. For example, suppose you've created a worksheet to measure the sales results for each of your company's products, as shown in Figure 7-1. Looking at the February sales totals tells you that sales went down.

Pop quiz! If you want your February sales results to equal $45,000, how much extra do sales of Hormone-laced beef have to increase to meet your goal? Rather than try to figure this out yourself, just tell Excel 2000 what results you want and which cell values to change to get those results.

Microsoft Excel - SalesResults

File Edit View Insert Format Tools Data Financial Manager Window Help

C7 = 9685.36

	A	B	C	D	E	F	G	H	I
1	Monthly Sales of Pseudo-Nutritious Foods								
2									
3		January	February	March	April				
4	Fake orange juice	$7,936.11	$2,451.24	$6,358.92	$2,751.66				
5	Lumpy gravy and meatballs	$6,358.72	$3,375.16	$6,473.24	$7,635.10				
6	Dead fish w/mercury flavor	$8,896.30	$9,635.26	$8,754.30	$3,241.08				
7	Hormone-laced beef	$4,658.21	$9,685.36	$4,789.58	$2,587.79				
8	Genetically altered apples	$3,785.24	$1,147.25	$1,547.36	$7,856.32				
9	Pears with pesticide	$8,678.11	$9,713.55	$4,125.20	$2,689.57				
10	Sawdust (for added fiber)	$5,698.67	$7,414.25	$7,459.99	$4,879.56				
11	Total =	$46,011.36	$43,422.07	$39,508.59	$31,641.08				

Sheet1 / Sheet2 / Sheet3 /

Ready   NUM

Figure 7-1:
Using goal
seeking in a
real-life
example.

To use Goal Seek to find an answer that you've been seeking, follow these
steps:

1. **Click on the cell where you want the new answer to appear. (This cell
   must contain a formula.)**

2. **Click on Tools⇔Goal Seek.**

   The Goal Seek dialog box appears, with the address of the selected cell
   in the Set cell text box, as shown in Figure 7-2.

   Dollar signs indicate that the cell reference is *absolute* instead of *relative*.
   (Absolute means that you're tagging a specific cell or range of cells.
   Relative means that you're specifying the data stored in a cell or range
   of cells but not the cell addresses themselves.)

3. **Click on the To value text box and then type the answer that you
   want.**

   For example, you may want to find out how to create a February sales
   total of $45,000. Type **45000** in the To value text box.

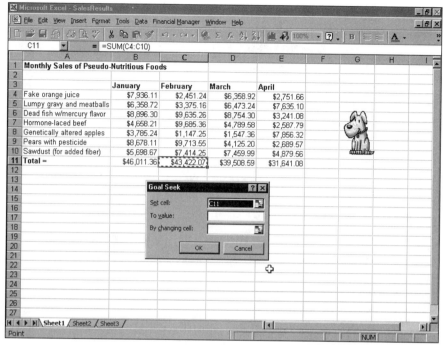

Figure 7-2:
The Goal
Seek dialog
box.

4. Click on the By changing cell text box.

This box is where you tell Excel 2000 what value to change to reach your goal.

5. Click on the cell containing the value that you want Excel to change to get to your answer.

The cell to be changed must contain a value (a number), not a formula. Excel 2000 automatically types the cell address in the By changing cell box.

6. Click on OK.

Excel automatically changes your chosen cell to provide the result that you requested. The Goal Seek Status dialog box shows the target value and the current value, which should be the same, as shown in Figure 7-3.

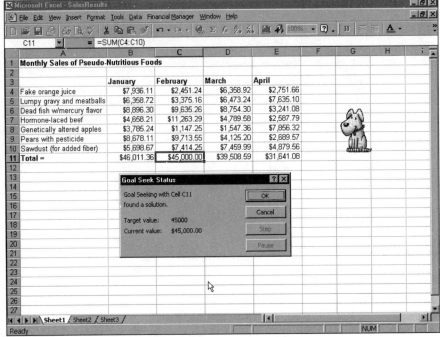

Figure 7-3:
The Goal
Seek Status
dialog box
letting you
know that a
solution is
found.

7. **Click on OK to accept the changes or click on Cancel to have the numbers revert to their original state.**

Goal seeking can only change the values in a single cell.

If you click on the OK button in the Goal Seek Status dialog box by mistake and want the numbers back the way they were, then press Ctrl+Z before you do anything else.

Storing Stuff in Tables

Although Microsoft Excel 2000 is a spreadsheet, many people have tortured Excel into a simple database rather than learn how to use a separate database program, such as Access 2000. To Excel 2000, a database is nothing more than a bunch of information in rows and columns (called a table) that you can store and manipulate.

To create an Excel 2000 database table, you start by typing headings in one row that labels the columns of information that you plan to include.

You may create a customer list, for example, with headings such as FIRST NAME, LAST NAME, and MONEY THEY OWE US.

In database terms, each item in a column is called a *field*. All the items in a single row of the table are called a *record*. So, the database is nothing more than a bunch of records that consist of a bunch of fields.

Type the data for each record just as you enter data in a normal worksheet, directly below the field-name labels, as shown in Figure 7-4.

Type the field names (column headings) in UPPERCASE, but type the actual data in lowercase. Using upper- and lower-case type makes recognizing your column headings from your data easier.

Typing data in a table

Typing data directly into a database table is easy enough, but it does have some drawbacks. If you have lots of fields, you'll be scrolling left and right an awful lot, which means you may not be able to see the first fields in the record as you enter the last field.

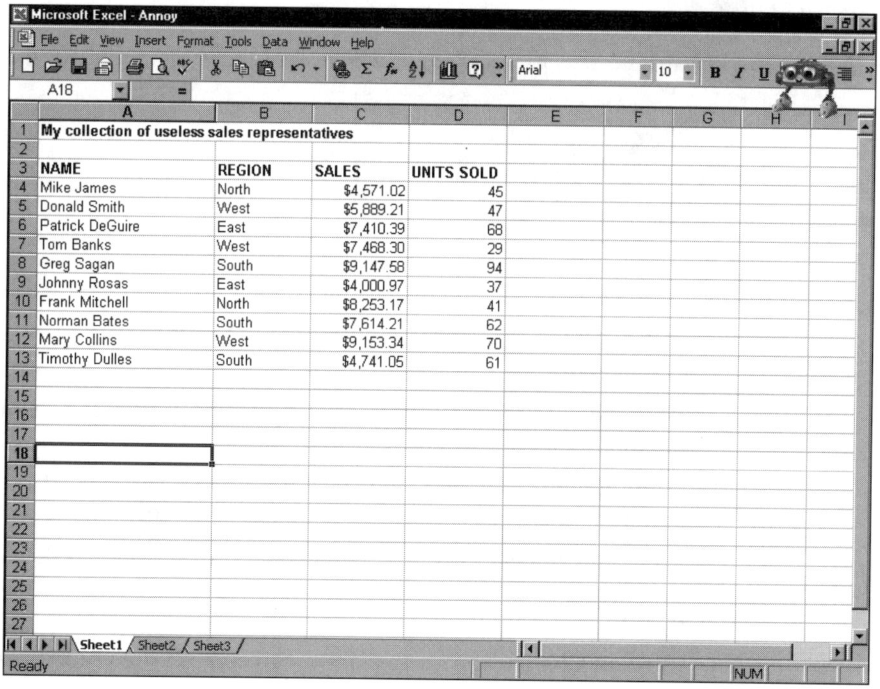

Figure 7-4:
The typical appearance of a database table in Microsoft Excel 2000.

	A	B	C	D
1	My collection of useless sales representatives			
2				
3	**NAME**	**REGION**	**SALES**	**UNITS SOLD**
4	Mike James	North	$4,571.02	45
5	Donald Smith	West	$5,889.21	47
6	Patrick DeGuire	East	$7,410.39	68
7	Tom Banks	West	$7,468.30	29
8	Greg Sagan	South	$9,147.58	94
9	Johnny Rosas	East	$4,000.97	37
10	Frank Mitchell	North	$8,253.17	41
11	Norman Bates	South	$7,614.21	62
12	Mary Collins	West	$9,153.34	70
13	Timothy Dulles	South	$4,741.05	61

To make typing data easier, Microsoft Excel 2000 gives you something to use called a data form. All you do is type the information that you want organized in a table into a dialog box. When you're done, Excel 2000 takes the time to put the data into your actual worksheet cells.

You can use the data form to type all sorts of data — not just database information — into an Excel 2000 worksheet.

To use a data form, follow these steps:

1. **Click on one of the cells in your data table.**

2. **Choose Data⇨Form.**

   The data form dialog box appears, with the name of the current worksheet in the title bar, as shown in Figure 7-5.

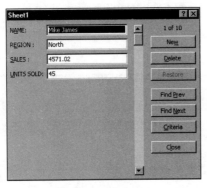

Figure 7-5:
The data
form dialog
box that
makes
organizing
data easier.

3. **Click on New.**

   All the fields in the dialog box are cleared so that you can start entering a new record.

4. **Type the data for the first field and then press the Tab key to move to the next field.**

5. **Continue entering data until all the fields for the record are entered and then click on New again (or just press Enter).**

   Each time you click on New, the new record is placed at the bottom of the table, the text boxes are cleared, and you can start entering the next record.

6. **Click on Close when you're done entering all the records that you want.**

   See how easy entering data in records is, without having to use the scroll bar even once?

Before using the data form, first format the cells in your database table. That way, Excel 2000 automatically formats your data as you type it.

If you're typing numbers that should be treated as text (such as zip codes), be sure to type an apostrophe (') before typing the rest of the number.

Sorting your tables

Sorting databases is something that you do frequently. You may want to sort the list by last name to make finding a particular person in the list easier; or you may want to sort by zip code (if you're creating mailing labels, for example).

To sort a table, follow these steps:

1. **Click on any cell in the column by which you want to sort the table.**

   For example, if you want to sort the table by name, click on any cell in the column that contains a name.

2. **Choose Data⇨Sort.**

   A Sort dialog box appears, as shown in Figure 7-6.

3. **Click on the Sort by list box and then choose a field by which to sort.**

4. **Click on the Then sort by list box and then choose a second field by which to sort (optional).**

5. **Click on the second Then sort by list box and then choose a third field by which to sort (optional).**

6. **Click on the Ascending (or Descending) option buttons for each Sort by list box and then click on OK.**

If you need to sort one field, then just click on either the Sort Ascending or the Sort Descending icon on the Standard toolbar. You may have to view the Standard toolbar on its own row by choosing View⇨Toolbars⇨Customize and then clearing the Standard and Formatting toolbars share one row check box.

Sorting doesn't physically change your data, but sorting does change the way that data looks on-screen. To undo a sort, press Ctrl+Z right away.

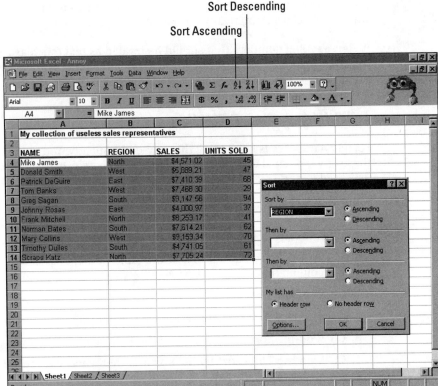

Figure 7-6:
The Sort
dialog box.

Analyzing Data with PivotTables

Database tables are supposed to be useful, but sometimes the information in a database table seems meaningless at first glance (or even after an extended period of time) if the data isn't organized well. So, to help you make sense of your database table, Microsoft Excel 2000 offers a unique feature called a PivotTable, which essentially converts an out-of-context dull list of information into a well-organized worksheet.

A PivotTable can rearrange data stored in a Microsoft Excel 2000 worksheet or from another database. A PivotTable consists of four parts, as shown in Figure 7-7:

> ✔ **Page field:** Filters the type of data displayed in the PivotTable, as shown in Figure 7-8
>
> ✔ **Row field:** Displays data in rows (such as products)

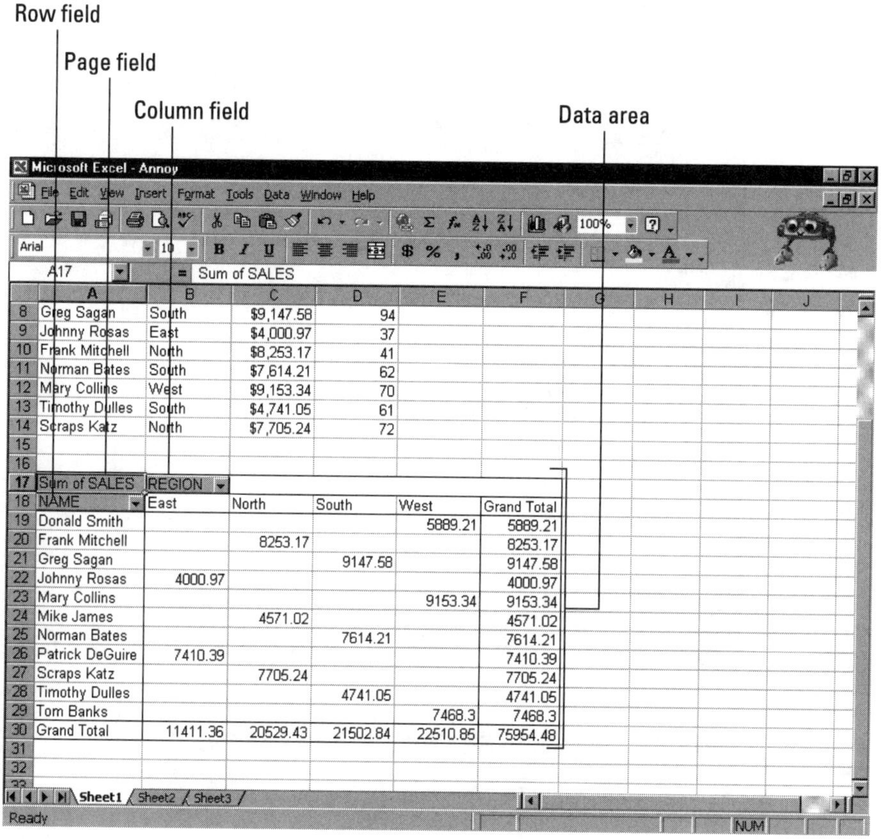

Row field

Page field

Column field

Data area

Figure 7-7:
A PivotTable
converts
a list of
information
into a
worksheet.

✔ **Column field:** Displays data in columns (such as months)

✔ **Data area:** Used to calculate totals for the PivotTable

Creating a PivotTable

To create a PivotTable with the PivotTable Wizard, follow these steps:

1. **Choose Data⇨PivotTable and PivotChart Report.**

   The first PivotTable Wizard dialog box appears, as shown in Figure 7-9.

2. **Click on the Microsoft Excel list or database option button, then click on the PivotTable option button, and finally click on Next.**

   The second PivotTable Wizard dialog box appears, as shown in Figure 7-10.

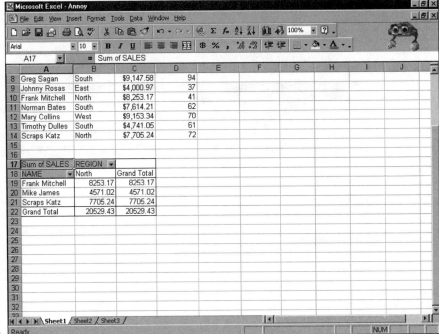

Figure 7-8:
The same
PivotTable
shown in
Figure 7-7
"filtered"
using the
Page field to
display only
data from
the North
region.

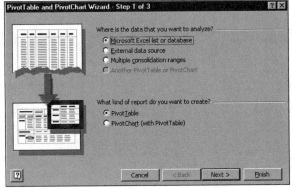

Figure 7-9:
The first
PivotTable
Wizard
dialog box
asking what
type of data
you want to
turn into a
PivotTable.

Figure 7-10:
The second
PivotTable
Wizard
dialog box
for choosing
data stored
in an Excel
database
table.

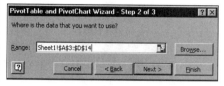

Figure 7-10:
The second
PivotTable
Wizard
dialog box
for choosing
data stored
in an Excel
database
table.

3. **Highlight your database table so that the Range box contains the headings and the data in your database table. Then click on Next.**

   The third PivotTable Wizard dialog box appears, as shown in Figure 7-11.

Figure 7-11:
The third
PivotTable
Wizard
dialog box
for
constructing
your
PivotTable.

4. **Click on the New worksheet or the Existing worksheet option button.**

   If you click on the Existing worksheet option button, then you have to specify a cell for the upper left-hand corner of your PivotTable.

5. **Click on Finish to finish creating the PivotTable.**

   An empty PivotTable appears, as shown in Figure 7-12.

6. **Drag the appropriate field-name buttons (such as NAME or REGION) to the row, column, or data portion of the PivotTable.**

   For example, drag the NAME button to Drop Row Fields Here, drag the REGION button to Drop Column Fields Here, and drag the SALES button to the Drop Data Items Here part of the PivotTable. Excel displays how your data looks, as shown in Figure 7-13.

7. **Click on the close box of the PivotTable toolbar to make the toolbar go away.**

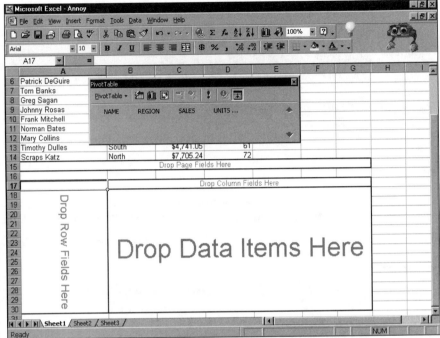

Figure 7-12:
An empty
PivotTable
waiting for
you to fill it
with data.

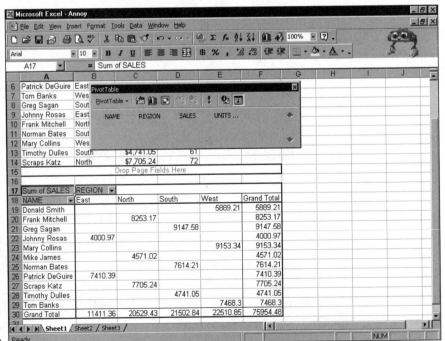

Figure 7-13:
A PivotTable
organizing
your data
for you.

Filtering a PivotTable

The main purpose of a PivotTable is to help you organize and understand your data. Since you may only be interested in part of your overall data, you can tell the PivotTable to "filter out" certain data.

For example, rather than have your PivotTable show you sales data from the East, North, South, and West sales regions (refer to Figure 7-7), you can view sales data from just the North sales region (refer to Figure 7-8). To choose a filter for your PivotTable, follow these steps:

1. **Click on the downward-pointing arrow of the row or column field that you want to filter.**

   A list appears, as shown in Figure 7-14.

2. **Click on the check boxes of the items that you want displayed in your PivotTable.**

3. **Click on OK.**

   Excel cheerfully displays your newly filtered PivotTable.

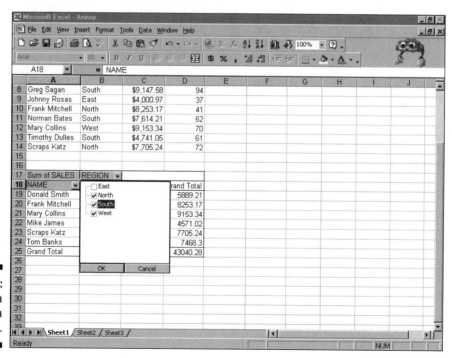

Figure 7-14: Choosing a filter for a PivotTable.

Formatting a PivotTable

If you don't like the way the PivotTable Wizard formats your data, you can always choose a different formatting style at any time. To format your entire PivotTable, follow these steps:

1. **Click on any cell inside your PivotTable.**

2. **Choose Format⇨AutoFormat.**

   An AutoFormat dialog box appears, as shown in Figure 7-15.

3. **Click on a format in the Table format list, and then click on OK.**

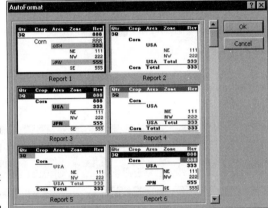

Figure 7-15:
The
AutoFormat
dialog box.

Deleting a PivotTable

If you decide that you don't need your PivotTable anymore, you can wipe it completely off your worksheet by following these steps:

1. **Right-click anywhere inside the PivotTable that you want to delete.**

   A pop-up menu appears.

2. **Choose Select⇨EntireTable.**

3. **Choose Edit⇨Delete.**

   A Delete dialog box appears.

4. **Click on OK.**

If you decide you've made a mistake and you don't really want to delete your PivotTable after all, press Ctrl+Z right away.

Chapter 8

Verifying Worksheet Formulas

. . . .

In This Chapter

▶ Tracing your formulas for problems

▶ Dealing with error messages

▶ Examining your cells in detail

▶ Looking for an oddball formula

▶ Correcting spelling errors

. . . .

*A*fter you type labels, numbers, and formulas into a worksheet, your job still isn't over. Now you have to make sure that your formulas calculate the correct answer. After all, you can create the best-looking spreadsheet in the world with fancy fonts, but if your spreadsheet consistently calculates wrong answers, no one can use it (except for the United States government).

To make sure that your spreadsheet calculates its formulas correctly, you may need to spend time examining each formula. Naturally, examining formulas can be a pain in the neck, but spending time checking your formulas is much easier than making a big mistake and going bankrupt because of your spreadsheet's faulty calculations.

How Microsoft Excel 2000 Helps Verify Your Formulas

To help you verify that your formulas are working correctly, Microsoft Excel 2000 comes with a special auditing feature that can identify

✔ Where a formula gets its data (so that you can see whether a formula is getting all the data it needs)

✔ How one formula may depend on the (possibly incorrect) calculation from another formula

If a formula isn't getting all the right data, the formula obviously can't calculate the correct results. Likewise, calculations from one formula can be used as data by another formula; so, if one formula calculates wrong answers, then any formulas that depend on that first formula are messed up as well.

Most of Microsoft Excel 2000's auditing features are hidden on the Auditing Toolbar, as shown in Figure 8-1. To display the Auditing Toolbar, choose Tools⇨Auditing⇨Show Auditing Toolbar.

Trace Precedents

Trace Dependents

Remove All Arrows

New Comment

Clear Validation Circles

Figure 8-1:
The Auditing
Toolbar.

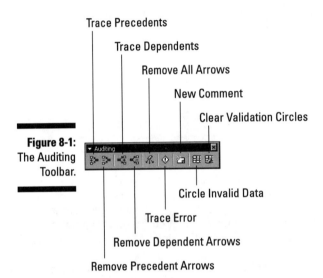

Circle Invalid Data

Trace Error

Remove Dependent Arrows

Remove Precedent Arrows

Tracing Your Formulas

The whole purpose of the Auditing Toolbar is to help you trace your formulas. To use auditing, you need to understand Microsoft Excel 2000's weird terminology. A *precedent* is a cell that contains data used by a formula, and a *dependent* is a cell that contains a formula.

For example, suppose that a formula appears in cell B7 like this:

```
=B5+B6
```

In this example, the cells B5 and B6 are called the precedents, and the cell B7 is the dependent. As long as you remember these definitions, you won't get confused between the Trace Precedents and the Trace Dependents icons on the Auditing Toolbar.

Understanding where a formula gets its data

A formula is only as good as the data it receives. Feed a formula the wrong data, and you always get the wrong answer. (This law of nature explains why governments are perpetually clueless: As long as they keep asking the wrong questions, they never come up with the right answers.)

If you want to know where your formula gets its data, follow these steps:

1. **Click on the cell that contains the formula that you want to examine.**

2. **Click on the Trace Precedents icon on the Auditing Toolbar.**

   Microsoft Excel 2000 draws one or more arrows to show all the cells from which your formula, chosen in Step 1, is getting its data, as shown in Figure 8-2.

If a formula uses data stored in an individual cell, then that cell is marked by a dot. If a formula doesn't use data in a cell, then no dot appears, even if the arrow is drawn over it.

Figure 8-2:
Tracing the
cells where
a formula
gets its
data.

	A	B	C	D
1	Thanks for shopping at Generic-Mart SuperStores			
2	"Putting local stores out of business since 1976"			
3				
4	Item	Quantity	Unit Price	Total
5	Politically-sanitized CDs	45	$16.95	$762.75
6	Middle class values	3	$5.00	$15.00
7	Non-controversial books	9	$9.95	$89.55
8	Maintenance of status quo	11	$4.95	$54.45
9	Censorship tutorials	26	$28.95	$752.70
10	Conservative opinions	4	$1.95	$7.80
11			Subtotal =	$1,682.25
12			Sales Tax Rate =	7.75%
13			Sales Tax =	$130.37
14			You Owe Us =	$1,812.62

Microsoft Excel - GenericMart

File Edit View Insert Format Tools Data Window Help

Arial 10 B I U $ % 100%

D7 = =C7*B7

Auditing

Sheet1 / Sheet2 / Sheet3 /

Ready NUM

Knowing which formulas a cell affects

The beauty of spreadsheets is that you can change one number in a cell and then watch that change ripple throughout the rest of your spreadsheet as the spreadsheet recalculates formulas from top to bottom. In case you want to know how the data stored in one cell may affect any formulas stored in other cells, you can use Excel 2000's auditing features to show you all the formulas that depend on a particular cell.

To identify which formulas a cell affects, follow these steps:

1. **Click on the cell that you want to examine.**

2. **Click on the Trace Dependents icon on the Auditing toolbar.**

   Excel draws one or more arrows that show which formulas your cell will change, as shown in Figure 8-3.

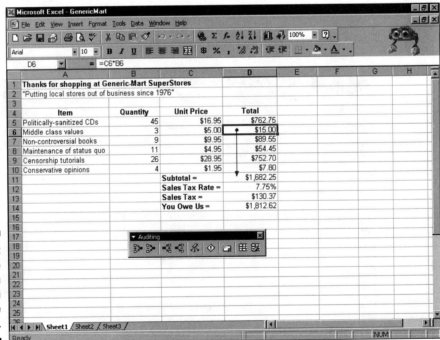

Figure 8-3:
Tracing to
see which
formulas a
change
affects.

Getting rid of those precedent and dependent arrows

After you trace your cells and formulas so that you know how they affect one another, you probably want to remove those silly arrows so that you can see what you're doing. Excel provides three ways to remove these arrows:

✔ Click on the cell that contains an arrowhead (the cell containing a formula), and then click on the Remove Precedent Arrows icon.

✔ Click on the cell that contains a dot and then click on the Remove Dependent Arrows icon. (You have to complete this step for each cell that contains a dot in the same arrow.)

✔ Click on the Remove All Arrows icon.

Knowing What to Do When a Formula Displays an Error Message

Sometimes you may create a formula and, rather than display a result, the cell displays an error message (#VALUE!, for example). Table 8-1 shows some of the most common error messages and a description of how you confused Excel 2000.

Table 8-1	Common Error Messages in Excel 2000 Formulas
Error Value	*What It Means*
#DIV/0!	Your formula is trying to divide by zero.
#VALUE!	Your formula isn't receiving the type of data it expects. For example, a formula may get a text string when it expects an integer.
#####	The cell width is too small to display the entire number. (To fix this problem, simply increase the width of your cell.)

Whenever your formula displays an error message rather than an actual result, you can hunt down and correct the mistake right away by following these steps:

1. **Click on the cell that contains the error message.**

2. **Click on the Trace Error icon on the Auditing toolbar.**

Excel draws a line that shows you all the cells that feed data to your formula, as shown in Figure 8-4. In this example, Excel is telling you that you're trying to multiply the text string stored in cell B6 by the number stored in C6. Because you can't multiply a number by a string, Excel 2000 displays an error message in cell D6 and D11.

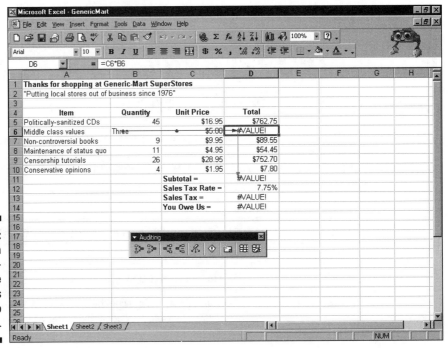

Figure 8-4: Tracing an error message to see which cells may be to blame.

Validating Your Data

When you're creating a formula, you usually have a good idea what type of data is not acceptable. For example, if you're calculating weekly paychecks by multiplying the hourly wage by the number of hours worked, then you know that nobody can work a negative number of hours (although many people try).

To catch such data entry errors, you can specify certain restrictions on the type of data that a cell should contain, such as a minimum and a maximum value. The moment someone tries to type data that doesn't meet your specified restrictions, Microsoft Excel 2000 pops up an error message.

Defining validation criteria for a cell

To define the type of data that a cell is allowed to contain, follow these steps:

1. **Click on the cell in which you want to specify the type of data the cell can contain.**

2. **Choose <u>D</u>ata⇨Va<u>l</u>idation.**

3. **Click on the Settings tab.**

   A Data Validation dialog box appears, as shown in Figure 8-5.

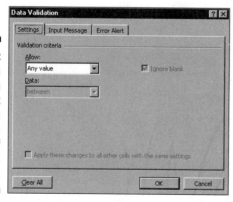

Figure 8-5:
The Data Validation dialog box lets you specify a range of valid data for a cell.

4. **Click on the Allow list box and then choose the type of data allowed in the cell, such as Whole numbers, Decimals, or Text.**

5. **Click on the Data list box and then choose a criterion, such as between, equal to, or greater than.**

6. **Click on the <u>M</u>inimum or Ma<u>x</u>imum list box and then type the minimum and maximum values allowed in your chosen cell.**

7. **Click on OK.**

Creating an input message

When you define a range of valid data for a cell, you may want to inform the user of the range of available data that the cell should contain. Although not necessary, such an input message can guide the user into typing valid data in a particular cell.

To create an input message for a cell, follow these steps:

1. **Click on the cell for which you have already defined a range of valid data.**

2. **Choose <u>D</u>ata⇨Va<u>l</u>idation.**

   A Data Validation dialog box appears.

3. **Click on the Input Message tab, as shown in Figure 8-6.**

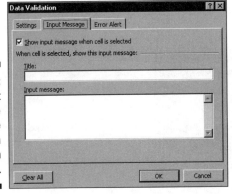

Figure 8-6:
The Input
Message
tab in the
Data
Validation
dialog box.

4. **Type a title for your input message dialog box in the <u>T</u>itle text box.**

5. **Type the message for your input message dialog box in the <u>I</u>nput message text box.**

6. **Click on OK.**

   From this point on, whenever the user highlights the cell chosen in Step 1, Excel 2000 displays a short input message dialog box, as shown in Figure 8-7.

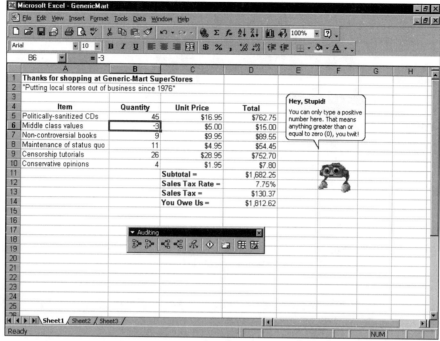

Figure 8-7:
The Input
Message
dialog box
popping up
whether the
user likes it
or not.

Creating an error message

If someone tries to type invalid data in a cell, then Microsoft Excel 2000 displays an error message dialog box, letting the person know the mistake.

To create an error message for a cell, follow these steps:

1. **Click on the cell for which you have already defined a range of valid data.**

2. **Choose Data⇨Validation.**

   A Data Validation dialog box appears.

3. **Click on the Error Alert tab, as shown in Figure 8-8.**

4. **Click on the Style list box and then choose the type of icon that you want displayed, such as Warning, Information, or Stop.**

5. **Type a title for your error message dialog box in the Title text box.**

6. **Type the message for your error message dialog box in the Error message text box.**

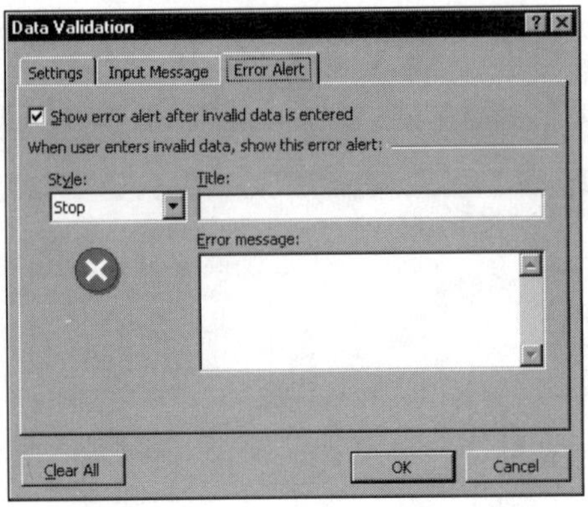

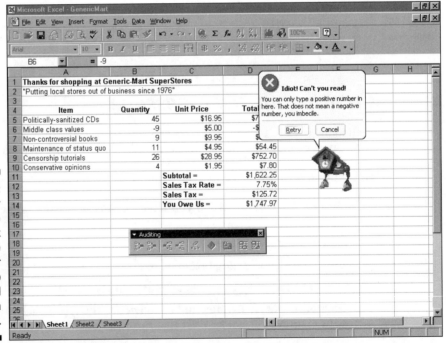

Figure 8-8: The Error Alert tab in the Data Validation dialog box.

7. Click on OK.

From this point on, Excel 2000 displays an error message dialog box if the user tries typing invalid data, as shown in Figure 8-9.

Figure 8-9: The Error Message dialog box scolding the user for trying to type invalid data in a cell.

Identifying invalid data in formulas

By using data validation, you can keep users from typing in nonsensical data, such as a negative number for an age. But what if you want to validate data for your cells that contain formulas as well?

It's perfectly possible for your users to type valid data in cells that feed information to a formula. Unfortunately, the data that the formula calculates may not make sense. For example, suppose you have a formula that calculates a subtotal. Normally the subtotal should add up to a positive number, but what if the subtotal adds up to zero? That should be a clear signal that

✔ Someone didn't type any data into the proper cells.

✔ Someone typed data in the proper cells, but your validation rules for those cells aren't correct.

To identify invalid data in a formula, follow these steps:

1. **Click on the cell containing the formula to which you want to apply data validation.**

2. **Follow Steps 2 through 7 in the "Defining validation criteria for a cell" section of this chapter.**

3. **Click on the Circle Invalid Data icon on the Auditing Toolbar.**

   If Excel 2000 finds any data that doesn't match your data validation criteria for a formula, then Excel 2000 circles (in red) the offending formula, as shown in Figure 8-10.

To remove any red circles around invalid formula data, click on the Clear Validation Circles icon on the Auditing Toolbar.

Finding the Oddball Formula

Often you need a row or column of nearly identical formulas, such as Row 7, as shown in Figure 8-11. In this example, all the cells in Row 11 should add the contents of the cells in Rows 4, 5, 6, 7, 8, 9, and 10.

But here's the dilemma. How do you know that one formula in that row isn't adding up all the rows as it's supposed to? Unless you relish the idea of examining each formula, one by one, Microsoft Excel 2000 has an easier method that lets you quickly find in a row or a column a formula that doesn't fit the other formulas in the same row or column.

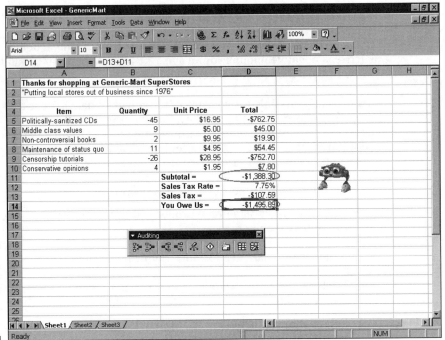

Figure 8-10:
Excel 2000
circles
invalid data
in a formula.

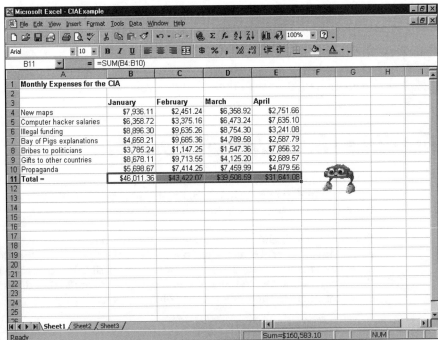

Figure 8-11:
A row of
nearly
identical
formulas.

To find an oddball formula in a row or a column, follow these steps:

1. **Highlight the row or column that contains the formulas that you want to check.**

2. **Choose Edit⇨Go To, or press Ctrl+G.**

   The Go To dialog box appears, as shown in Figure 8-12.

Figure 8-12:
The Go To dialog box.

3. **Click on Special.**

   The Go To Special dialog box appears, as shown in Figure 8-13.

Figure 8-13:
The Go To Special dialog box.

4. **Click on either the Row differences or the Column differences option button and then click on OK.**

   Excel 2000 highlights the cell or cells that contain formulas that are not similar to their neighboring cells.

Checking Your Spelling

Just because you don't know how to spell, that doesn't mean you're stupid. Unfortunately, misspellings and typos can make you look stupid even if your data is 100 percent accurate and up-to-date. If you want to prevent your boss from denying you a raise just because you titled your spreadsheet "Our 2001 Anual Budgett Report," then rest assured that Microsoft Excel 2000 can check your spelling before you print your spreadsheet for other people to see.

To check your spelling, follow these steps:

1. **Press F7, choose Tools⇨Spelling, or click on the Spelling icon on the Standard Toolbar.**

   The Spelling dialog box appears and highlights the first word that Excel suspects is misspelled, as shown in Figure 8-14.

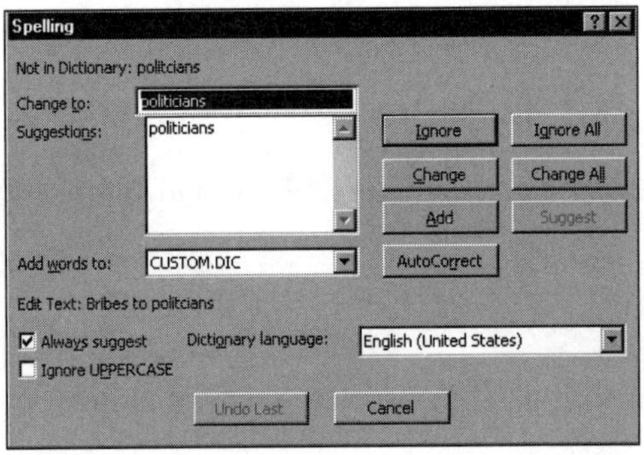

Figure 8-14:
The Spelling dialog box where you can correct misspelled words.

2. **Choose one of the following:**
   - **Ignore:** If you know that the word is spelled correctly
   - **Ignore All:** If you want Excel to ignore all occurrences of the word
   - **Change:** If you want Excel to correct your spelling with the word displayed in the Change To box
   - **Change All:** If you want Excel to correct all occurrences of the word
   - **Add:** To add the word to Excel's dictionary
   - **AutoCorrect:** To make Excel correct any misspellings as defined in its custom dictionary file

3. **Repeat Step 2 for each word Excel highlights as misspelled.**

   Click on Cancel if you want to stop checking before the spell checker is finished. Otherwise, Excel displays a dialog box to let you know when the spelling in your entire worksheet has been checked.

Chapter 9

Printing Pretty Pages

. . . .

In This Chapter

▶ Making cells look nice

▶ Fitting your work on a single page

▶ Messing with margins

▶ Placing headers and footers on a page

▶ Choosing paper size and changing its orientation

▶ Deciding whether to print gridlines, headings, and page orders

. . . .

After you type all your text and numbers, make sure your formulas work properly, and format your data to look nice, your next headache (if you choose to accept the assignment) is to make your pages look presentable when you print them.

Prettying Up Individual Cells

Normally, the cells in a worksheet look plain, dull, and ordinary — much like many of your relatives. Rather than force you to endure plain black-and-white cells, Microsoft Excel 2000 gives you the opportunity to spice up your cells with color, borders, and strange text manipulations.

Splashing cells with color

For your first step in beautifying your worksheet cells, throw some color in the cells. Color can serve purely aesthetic purposes, or color can highlight certain features of your worksheet — a red cell warning you of losses or a green cell emphasizing your profits.

To add color to a cell, follow these steps:

1. **Click on the cell to which you want to add color.**

2. **Choose Format⇨Cells, press Ctrl+1, or right-click and choose Format Cells.**

   The Format Cells dialog box appears.

3. **Click on the Patterns tab, as shown in Figure 9-1.**

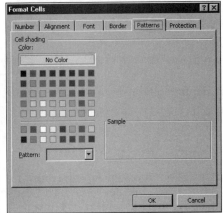

Figure 9-1:
The
Patterns tab
in the
Format Cells
dialog box
for choosing
a color.

4. **Click on a color.**

   Your chosen color appears in the Sample box so that you can get a better idea what the color actually looks like.

5. **Click on OK.**

If you want to change the color of the text inside a cell, click on a cell, then click on the Font Color icon on the Formatting toolbar, and then click on the color you want to use.

Putting a border around a cell

Besides adding color to a cell, you can also put borders around a cell. To add a border around a cell, follow these steps:

1. **Click on the cell to which you want to add a border.**

2. **Choose Format⇨Cells, press Ctrl+1, or right-click and choose Format Cells.**

   The Format Cells dialog box appears.

3. **Click on the Border tab, as shown in Figure 9-2.**

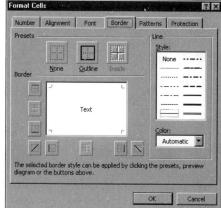

Figure 9-2:
The Border
tab in the
Format Cells
dialog box
for choosing
a border.

4. **Click on the Color list box and then choose a color for your border.**

5. **Click on a line style in the Style box to choose a thick, thin, or dotted line for your border.**

6. **Click on the border buttons in the Border group to choose a top, bottom, left, or right border for your chosen cell.**

7. **Click on OK.**

Cramming text in a cell

You can type a bunch of text in a cell, but if the cell isn't wide enough, Microsoft Excel 2000 mindlessly allows the text to spill across to any neighboring cells. At this point, you can increase the width of the cell that contains the text (so the entire text fits inside the wider cell).

Unfortunately, widening one cell automatically widens the entire column of cells at the same time. If you want text to appear in one cell without having to widen the cell too much, you can tell Excel 2000 to wrap text inside a cell.

Text-wrapping simply makes the cell taller (increases the row height) without adjusting the column width one bit.

To apply text-wrapping to a cell, follow these steps:

1. **Click on the cell to which you want to apply text-wrapping.**

2. **Choose Format⇨Cells, press Ctrl+1, or right-click and choose Format Cells.**

   The Format Cells dialog box appears.

3. **Click on the Alignment tab, as shown in Figure 9-3.**

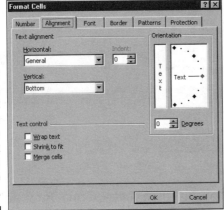

Figure 9-3:
The Alignment tab in the Format Cells dialog box for shoving text inside a cell.

4. **Click on the Wrap text check box so that a check mark appears.**

5. **Click on OK.**

   Microsoft Excel 2000 crams your text inside the chosen cell, as shown in Figure 9-4.

Merging text in multiple cells

You may find that two or more cells have identical information, such as a name. Rather than clutter up your worksheet with redundant labels, Microsoft Excel 2000 lets you merge cells with identical contents into one big cell. That way your worksheet can be easier to study and understand (hopefully).

To merge text in multiple cells, follow these steps:

1. **Highlight the cells that contain identical text.**

Cell with text-wrapping

Cell without text-wrapping

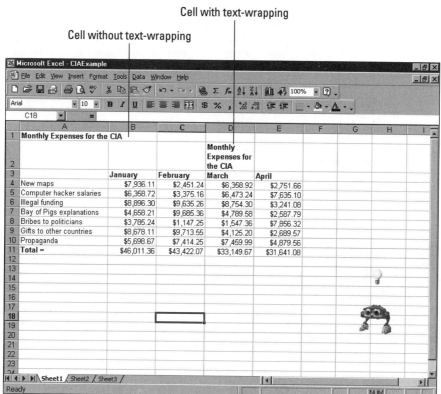

Figure 9-4:
Text-
wrapping in
a cell.

2. **Choose Format➪Cells, press Ctrl+1, or right-click and choose Format Cells.**

   The Format Cells dialog box appears.

3. **Click on the Alignment tab (refer to Figure 9-3).**

4. **Click on the Vertical list box and then choose Center (or Top, Bottom, or Justify).**

5. **Click on the Merge cells check box so that a check mark appears.**

   A dialog box appears, letting you know that Excel 2000 is about to merge all the text into one big cell.

6. **Click on OK.**

   Microsoft Excel 2000 merges your cells together, as shown in Figure 9-5.

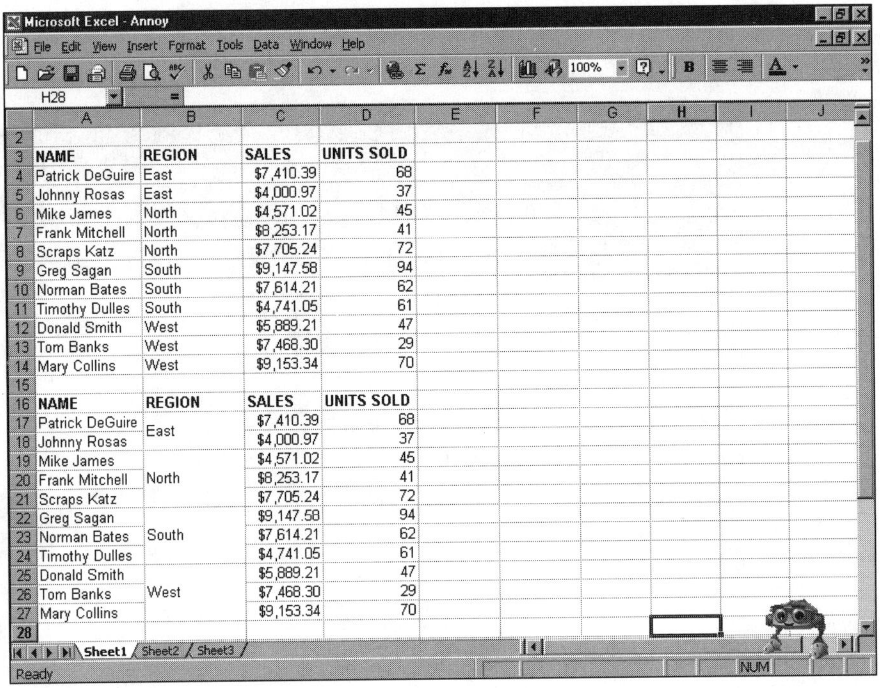

Figure 9-5:
Merging
multiple
cells
together.

Squeezing (Or Blowing up) Your Work

Nothing is more frustrating than creating a spreadsheet in which everything fits on one page — except for one or two lines that print on a second page, as shown in Figure 9-6. Rather than print your spreadsheet on two pages and leave the second page mostly blank, you can tell Excel to squeeze all your work onto a single page.

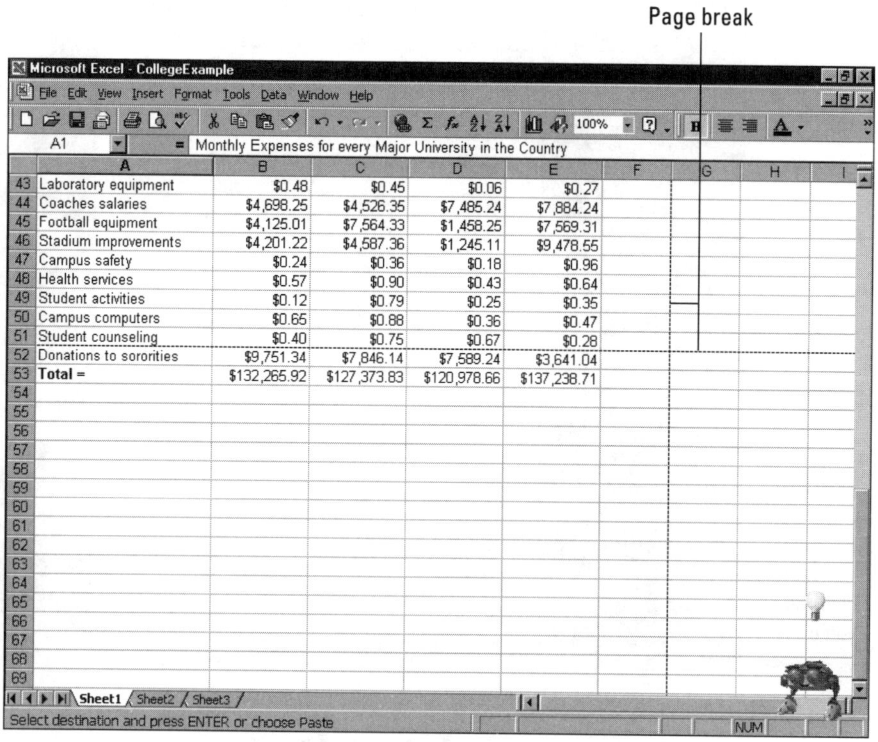

Page break

Figure 9-6:
A typical
worksheet
inconve-
niently
divided by a
page break.

To shrink or expand your spreadsheet, follow these steps:

1. **Choose File⇨Print Preview.**

   Excel displays your worksheet exactly as the worksheet will look when
   you print it, as shown in Figure 9-7.

2. **Click on Setup.**

   The Page Setup dialog box appears, as shown in Figure 9-8.

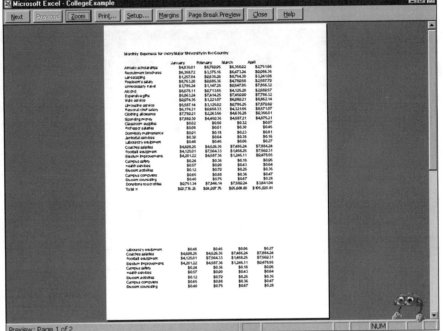

Figure 9-7:
Print
Preview
shows what
your work-
sheet will
look like if
you print it.

Figure 9-8:
The Page
Setup dialog
box for
adjusting
your work-
sheet
pages.

3. **Click on the Fit to option button and then click on the page(s) wide by list box and the tall list box to specify how you want Excel to squeeze your spreadsheet onto your pages.**

   For example, if you want to squeeze everything onto one page, then both the "page(s) wide by" and the "tall" list boxes should have 1 in them.

4. **Click on OK.**

   Excel 2000 displays your newly scaled worksheet.

5. **Click on Close when you're happy with the way your worksheet will look when it's printed.**

As an alternative to clicking on the Fit to option button in Step 3, you can click on the Adjust to option button and then click on the % normal size list box to change the scaling of your worksheet.

This option lets you specify an exact percentage to shrink or expand your worksheet. To shrink your worksheet, choose a percentage less than 100 (90, for example). To expand your worksheet, choose a percentage larger than 100 (120, for example).

Shrinking or expanding your worksheet lets you change the way page breaks separate your worksheet. If you already know where you want to put a page break, you can easily tell Excel 2000, "See that row? Put a page break right there."

To place a page break, follow these steps:

1. **Click on the row label that you want to appear directly below the page break.**

   If you want to put a page break between Rows 6 and 7, then click on Row label 7.

2. **Choose Insert⇨Page Break.**

To remove a page break, follow these steps:

1. **Click on any cell in the row directly beneath the page break.**

2. **Choose Insert⇨Remove Page Break.**

Setting Page Margins

Nothing is more annoying than printing your entire worksheet, binding it together, and then suddenly realizing that your margins are so narrow that you have to pry apart the binding just to see the left-hand column of your worksheet. To prevent this problem and to give you another way to make your worksheets look aesthetically pleasing, Microsoft Excel 2000 lets you adjust the top, bottom, right, and left margins.

Adjusting page margins the fast way

If you're in a hurry and want to adjust your page margins quickly, then using your mouse is the easiest route. Although using the mouse isn't precise, the mouse is fast and easy, which is a rare commodity in anything involving personal computers.

To adjust your page margins quickly, follow these steps:

1. **Choose <u>F</u>ile⇨Print Pre<u>v</u>iew.**

   Excel displays your worksheet exactly as it will look when you print it (refer to Figure 9-7).

2. **Click on <u>M</u>argins.**

   Excel 2000 displays your worksheet's margins, as shown in Figure 9-9.

3. **Move the mouse pointer over any of the page margins so that the pointer turns into a double-pointing arrow, as shown in Figure 9-9.**

Figure 9-9:
Page
margins as
seen in Print
Preview.

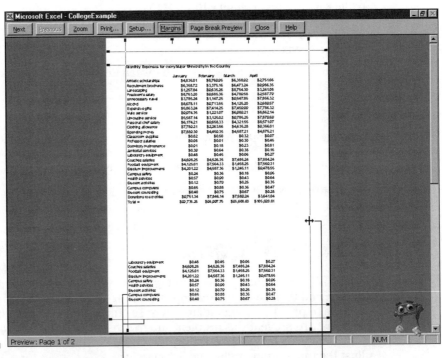

Page margins   Double-pointing arrow

4. **Hold down the left mouse button and drag the mouse to where you want the new margin to appear.**

   The original page margin line remains visible, and a new dotted line appears under the mouse pointer so that you know where the new page margin will appear.

5. **When you're happy with the page margin position, release the left mouse button.**

6. **Click on Close.**

Adjusting page margins the slower, more precise way

In case you absolutely must have page margins narrowed to two decimal places, you can specify exact values rather than just move the page margins around and guess where they should appear.

To adjust your page margins by typing values, follow these steps:

1. **Choose File⇨Page Setup.**

   The Page Setup dialog box appears (refer to Figure 9-8).

2. **Click on the Margins tab, as shown in Figure 9-10.**

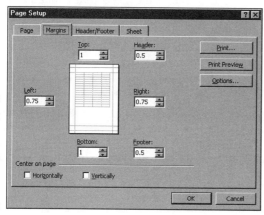

Figure 9-10:
Defining
precise
values for
your page
margins.

3. **Click on the Top, Bottom, Left, or Right list boxes and then choose a value for your page margins.**

4. **Click on the Horizontally and Vertically check boxes in the Center on page group if you want your worksheet neatly centered on the page.**

5. **Click on OK.**

Playing with Headers and Footers

A *header* consists of text that appears at the top of every page in your worksheet, but only when you print it. Here are some typical examples of headers:

- ✔ Annual 2000 Report
- ✔ Prepared by John Doe (who deserves a fat raise)
- ✔ Top Secret: Destroy before reading

A *footer* consists of text that appears at the bottom of every page in your worksheet, but only when you print it. Here are some typical examples of footers:

- ✔ Page 5
- ✔ Copyright © 2001
- ✔ Warning: Profit margins seem larger than they really are

To help make the process of choosing a header or a footer as mindless as possible, Microsoft Excel 2000 provides a list box that contains some common types of headers and footers. You can also create your own headers and footers and get as creative as you want.

Choosing a header and a footer

If you don't want to think for yourself, the simplest solution is to choose a header or a footer that Microsoft Excel 2000 has already created for you.

To choose one of the default headers or footers, follow these steps:

1. **Choose File➪Page Setup.**

   The Page Setup dialog box appears (refer to Figure 9-8).

2. **Click on the Header/Footer tab, as shown in Figure 9-11.**

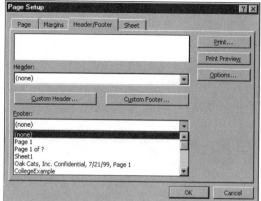

Figure 9-11:
The Header/
Footer tab
in the
Page Setup
dialog box.

3. **Click on the Header list box and then choose a header.**

4. **Click on the Footer list box and then choose a footer.**

5. **Click on OK.**

Making your own headers and footers

Unfortunately, being forced to choose from one of Microsoft Excel 2000's default headers or footers can seem as limiting as choosing between two equally obnoxious and unappealing politicians. To give you even greater freedom, Excel 2000 lets you create your own custom headers and footers.

To create a custom header or footer, follow these steps:

1. **Choose File⇨Page Setup.**

   The Page Setup dialog box appears (refer to Figure 9-8).

2. **Click on the Header/Footer tab (refer to Figure 9-11).**

3. **Click on Custom Header.**

   The Header dialog box appears, as shown in Figure 9-12.

4. **Click on the text box displayed in the Left Section box.**

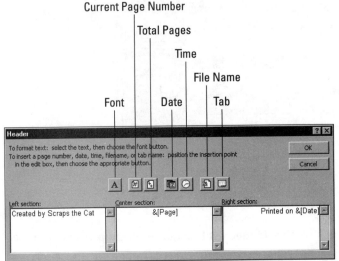

Figure 9-12:
The Header
dialog box
for creating
your own
header.

5. **Type the text that you want to display as your header. If you want Excel 2000 to insert or format text for you, click on one of the following buttons:**

   • **Font:** Lets you change your header/footer's font and font size

   • **Current Page Number:** Displays the current page number

   • **Total Pages:** Displays the total number of pages in your worksheet

   • **Date:** Inserts the date on which you print the worksheet

   • **Time:** Inserts the time at which you print the worksheet

   • **File Name:** Inserts the file name of your worksheet

   • **Tab:** Inserts the worksheet name

6. **Click on the Center Section box, type more text, and then click on the Right Section box to type even more text, if you want.**

7. **Click on OK.**

   The Page Setup dialog box appears again.

8. **Click on Custom Footer.**

   The Footer dialog box that appears looks suspiciously similar to the Header dialog box (refer to Figure 9-12).

9. **Repeat Steps 5 through 7 and fill in the information for your footer.**

10. **Click on OK.**

   The Page Setup dialog box appears again.

11. **Click on OK.**

Changing the Paper Size and Orientation

Sometimes a worksheet won't fit within the confines of a typical piece of paper. When this situation occurs, you can tell Microsoft Excel 2000 to print your worksheets sideways or on legal-size paper so that everything fits on a single page.

Changing the page orientation

The two types of page orientation are portrait and landscape. In *portrait orientation,* a page is taller than it is wide. Think about how you would orient a canvas to paint a person's portrait. Because most people are taller than they are wide, height is more important.

In *landscape orientation,* a page is wider than it is tall. If you paint a landscape, width is more important than height, so you use landscape orientation when you want to print your worksheets sideways on a sheet of paper.

To change the page orientation of your worksheet, follow these steps:

1. **Choose File⇨Page Setup.**

   The Page Setup dialog box appears (refer to Figure 9-8).

2. **Click on the Page tab, as shown in Figure 9-13.**

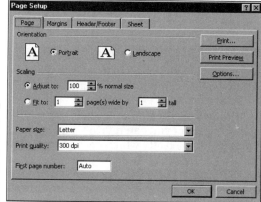

Figure 9-13:
The Page
tab in the
Page Setup
dialog box.

3. **Click on the Portrait or Landscape option button.**
4. **Click on OK.**

Choosing the size of your paper

Many people use paper that measures 8½ x 11 inches. If you want to cram more of your worksheet on a single page, you can just stuff your printer with different sizes of paper. Immediately after you load your printer with a different size of paper, you have to tell Microsoft Excel 2000 the size of the new paper so that it correctly prints your worksheets on the paper.

To tell Microsoft Excel 2000 the size of the paper on which to print, follow these steps:

1. **Choose File➪Page Setup.**

   The Page Setup dialog box appears (refer to Figure 9-8).
2. **Click on the Page tab (refer to Figure 9-13).**
3. **Click on the Paper size list box and then choose a paper size.**
4. **Click on OK.**

Printing Gridlines, Headings, and Page Orders

The entire purpose of displaying gridlines and row/column headings is to help you place your labels, numbers, and formulas. Normally, when you print a worksheet, you don't want your gridlines and row or column headings to appear, because they can be as distracting as the wires holding up a marionette during a puppet show.

Because Excel 2000 gives you options for practically everything imaginable, you can also choose to print your gridlines and headings. Then you can see exactly which cells contain labels, numbers, and formulas.

One good time to print gridlines and headings is when you're printing a worksheet with all its formulas revealed (you can reveal your formulas by pressing Ctrl+'). Then you can see exactly which cells contain data and which cells contain formulas.

If you have a particularly large worksheet (three pages or more), then you can even tell Excel 2000 in which order you want to print everything. Then you don't have to re-sort your worksheets by hand after printing them. The two choices for printing your worksheets are

✔ Down, then over (Prints from top to bottom, then from right to left)

✔ Over, then down (Prints from right to left, then top to bottom)

Which method you choose depends on your personal preferences and how you organize your data in a worksheet. For example, you may want to print Over, then down, if your data is organized as follows:

1st Quarter sales   *2nd Quarter sales*

       Jan.   Feb.   Mar.   Apr.   May   Jun.

Cat food   Cat food

Dog food   Dog food

Fish food   Fish food

3rd Quarter sales   *4th Quarter sales*

       Jul.   Aug.   Sep.   Oct.   Nov.   Dec.

Cat food   Cat food

Dog food   Dog food

Fish food   Fish food

But, suppose your worksheets are organized this way, in which case you probably want to print Down, then over, to make sure that your data appears in the right order.

1st Quarter sales   *3rd Quarter sales*

       Jan.   Feb.   Mar.   Jul.   Aug.   Sep.

Cat food   Cat food

Dog food   Dog food

Fish food   Fish food

2nd Quarter sales   *4th Quarter sales*

       Apr.   May   Jun.   Oct.   Nov.   Dec.

Cat food   Cat food

Dog food   Dog food

Fish food   Fish food

To change the print order of your worksheet or to make Excel 2000 print gridlines and headings, follow these steps:

1. **Choose File⇨Page Setup.**

   The Page Setup dialog box appears (refer to Figure 9-8).

2. **Click on the Sheet tab, as shown in Figure 9-14.**

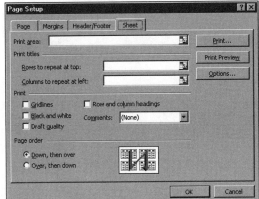

Figure 9-14:
The Sheet tab in the Page Setup dialog box.

3. **Click on the Gridlines check box so that a check mark appears if you want to print gridlines.**

4. **Click on the Row and column headings check box so that a check mark appears if you want to print row and column headings.**

5. **Click on either the Down, then over option button or the Over, then down option button in the Page order group.**

6. **Click on OK.**

Chapter 10

Sharing Your Microsoft Excel Worksheets

*E*ven though you can work happily by yourself with a copy of Microsoft Excel 2000 on your computer, you may need to share your worksheets with other people so that they can add new data or stare at the wonderful calculations that you've created. So, the next time you create an Excel 2000 worksheet, feel free to share your worksheet with others. This chapter shows you how.

Adding Comments to Cells

When you share your Microsoft Excel 2000 worksheets with other people, you may want to add comments to your worksheets to ask for more help, question certain formula assumptions, or tell your coworker what a jerk your boss was last Friday afternoon. You can print your worksheets and attach comments to them with a paper clip, but Excel 2000 includes a neat feature for attaching comments directly to your individual worksheet cells.

Attaching a comment

Notes can come in handy when you want to remind yourself about the contents of a certain cell ("January sales were down because Bob messed up") or if you're sharing Microsoft Excel 2000 worksheets with others ("Jane, verify that this figure is accurate; if it's not, you'll be suspected of embezzlement").

To attach a comment to a cell, follow these steps:

1. **Click on the cell to which you want to attach your comment.**

2. **Choose Insert⇨Comment, or right-click and choose Insert Comment.**

   The Comment window appears, as shown in Figure 10-1.

3. **Type your comment and then click anywhere on the worksheet when you're done.**

   Excel 2000 draws a little red dot in the upper-right corner of the cell to let you know that the cell contains a comment, as shown in Figure 10-2. (Obviously the red dot looks black in the figure.)

The comment window automatically includes the name that you gave Microsoft Office 2000 when you first installed the program. If you want to change the name that appears in the comment window, then choose Tools⇨ Options, click the General tab, type a new name in the User name box, and then click on OK.

Figure 10-1: The Comment window for typing additional text to a cell.

	A	B	C	D
2				
3	NAME	REGION	SALES	UNITS SOLD
4	Patrick DeGuire	East	$7,410.39	68
5	Johnny Rosas	East	$4,000.97	37
6	Mike James	North	$4,571.02	45
7	Frank Mitchell	North	$8,253.17	41
8	Scraps Katz		24	72
9	Greg Sagan		58	94
10	Norman Bates		21	62
11	Timothy Dulles		05	61
12	Donald Smith		21	47
13	Tom Banks	West	$7,468.30	29
14	Mary Collins	West	$9,153.34	70
15				
16	NAME	REGION	SALES	UNITS SOLD
17	Patrick DeGuire	East	$7,410.39	68
18	Johnny Rosas		$4,000.97	37
19	Mike James		$4,571.02	45
20	Frank Mitchell	North	$8,253.17	41
21	Scraps Katz		$7,705.24	72
22	Greg Sagan		$9,147.58	94
23	Norman Bates	South	$7,614.21	62
24	Timothy Dulles		$4,741.05	61
25	Donald Smith		$5,889.21	47
26	Tom Banks	West	$7,468.30	29
27	Mary Collins		$9,153.34	70
28				

Microsoft Excel - Annoy

File Edit View Insert Format Tools Data Window Help

Comment 20

Scraps the Cat:

Sheet1 / Sheet2 / Sheet3 /

Cell A9 commented by Scraps the Cat

NUM

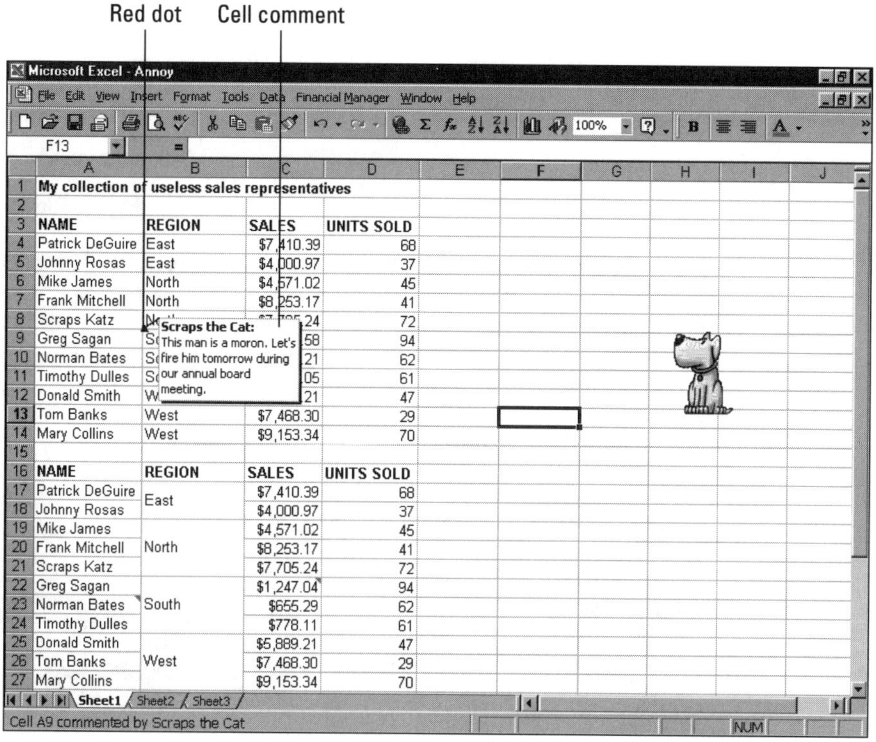

Red dot   Cell comment

Figure 10-2:
A cell
comment
appears
whenever
you move
the mouse
pointer over
a cell that
contains a
red dot.

Finding all comments in a worksheet

After you or someone else has scattered various comments in different cells, the hard part may be finding them so that you can read them. If you want, you can look for every red dot that appears in a cell, but if you have that much time on your hands, then you probably need a hobby to soak up your free time. For an easier method, just have Microsoft Excel 2000 show you a list of all the cell comments in a worksheet.

To find all the cell comments buried throughout a worksheet, follow these steps:

1. **Choose View⇨Comments.**

   All the comment windows appear along with the Reviewing toolbar, as shown in Figure 10-3.

2. **Click on the Hide All Comments icon on the Reviewing toolbar to make your comment windows disappear again.**

3. **Click on the close box in the Reviewing toolbar to make the Reviewing toolbar disappear.**

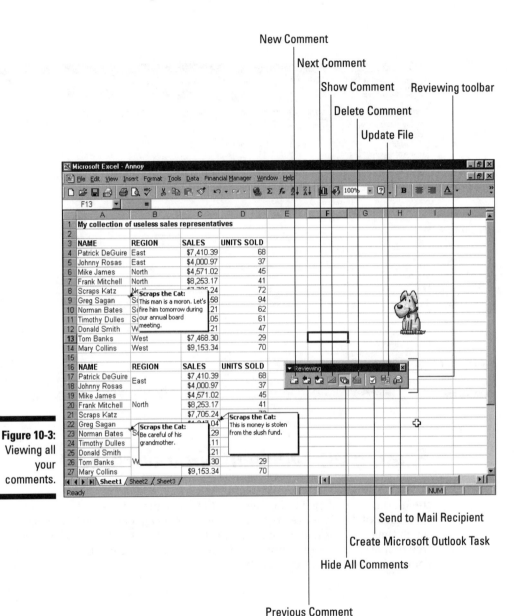

Figure 10-3: Viewing all your comments.

Editing a comment

Whenever you want, you can edit a comment in case you need to add more information or just feel like typing a dirty joke in place of a useful comment. To edit a comment, follow these steps:

1. **Click on the cell that contains the comment that you want to edit.**

2. **Choose Insert⇨Edit Comment, or right-click and choose Edit Comment.**

   The comment window pops up.

3. **Click anywhere inside the comment window and then type or edit your comment.**

4. **Click anywhere outside the comment window when you're done.**

Printing comments

When you print your worksheets, Microsoft Excel 2000 normally refuses to print any cell comments. In case you want (or need) to print your comments along with your worksheets, you can do so by following these steps:

1. **Choose File⇨Page Setup.**

   The Page Setup dialog box appears.

2. **Click on the Sheet tab.**

3. **Click on the Comments list box and then choose one of the following:**

   • (None).

   • At end of sheet.

   • As displayed on sheet. Make sure that you choose View⇨Comments before printing your worksheet.

4. **Click on OK.**

Deleting comments

After littering a worksheet with comments, you eventually want to get rid of the comments so that the cells don't keep sprouting messages whenever you move the mouse pointer over the red dots.

To delete a comment, follow these steps:

1. **Right-click on the cell containing the comment that you want to delete.**

   A pop-up menu appears.

2. **Click on Delete Comment.**

If you delete a comment by mistake, then press Ctrl+Z to recover it.

Playing with Scenarios

Creating a worksheet and plugging in numbers can give you an accurate calculation, but what if you aren't sure which values you should use? Suppose you're creating a report that lists how much money your company has lost in the past year but not all the sales results for the fourth quarter are available yet.

Rather than just give up and go home (which is probably the more appealing option), Microsoft Excel 2000 lets you create your worksheet anyway and then display separate scenarios. A *scenario* is just an identical copy of a worksheet with slightly different numbers plugged into it.

One scenario may contain numbers that show a highly optimistic possibility, and another scenario may contain numbers that show a more pessimistic (and probably more realistic) result. By plugging different numbers into the same worksheet and storing separate copies of the calculations, you can forecast the range of possible outcomes that might occur. If fourth quarter sales are high, for example, you can pay off your bills; if fourth quarter sales are lower than expected, you can start looking for another job tomorrow.

Creating a scenario

Before you create a scenario, you have to create your worksheet. Then you have to specify which cells will contain different numbers between your scenarios. The cells that you choose are called *changing cells,* because the contents of these cells will — obviously — vary between your multiple scenarios.

To create a scenario, follow these steps:

1. **Choose Tools⇨Scenarios.**

   The Scenario Manager dialog box appears, as shown in Figure 10-4.

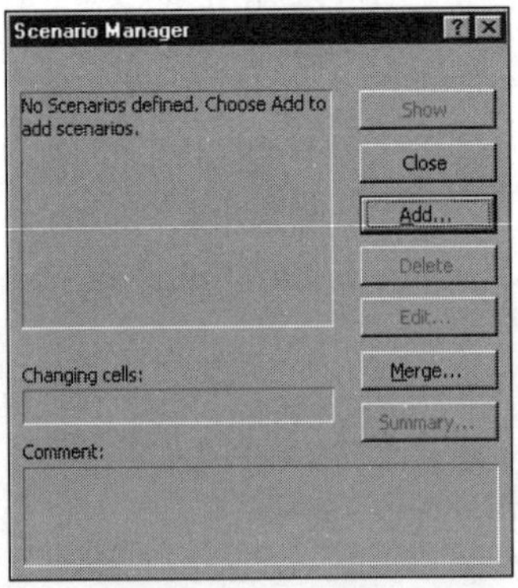

Figure 10-4:
The
Scenario
Manager
dialog box.

2. **Click on Add.**

   The Add Scenario dialog box appears, as shown in Figure 10-5.

3. **In the Scenario name box, type a descriptive name for your scenario (Best-Case Scenario if Bob Doesn't Ruin Our Latest Deal, for example).**

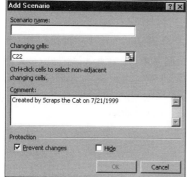

Figure 10-5:
The Add
Scenario
dialog box.

4. **Click on the Changing cells box.**

5. **Highlight or click on all the cells that will contain varying data.**

   To choose more than one cell, drag the mouse over the cells you want, or hold down the Ctrl key and then click on the cells you want to choose.

6. **Click on OK.**

   The Scenario Values dialog box appears, as shown in Figure 10-6.

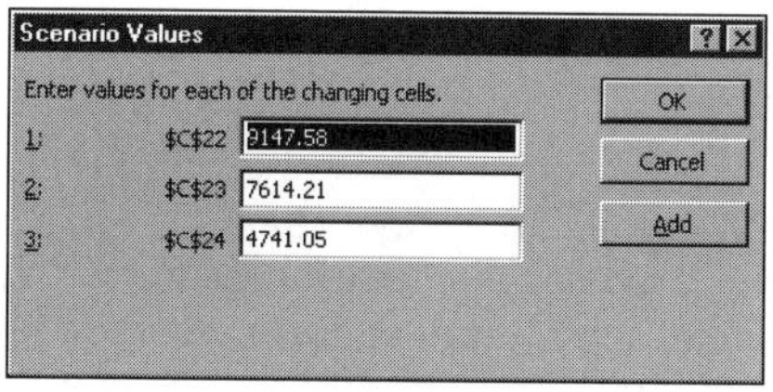

Figure 10-6:
The
Scenario
Values
dialog box.

7. **Type a value for each of your changing cells and then click on OK.**

   The Scenario Manager dialog box appears.

8. **Repeat Steps 2 through 7 for each scenario that you want to create.**

9. **Click on Close.**

Viewing a scenario

After you create two or more scenarios, you can view them and see how the different numbers may affect the rest of your worksheet.

To view your scenarios, follow these steps:

1. **Choose Tools➪Scenarios.**

   The Scenario Manager dialog box appears (refer to Figure 10-4).

2. **Click on the scenario name that you want to view, shown in Figure 10-7, and then click on Show.**

   Microsoft Excel 2000 shows you how the numbers stored in your chosen scenario affect the rest of your worksheet.

3. **Click on Close.**

Figure 10-7: The Scenario Manager dialog box listing different scenarios to choose from.

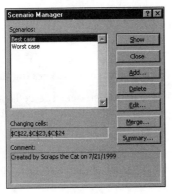

Editing a scenario

A scenario contains numbers that you can always change later, just in case your first guess was wrong or you eventually get more accurate numbers. If your numbers change, then just go over your scenario and plug in the new numbers. Another reason that you may want to edit your scenario is to modify the number of changing cells in the scenario.

To edit a scenario, follow these steps:

1. **Choose Tools➪Scenarios.**

   The Scenario Manager dialog box appears (refer to Figure 10-4).

2. **Click on the scenario name that you want to edit and then click on Edit.**

   The Edit Scenario dialog box appears.

3. Type a new scenario name in the Scenario <u>n</u>ame box (optional).

4. Click on the Changing <u>c</u>ells box, highlight or click on all the cells that you want your scenario to change, and then click on OK.

5. Type the new values for your scenario's changing cells and then click on OK.

6. Click on Close.

Deleting a scenario

Scenarios are great for playing around with different numbers, but you probably won't want to keep your scenarios around forever.

If you delete a scenario, then you cannot undelete it. Make sure that you really want to delete a scenario, because when a scenario's gone, it's gone for good.

To delete a scenario, follow these steps:

1. Choose <u>T</u>ools⇨Sc<u>e</u>narios.

   The Scenario Manager dialog box appears (refer to Figure 10-4).

2. Click on the scenario name that you want to delete and then click on <u>D</u>elete.

3. Click on Close.

Protecting Your Worksheets from Others

If you plan to share your Microsoft Excel 2000 files with others, then you probably don't want people to enter different values, edit your labels, or mess around with your formulas. To keep others from messing up your carefully crafted worksheets, Excel 2000 gives you two ways to protect them from modification:

✔ Protect individual sheets

✔ Protect an entire workbook

A workbook consists of one or more sheets. If you protect only one sheet in your workbook, then other people can still modify the other sheets.

When you protect an individual sheet, no one can modify the contents of that sheet. When you protect an entire workbook, no one can add or delete a sheet from the workbook. People can still edit the contents of your individual sheets, however. If you want complete protection from modifications, then protect both your individual sheets and your entire workbook.

Protecting your work

Protecting your work is a good idea whenever you plan to let anyone else look at your Excel files.

To protect a sheet or a workbook, follow these steps:

1. **Choose Tools⇨Protection and then choose one of the following:**

   • **Protect Sheet:** Protects an individual sheet in a workbook

   • **Protect Workbook:** Protects all sheets in a workbook

   • **Protect and Share Workbook:** Tracks editing changes but won't allow anyone (but you) to remove or accept editing changes

   The Protect Sheet (shown in Figure 10-8), Protect Workbook, or Protect and Share Workbook dialog box appears.

Figure 10-8:
The Protect
Sheet dialog
box.

2. **Type a password in the Password box to password-protect your sheet or workbook.**

   Typing a password is optional, but highly recommended. If you don't type a password, anyone can use the Unprotect command to unprotect your work and modify your worksheet. Ideally, you should pick a password that's easy for you to remember but difficult for someone else to guess. For example, using your name as a password isn't smart (although doing so may keep your boss from guessing it). A combination of letters and numbers may be best, such as RU4REAL.

3. Click on OK.

The Confirm Password dialog box appears, asking you to type your password again, as shown in Figure 10-9.

Figure 10-9: The Confirm Password dialog box.

4. Type your password again and then click on OK.

If you have multiple sheets in a workbook, then you can protect each sheet with a different password. That way you can share your passwords with other people so that only certain people can edit specific sheets.

If you password-protect your sheet or workbook and then forget your password, you're locked out from editing your own work. The good news is that many third-party programs (available from www.crak.com or www.accessdata.com) can crack protected Excel files and retrieve your password. The bad news is that thieves can use these same programs to find your password and modify your Excel files. So don't expect a simple password to keep out determined intruders.

Unprotecting your work

After you let hordes of other people paw over your work, you can unprotect your files so that you can edit them again.

To unprotect a sheet or workbook, follow these steps:

1. Choose Tools⇨Protection and then choose either Unprotect Sheet, Unprotect Workbook, or Unprotect Shared Workbook.

An Unprotect Sheet or Unprotect Workbook dialog box appears.

2. Type your password in the Password box and then click on OK.

Part III
The Microsoft PowerPoint 2000 Dog-and-Pony Show

The 5th Wave   By Rich Tennant

YEAH, BUT YOU SHOULD SEE HOW NICELY IT CENTERED EVERYTHING.

In this part . . .

The number one fear of most Americans is public speaking. However, the number one fear of most audiences is wasting their time and being bored to death during a presentation.

Fortunately, Microsoft PowerPoint 2000 can tackle both ends of the problem by helping you create dazzling presentations so that you don't have to say a word and your audience doesn't have to do anything but stare mindlessly at your slide show. By learning how to add sound and video, you can give your slide-show presentation a feeling of importance when you may really have nothing of substance to offer.

To help you create and give your slide-show presentation, PowerPoint 2000 can create notes (so you know what you're supposed to be talking about at any give time) and handouts (so your audience doesn't have to take notes themselves, which frees them to daydream instead of paying attention to what you're saying).

With PowerPoint 2000 as your presentation tool, you'll never be at a loss for words again. Unless, of course, the power goes out during your presentation.

Chapter 11

Prettying Up Your Presentations

• •

In This Chapter

▶ Displaying charts

▶ Adding headers and footers

▶ Playing with WordArt

• •

Microsoft PowerPoint 2000 can present information in a visually pleasing manner so that you can convince others that you're right (even if
you're wrong). To achieve this noble goal, PowerPoint 2000 provides several
features to help make your presentations as neat, organized, and pretty as
possible. Because nothing is more convincing than facts (even if you have to
make them up), PowerPoint 2000 lets you create pie, line, or bar charts that
you can plug into a presentation.

Although people like to believe that looks aren't everything, one glance at the
paychecks that supermodels receive for posing in bikinis should be enough
to convince you otherwise.

Creating and Displaying Charts

Charts can condense globs of information into easy-to-see pictures, so that
your audience can understand your presentation without having to think.
That way, instead of listing boring lines of text for your audience to read, you
can just display a fancy and colorful chart that communicates your message
right away.

Putting a chart on a slide

To be effective, charts need to be fairly large, so you may want to put a chart
on a slide by itself, rather than try to cram the chart on a slide already filled
with text and graphics.

To put a chart on a slide, follow these steps:

1. **Display the slide where you want the chart to appear. (You may want to create a new slide by pressing Ctrl+M.)**

2. **Choose Insert⇨Chart, or click the Insert Chart icon on the Standard toolbar.**

   PowerPoint 2000 displays a sample chart along with a datasheet window for storing the data used to plot points on your chart, as shown in Figure 11-1.

3. **Choose Chart⇨Chart Type.**

   A Chart Type dialog box appears, as shown in Figure 11-2.

4. **Click on the chart type that you want (such as a bar chart or line chart) in the Chart type group.**

5. **Click on the variation of the chart that you want in the Chart sub-type group and then click on OK.**

6. **Click on the datasheet window and then type the data that you want to plot on your chosen chart. (If you want to use data stored in a Microsoft Excel 2000 worksheet, click on the Import File icon and then choose the Excel 2000 file that you want to use.)**

Import File

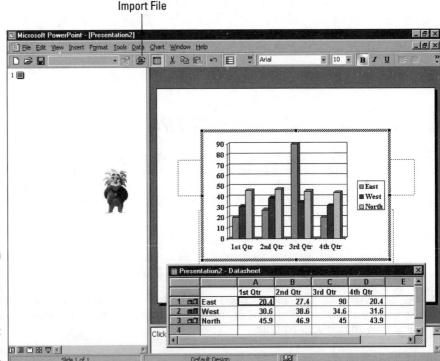

Figure 11-1:
A sample chart and data in the Datasheet window.

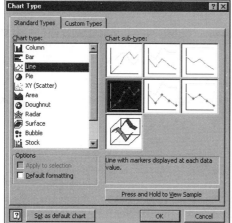

Figure 11-2:
The Chart
Type dialog
box for
choosing a
different
looking
chart.

7. **Click anywhere outside the chart. PowerPoint 2000 displays your chart on the slide.**

   You may have to move the chart to keep it from overlapping any existing text or graphics on the slide.

Editing and deleting data in the datasheet window

A datasheet contains rows and columns of data used to create your chart. However, you may want to edit or delete data in a particular cell.

To edit data in a cell, follow these steps:

1. **Double-click on the cell that contains the data that you want to edit.**

2. **Press the arrow keys, Backspace, or Delete keys to delete characters and then type any new numbers or text that you want to add.**

To replace data in a cell, just click on that cell and type any new data that you want to use.

To delete data in a cell, follow these steps:

1. **Click on the cell that contains the data that you want to delete.**

2. **Press Delete.**

To delete an entire row or column of data, follow these steps:

1. **Click on the gray row or column label containing the data that you want to delete.**

2. **Press Delete.**

If you delete a row or column accidentally, press Ctrl+Z to get your row or column back again.

Moving your chart

Unless you're really lucky, Microsoft PowerPoint 2000 probably won't put your chart in the exact location where you want it to appear on your slide. To fix this problem, you can move or resize your chart at any time.

To move a chart, follow these steps:

1. **Move the mouse pointer over the chart and then click the left mouse button once. White handles appear around the chart borders, as shown in Figure 11-3.**

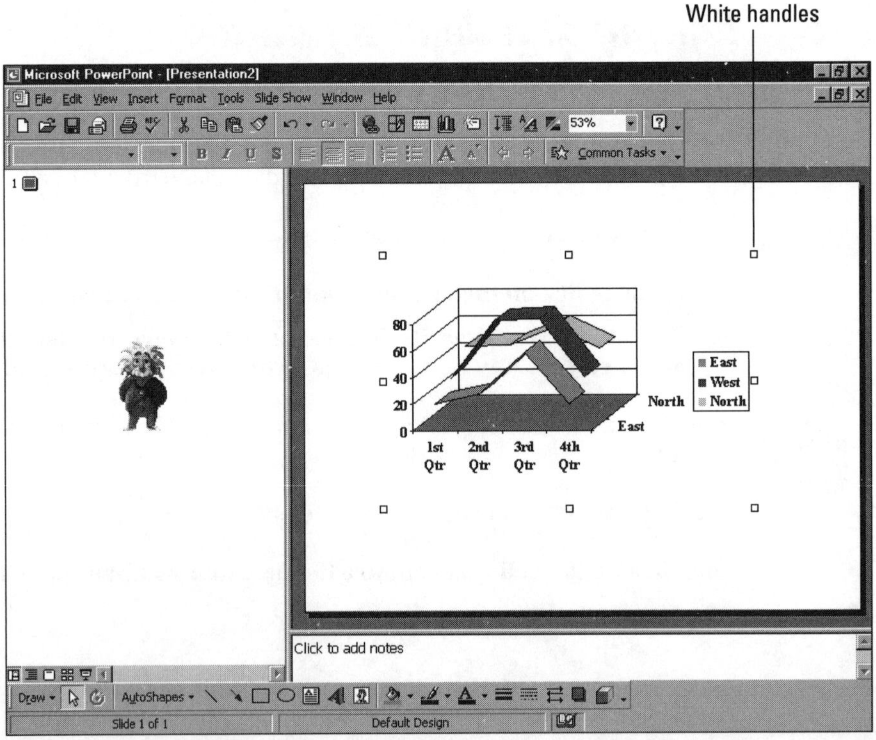

White handles

Figure 11-3:
Choosing a
chart to
move.

2. **Hold down the left mouse button and drag the mouse to move the chart to a new location.**

3. **Release the left mouse button when you're happy with the chart's new location.**

To resize a chart, follow these steps:

1. **Click on the chart.**

   White handles appear around the chart.

2. **Move the mouse pointer over a white handle. The mouse pointer turns into a double-pointing arrow.**

3. **Hold down the left mouse button and drag the mouse to adjust the size of the chart.**

4. **Release the left mouse button when you're happy with the new size of the chart.**

If you drag one of the corner handles, then you can resize the height and width at the same time.

Editing your chart

After you've created a chart, you may want to alter your chart's appearance by picking a new chart, modifying your chart, or changing the data used to plot the points on your chart.

Picking a new chart

In case you want to pick an entirely new chart, you can do so by following these steps:

1. **Move the mouse pointer over the chart and then double-click the left mouse button.**

   Gray borders appear around the chart, and the datasheet window pops up.

2. **Choose Chart⇨Chart Type.**

   A Chart Type dialog box appears (refer to Figure 11-2).

3. **Click on the chart type that you want (such as a bar chart or a line chart) in the Chart type group.**

4. **Click on the variation of the chart that you want in the Chart sub-type group and then click on OK.**

Modifying your chart

To give you some semblance of control over your charts, you can change the following:

- ✔ X- and Y-axis gridlines to make your charts easier to read
- ✔ A chart legend to identify specific points on your chart
- ✔ Whether to chart data by row or column
- ✔ Whether to display data (in a table format) on the chart or not

To modify your chart in any of the preceding ways, follow these steps:

1. **Move the mouse pointer over the chart and then double-click the left mouse button.**

   Gray borders appear around the chart, and the datasheet window pops up.

2. **Choose Chart⇨Chart Options.**

   A Chart Options dialog box appears, as shown in Figure 11-4.

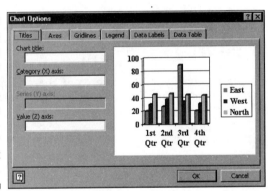

Figure 11-4:
The Chart Options dialog box allows you to change the appearance of your PowerPoint charts.

3. **Click on one of the following tabs and then choose an option.**
   - **Titles:** For typing a chart title or X-axis or Y-axis labels
   - **Axes:** For changing the data used to plot along the X-, Y-, and Z-axes
   - **Gridlines:** For displaying lines on the chart
   - **Legend:** For defining the location of the chart legend
   - **Data Labels:** For displaying labels to identify data on a chart
   - **Data Table:** For displaying data directly on the chart, as shown in Figure 11-5

4. **Click on OK.**

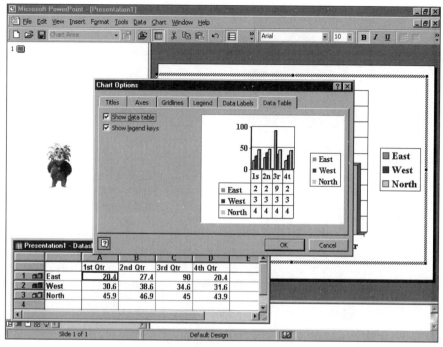

Figure 11-5:
A Data
Table can
display your
numeric
data directly
on a chart.

Plotting Microsoft Excel 2000 data

Rather than create a chart from data typed into the datasheet, you can just
plot data stored in a Microsoft Excel 2000 file instead.

To plot Microsoft Excel 2000 data, follow these steps:

1. **Move the mouse pointer over the chart and then double-click on the left mouse button.**

   Gray borders appear around the chart, and the datasheet window pops up.

2. **Click on the Import File icon.**

   An Import File dialog box appears.

3. **Click on the Excel 2000 file that you want to use and then click on Open.**

   An Import Data Options dialog box appears, as shown in Figure 11-6.

4. **Click on the worksheet name that contains the data that you want to plot. (You may also want to specify the exact cell range as well.)**

5. **Click on OK.**

Figure 11-6:
The Import
Data
Options
dialog box
for choosing
specific
worksheets
to use.

Adding Footers

A footer can display identical text on all your slides. That way you can always display your company's motto ("We treat everyone equally poorly regardless of race, sex, or age"), slide numbers, or date on every slide of your presentation.

To add a footer to your slides, follow these steps:

1. **Choose View⇨Header and Footer.**

   The Header and Footer dialog box appears.

2. **Click on the Slide tab, as shown in Figure 11-7.**

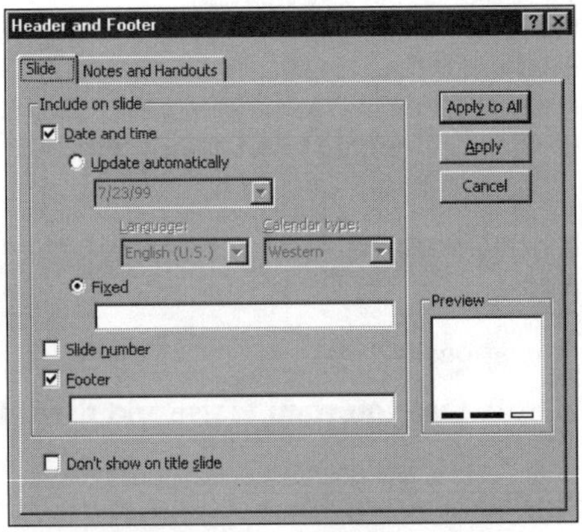

Figure 11-7:
The Slide
tab in the
Header and
Footer
dialog box.

3. **Click on the Date and time check box (so that a check mark appears) if you want to display the date and time.**

4. **Click on the Update automatically option button (and then click on the Update automatically list box to choose a time and date style to display) or click on the Fixed option button and then type any text.**

5. **Click on the Slide number check box (so that a check mark appears) to display the current slide number.**

6. **Click on the Footer check box (so that a check mark appears) and then type any text.**

7. **Click Apply to All (to display your choices on all slides) or Apply (to display your choices on the currently displayed slide).**

Playing with WordArt

To give you yet another way to display text on a slide, Microsoft PowerPoint 2000 lets you use WordArt, which lets you display text in a variety of odd shapes and colors, as shown in Figure 11-8. WordArt serves no functional purpose other than to let you express your creativity and goof around at your computer while pretending to be hard at work creating an important PowerPoint 2000 presentation.

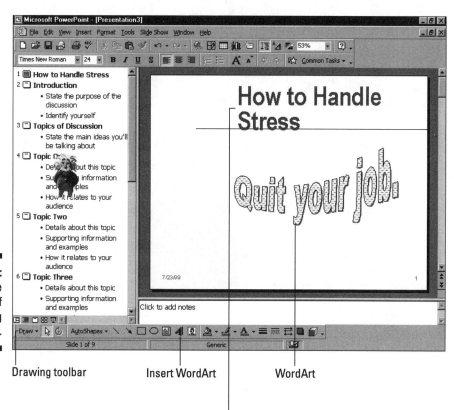

Figure 11-8: A creative example of using WordArt.

Drawing toolbar   Insert WordArt   WordArt

Ordinary text

Creating WordArt

To create WordArt, follow these steps:

1. **Choose <u>V</u>iew⇨<u>T</u>oolbars and then choose Drawing. (If a check mark already appears in front of the Drawing toolbar, skip this step.)**

   The Drawing toolbar appears (refer to Figure 11-8).

2. **Click on the Insert WordArt icon on the Drawing toolbar.**

   The WordArt Gallery appears, as shown in Figure 11-9.

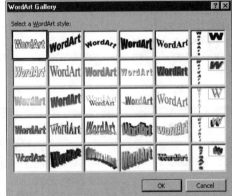

Figure 11-9: The WordArt Gallery.

3. **Click on the WordArt style that you want to use and then click on OK.**

   An Edit WordArt Text dialog box appears, as shown in Figure 11-10.

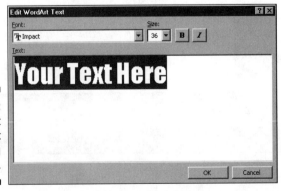

Figure 11-10: The Edit WordArt Text dialog box.

4. **Type your text and then click on OK. (Any changes that you make to the font, size, bold, or italics affects all your WordArt text.)**

PowerPoint 2000 displays your WordArt on the current slide.

You can move WordArt by clicking on the WordArt and then dragging the mouse. Or you can resize WordArt by clicking on the WordArt and then dragging one of the WordArt handles.

Editing WordArt

After you've created some WordArt, you may want to modify your WordArt by changing its shape, color, or text.

Editing the WordArt text

No matter how wonderful your WordArt may look, the whole point of using WordArt is to display text. To edit WordArt text, follow these steps:

1. **Click on the WordArt that you want to edit.**

A WordArt toolbar appears, as shown in Figure 11-11.

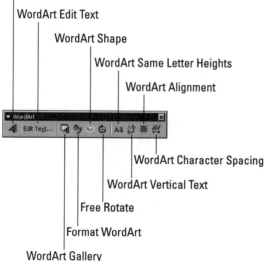

Insert WordArt
WordArt Edit Text
WordArt Shape
WordArt Same Letter Heights
WordArt Alignment

Figure 11-11: The WordArt toolbar.

WordArt Character Spacing
WordArt Vertical Text
Free Rotate
Format WordArt
WordArt Gallery

2. **Click on the WordArt Edit Text button on the WordArt toolbar.**

   The Edit WordArt Text dialog box appears (refer to Figure 11-10).

3. **Edit your text and then click on OK when you're done.**

If you double-click on WordArt, you can access the Edit WordArt Text dialog box right away.

Changing the shape of WordArt

Once you've typed text to display as WordArt, you may want to change its shape so that the WordArt appears as a wavy line, a triangle, or a square. To change the shape of WordArt, follow these steps:

1. **Click on the WordArt that you want to edit.**

   A WordArt toolbar appears (refer to Figure 11-11).

2. **Click on the WordArt Shape icon on the WordArt toolbar.**

   A pop-up menu of different shapes appears for you to choose from, as shown in Figure 11-12.

Figure 11-12: The different shapes you can choose for your WordArt.

3. **Click on the shape that you want to use.**

Rotating WordArt

Rotating WordArt lets you (what else?) rotate your WordArt so that your WordArt can appear in different angles. To rotate WordArt, follow these steps:

1. **Click on the WordArt that you want to edit.**

   A WordArt toolbar appears (refer to Figure 11-11).

2. **Click on the Free Rotate icon on the WordArt toolbar.**

3. **PowerPoint 2000 displays green dots on each corner of your WordArt.**

4. **Move the mouse pointer over one of the green dots, hold down the left mouse button, and then drag the mouse.**

   PowerPoint 2000 displays the new location of your WordArt as two parallel dotted lines.

5. **Release the left mouse button when you're happy with the new position of your WordArt.**

Changing the appearance of characters in WordArt

For those who must have absolute control over the appearance of the text that appears in WordArt, Microsoft PowerPoint 2000 lets you adjust the height, spacing, alignment of your text, and whether you want your text laid out vertically.

To change the appearance of text, follow these steps:

1. **Click on the WordArt that you want to edit.**

   A WordArt toolbar appears (refer to Figure 11-11).

2. **Click on one of the following icons on the WordArt toolbar:**

   • WordArt Same Letter Heights

   • WordArt Vertical Text

   • WordArt Alignment

   • WordArt Character Spacing

Figure 11-13 shows what WordArt looks like as vertical text and with all letters the same height.

Changing the text color of your WordArt

To get really creative, you can change the color of your WordArt so that text appears in bright orange or hard-to-see yellow. You can change three details of your WordArt text:

✔ The text color

✔ The text border color (the color of the line that defines the outline of each character)

✔ The text border line style (the line appearance that defines the outline of each character)

Vertical text WordArt　　　　Same letter height WordArt

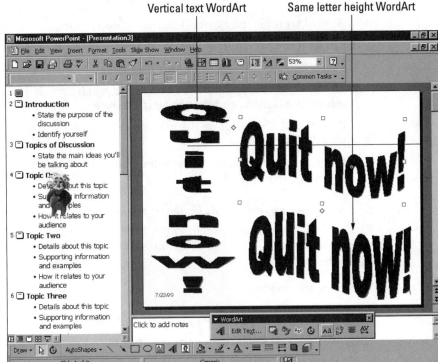

Figure 11-13:
WordArt
appearing in
different
ways.

To change the color of your WordArt, follow these steps:

1. **Click on the WordArt that you want to edit.**

   A WordArt toolbar appears (refer to Figure 11-11).

2. **Click on the Format WordArt icon on the WordArt toolbar.**

   The Format WordArt dialog box appears.

3. **Click on the Colors and Lines tab, as shown in Figure 11-14.**

4. **Click on the Color list box in the Fill group and then choose the color to appear inside your WordArt characters.**

5. **Click on the Color list box in the Line group and then choose the color to appear on the border of your text.**

6. **Click on the Dashed list box in the Line group and then choose a line style to appear as the border of your text.**

7. **Click on the Weight list box and then choose a point size for the border of your text.**

8. **Click on OK.**

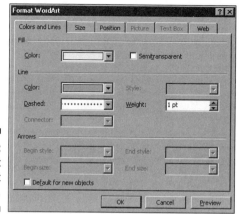

Figure 11-14:
The Format
WordArt
dialog box.

You can also use the Format WordArt dialog box to define the position, height, and rotation angle of your WordArt by clicking on the Size or Position tabs of the format WordArt dialog box.

Deleting WordArt

In case you want to get rid of your WordArt, follow these steps:

1. **Click on the WordArt that you want to delete.**

2. **Press Delete.**

If you accidentally delete WordArt, press Ctrl+Z to retrieve it right away.

Chapter 12

Making Notes and Handouts

In This Chapter

▶ Jotting down notes for yourself

▶ Making notes for yourself or recording comments from audience members

▶ Giving handouts to your audience

*Y*ou can use Microsoft PowerPoint 2000 not only to make slides but also to create notes and handouts as well. *Notes* are for your benefit so that you can jot down ideas, statistics, or alibis that you can see while you're making a presentation. *Handouts* let you pass out printed copies of your presentation so that members of your audience can jot down their ideas or questions.

Neither notes nor handouts are necessary. By creating notes to yourself, you can avoid forgetting something and looking foolish during that all-important business meeting that most people won't pay attention to anyway. By creating handouts, you can give your audience members something to remember (or throw away) after they leave your presentation.

Designing Your Notes Page

Before writing any notes or handouts, you may want to take some time to design their layout. Then you can ensure that your notes and handouts look consistent (even if the text that's written on them doesn't make any sense).

Microsoft PowerPoint 2000 provides a Note Master that lets you design a uniform layout and appearance for your notes. A note typically contains one slide along with any explanatory text underneath it. By printing your notes and keeping them nearby while you're giving a presentation, you can make sure that you don't forget any relevant points.

Because your notes are likely to be seen only by you, you can be as wildly creative and outrageous or as sparse and minimal as you want, without worrying about annoying other people.

The purpose of the Notes Master Page is to design the layout for all your notes. The Notes Master Page is not for typing your notes.

To design the Notes Master, follow these steps:

1. **Choose <u>V</u>iew⇨<u>M</u>aster⇨<u>N</u>otes Master.**

   PowerPoint 2000 displays your notes page, as shown in Figure 12-1.

2. **Choose <u>V</u>iew⇨<u>Z</u>oom.**

   The Zoom dialog box appears, as shown in Figure 12-2.

3. **Click on an option button to choose a resolution (such as <u>1</u>00%) and then click on OK.**

4. **Draw any borders, lines, or shapes that you want PowerPoint 2000 to insert on all your notes pages.**

5. **Highlight and format any text styles, such as the Master text style or the Second level style, as shown in Figure 12-3.**

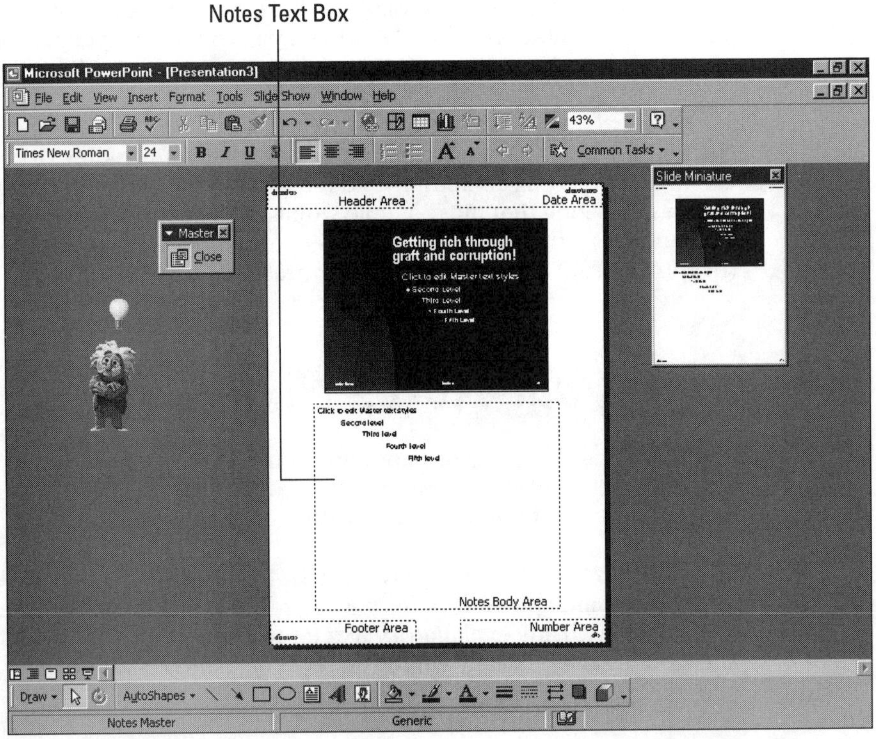

Notes Text Box

Figure 12-1: Designing a Notes Master page.

Figure 12-2:
The Zoom dialog box for expanding or shrinking the appearance of your notes page.

Figure 12-3:
The Notes Master page lets you modify the text styles used for all your notes.

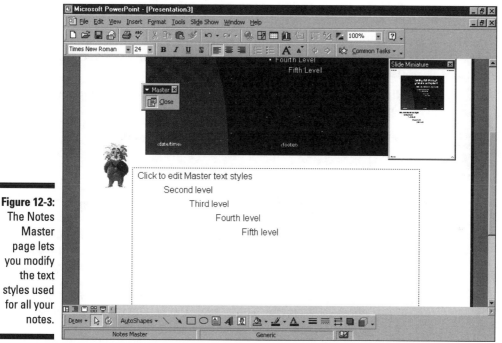

Jotting Down Notes for Posterity

Because you're the only one to see your notes, you can write anything on them that you want (points you want to make during your presentation, stories or statistics to support a particular slide, or tasteless jokes to keep yourself amused while you're giving a presentation to a captive audience).

You can create a separate notes page for each slide in your presentation either before you present your PowerPoint 2000 slides to an audience (so that you can jot down notes ahead of time) or during your presentation (so that you can write comments from audience members who are paying attention).

Creating notes for yourself

To create a note before giving a presentation, follow these steps:

1. **Choose View➪Notes Page.**

   Microsoft PowerPoint displays the current slide on a notes page, as shown in Figure 12-4. You may want to choose View➪Zoom to change the resolution of the notes page to make the text bigger (or smaller) so that you can see the text better.

2. **Click on the notes page text box and then type any ideas, stories, statistics, or funny jokes that you want.**

3. **Highlight any text and then click on the Promote or Demote icons if you want to indent blocks of text.**

If you choose View➪Normal, then you can type notes directly into the note pane, which appears underneath the slide pane.

Writing notes during a presentation

The notes page is also a great place to jot down any comments, questions, or ideas that you may get from the audience. For example, you may show a slide that proves that your company really isn't going bankrupt, and then someone asks for facts. Rather than jot down this request on a separate piece of paper, you can jot the request on your notes page instead. That way you won't risk losing any audience comments (unless, of course, you lose your computer).

When you're writing comments during a presentation, you can store the comments in one of three places:

- ✔ On the notes page of the currently displayed slide
- ✔ On a temporary page called the Meeting Minutes page
- ✔ As a separate slide titled Action Items

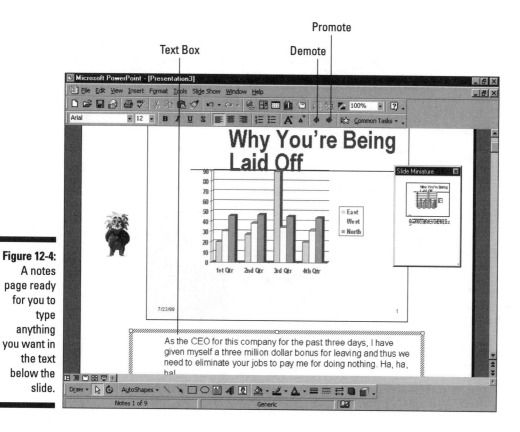

Figure 12-4:
A notes page ready for you to type anything you want in the text below the slide.

Typing comments on the notes page of the current slide

While you're giving a presentation, you may come up with an idea that you want to save directly on your notes page. To type a comment on a notes page during a presentation, follow these steps:

1. **Click on the right mouse button.**

   A pop-up menu appears.

2. **Click on Speaker Notes.**

   The Speaker Notes dialog box appears.

3. **Type any text that you want to include on your notes page and then click on Close.**

Typing meeting minutes

Every boring meeting that won't affect society one bit usually demands that someone keep track of the meeting minutes. That way, if anyone really cares what was discussed in a meeting three weeks ago, he or she can just review the meeting minutes.

To type meeting minutes during a presentation, follow these steps:

1. Click on the right mouse button.

A pop-up menu appears.

2. Click on Meeting Minder.

The Meeting Minder dialog box appears.

3. Click on the Meeting Minutes tab, as shown in Figure 12-5.

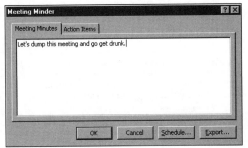

Figure 12-5:
The Meeting
Minutes tab
in the
Meeting
Minder
dialog box.

4. Type any text that you want to save as part of your meeting minutes.

5. Click on OK.

If you want to see any text previously stored in the Meeting Minder, then choose Tools⇨Meeting Minder and then click on the Meeting Minutes tab.

If you click on the Export button in Step 5, then you can save your meeting minutes in Microsoft Outlook 2000 and as a separate Microsoft Word 2000 document.

If you click on the Schedule button in Step 5, then you can store your text as a Microsoft Outlook 2000 appointment.

Creating a list of action items

While you're giving a presentation, some bozo (your boss, for example) probably wants to know what type of action he or she can assign someone else to do. For these types of unwelcome comments, Microsoft PowerPoint 2000 provides a special Action Items text box.

To type text in the Action Items box during a presentation, follow these steps:

1. **Click on the right mouse button.**

   A pop-up menu appears.

2. **Click on Meeting Minder.**

   The Meeting Minder dialog box appears.

3. **Click on the Actions Items tab, as shown in Figure 12-6.**

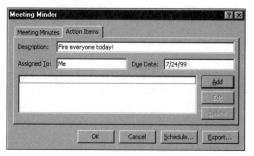

Figure 12-6: The Action Items tab in the Meeting Minder dialog box.

4. **Type a task description in the Description text box.**

5. **Type the name of a person assigned to the task in the Assigned To text box.**

6. **Click on Add.**

   Repeat Steps 4 through 6 for each action item that you want to add.

7. **Click on OK.**

   If you want to see any previously typed action items, then choose Tools⇨Meeting Minder and then click on the Action Items tab.

If you click on the Export button in Step 6, then you can save your meeting minutes in Microsoft Outlook 2000 and as a separate Microsoft Word 2000 document.

If you click on the Schedule button in Step 6, then you can store your text as a Microsoft Outlook 2000 appointment.

Printing your notes pages

After you write and save text on your notes pages, you may want to print the notes pages so that you don't have to turn on your computer every time you want to read your notes.

To print your notes pages, follow these steps:

1. **Choose File⇨Print, or press Ctrl+P.**

   The Print dialog box appears.

2. **Click on the Print what list box and then choose Notes Pages.**

3. **Click on OK.**

Providing Distracting Handouts to Your Audience

Unlike notes, handouts are meant for others to see. Rather than expecting others to memorize your slides or take notes, you can print your entire slide show on paper so that audience members can walk away with printed copies of every slide in your presentation.

To print handouts of your slides, follow these steps:

1. **Choose File⇨Print, or press Ctrl+P.**

   The Print dialog box appears.

2. **Click on the Print what list box and then choose Handouts.**

3. **Click on the Slides per page list box and then choose the number of slides that you want to print on each page (such as 2 or 6).**

4. **Click on OK.**

If you choose to print three slides per page in Step 3, Microsoft PowerPoint 2000 prints three slides to the left of each page and prints blanks to the right of each slide where people can write their comments.

Chapter 13

Adding Animation and Sound Effects

• •

• •

Most business presentations tend to be dry, dull, and utterly useless. Although the information presented may be valuable, the presentation itself resembles nothing more exciting than watching someone fumble with poorly drawn charts and graphs.

To avoid making a boring presentation, Microsoft PowerPoint 2000 gives you the chance to spice up your slide shows with animation and sound. By adding sound to your presentations, you can wake up your audience with a siren or rooster crowing. By adding animation, you can make your presentations more visually interesting to watch, much like a Saturday morning cartoon.

Playing Videos in a Presentation

Because most people would rather watch TV than read or listen to you, adding video can give your Microsoft PowerPoint 2000 presentations that extra bit of stimulus necessary to keep a roomful of executives interested in what you're trying to say. That's why PowerPoint 2000 can play animated files stored in the GIF or AVI file format.

You can also find many animated GIF and AVI files on the Internet or on your favorite online service, such as America Online.

Adding animated GIF files

To add an animation file to a slide, follow these steps:

1. **Insert disk 2 of the Microsoft Office 2000 CD collection in your CD-ROM drive.**

2. **Choose Insert⇨Movies and Sounds and then choose Movie from Gallery.**

   An Insert Movie dialog box appears, as shown in Figure 13-1.

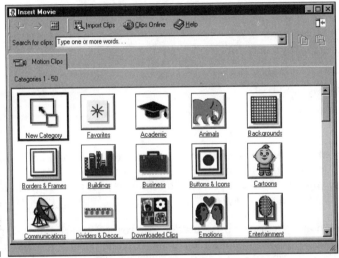

Figure 13-1:
The Insert Movie dialog box where you can pick from a gallery of clip art images.

3. **Click on a category (such as Animals or Buildings) and then click on an image.**

   A pop-up menu appears, as shown in Figure 13-2. (Not all categories may contain animated GIF files.)

4. **Click on an image and then click on the Insert clip icon.**

   If you click on the Play clip icon, then PowerPoint 2000 shows you what the animated GIF file looks like.

5. **Click on the close box of the Insert Movie dialog box.**

   PowerPoint 2000 displays your chosen GIF file on the current slide along with the Picture toolbar.

6. **To adjust the size or location of the GIF file, choose one of the following:**

   • Move the mouse pointer over the animated GIF, hold down the left mouse button, and then drag the mouse to move the GIF to a new location.

- Move the mouse pointer over a white handle around the edge of the GIF until the mouse pointer turns into a double-pointing arrow, hold down the left mouse button, and then drag the mouse to resize the video icon.

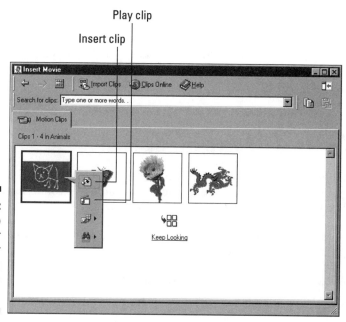

Play clip

Insert clip

Figure 13-2:
A pop-up menu for inserting or viewing your chosen image.

You can type a word in the Search for clips text box to help quickly find the image you want. For example, if you're looking for animated pictures involving computers, then type **computer** in the Search for clips text box of the Insert Movie dialog box in Step 2 and then press Enter.

Adding an AVI video file

To add an AVI video file to a slide, follow these steps:

1. **Choose Insert⇨Movies and Sounds and then choose Movie from File.**

   An Insert Movie dialog box appears.

2. **Click on the file that you want to use and then click on OK.**

   Microsoft PowerPoint 2000 displays your chosen video file icon on the current slide. A dialog box appears, asking if you want to play the movie automatically in your slide show.

3. **Click on** <u>Y</u>**es or** <u>N</u>**o.**

4. **To adjust the size or location of the video file icon, choose one of the following:**

   - Move the mouse pointer over the video file icon, hold down the left mouse button, and then drag the mouse to move the video file icon to a new location.

   - Move the mouse pointer over a white handle around the edge of the video file icon until the mouse pointer turns into a double-pointing arrow, hold down the left mouse button, and then drag the mouse to resize the video file icon.

Adding Sounds to a Slide

Sound effects can highlight an important point, wake up your audience, or just provide additional stimulus to keep your audience wondering what sound or video file you're going to show them next.

Microsoft PowerPoint 2000 can use sound files (stored in the WAV or MIDI file format) from four different sources:

- The Microsoft Office 2000 sound clip library

- Any WAV or MIDI file stored on your hard disk, floppy disk, or CD

- Songs from an audio CD, such as your favorite Beatles, King Crimson, or Pink Floyd album

- WAV or MIDI files that you've recorded yourself

To record your own WAV or MIDI sound files, you need the proper equipment, such as a microphone and sound recording software. Just yelling at your computer won't be enough to record a sound file no matter how loudly you scream.

Adding a Microsoft Office 2000 sound clip

To add a sound file to your slide, follow these steps:

1. **Choose** <u>I</u>**nsert**⇨**Mo**<u>v</u>**ies and Sounds and then choose** <u>S</u>**ound from Gallery.**

   An Insert Sound dialog box appears, as shown in Figure 13-3.

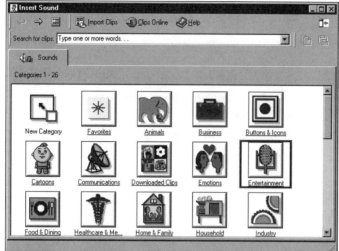

Figure 13-3:
The Insert
Sound
dialog box
where you
can pick a
sound file.

2. **Click on the Entertainment or Music category and then click on a sound file.**

   A pop-up menu appears.

3. **Click on Insert clip.**

   PowerPoint displays your chosen sound file as a tiny icon on the current slide. If you click on Play clip, then you can hear the sound file before adding the sound file to your slide.

4. **Click on the close box to make the Insert Sound dialog box go away.**

   A dialog box appears, asking if you want the sound file to play automatically.

5. **Click on Yes or No.**

   PowerPoint 2000 displays your sound file as an icon on the currently displayed slide.

6. **To adjust the size or location of the sound file icon, choose one of the following:**

   - Move the mouse pointer over the sound file icon, hold down the left mouse button, and then drag the mouse to move the sound file icon.

   - Move the mouse pointer over a white handle around the edge of the sound file icon until the mouse pointer turns into a double-pointing arrow, hold down the left mouse button, and then drag the mouse to resize the sound file icon.

Adding a WAV or MIDI sound file

To add a sound file to your slide, follow these steps:

1. **Choose Insert⇨Movies and Sounds and then choose Sound from File.**

   An Insert Sound dialog box appears, where you can choose the specific WAV file that you want to use.

2. **Click on a sound file and then click on OK.**

   A dialog box appears, asking if you want to play the sound file automatically.

3. **Click on Yes or No.**

   PowerPoint 2000 displays the sound file icon on the currently displayed slide.

4. **To adjust the size or location of the sound file icon, choose one of the following:**

   • Move the mouse pointer over the sound file icon, hold down the left mouse button, and then drag the mouse to move the sound file icon.

   • Move the mouse pointer over a white handle around the edge of the sound file icon until the mouse pointer turns into a double-pointing arrow, hold down the left mouse button, and then drag the mouse to resize the sound file icon.

Playing songs from an audio CD

Rather than use WAV or MIDI sound files, you may be more interested in playing songs directly off audio CDs instead. In this way you can play your favorite songs during your presentation to emphasize the point that you're making, to provide pleasant background music so that you don't have to keep talking, or to send a subtle message to your audience (such as playing the song, "Take This Job and Shove It").

To play an audio CD track to a slide, follow these steps:

1. **Insert your audio CD in your CD-ROM drive.**

2. **Choose Insert⇨Movies and Sounds⇨Play CD Audio Track.**

   The Play Options dialog box appears, as shown in Figure 13-4.

3. **Click on the Track list box (under the Start group) to define the first audio track to play.**

4. **Click on the Track list box (under the End group) to define the last audio track to play.**

Figure 13-4:
The Play
Options
dialog box
for playing a
song from
an audio CD.

5. **Click on the At list box (under the Start group) to define what part of the song you want to start playing. (If you want to start the song at the beginning, then choose 00:00.)**

6. **Click on the At list box (under the End group) to define what part of the song you want to stop playing. (If you want to stop at the end of the song, then don't change the time listed in the At list box.)**

7. **Click on OK.**

   A dialog box appears, asking if you want to play the song automatically.

8. **Click on Yes or No.**

   Microsoft PowerPoint 2000 displays a CD file icon on the current slide.

9. **To adjust the size or location of the audio CD file icon, choose one of the following:**

   • Move the mouse pointer over the audio CD file icon, hold down the left mouse button, and then drag the mouse to move the audio CD file icon.

   • Move the mouse pointer over a white handle around the edge of the audio CD file icon until the mouse pointer turns into a double-pointing arrow, hold down the left mouse button, and then drag the mouse to resize the audio CD file icon.

If you want to play a song from an audio CD during your presentation, you must have that particular audio CD in your CD-ROM drive. Because most computers have only one CD-ROM drive, you probably won't be able to use sound from more than one audio CD.

Deleting Sound and Video Files

In case you want to delete a sound or video file from a slide, follow these steps:

1. **Click on the sound or video file so that white handles appear around the file's edges.**

2. **Press Delete.**

When you delete a sound or video file from a slide, the file still physically exists in its original location.

Part IV

Getting Organized with Microsoft Outlook 2000

The 5th Wave By Rich Tennant

"Now take your time and see if you can identify the person who attacked you on e-mail."

In this part . . .

Time is money, which means that if you use your time wisely, you can make more money than individuals who squander every day until they're left wondering why they're not getting anything important done in their lives.

This part of the book helps you become one of those few people who tracks his or her activities during the day by learning to use Microsoft Outlook 2000 to monitor your time and help you jot down any sudden inspirational ideas that may hit you on the spur of the moment. This part also contains tips for using Outlook 2000 instead of the Windows Explorer.

By using Outlook 2000, you can take responsibility for your own life and pursue the goal of your dreams, which immediately puts you in the minority of the people who know what they want out of life.

Chapter 14

Organizing Your Stuff with Microsoft Outlook 2000

. . . .

In This Chapter

▶ Loading Microsoft Outlook 2000 at start-up

▶ Organizing your hard disk

▶ Deleting and renaming files

. . . .

*B*elieve it or not, you can actually run your entire computer from within Microsoft Outlook 2000. In Microsoft Outlook 2000 you can load and run other programs (such as Word 2000 or Excel 2000), create directories, or delete files. So browse through this chapter and look for tips to help you use Outlook 2000 more effectively.

Loading Microsoft Outlook 2000 Automatically

Microsoft Outlook 2000 lets you read and send e-mail, organize your daily tasks, plan appointments in advance, or jot down notes, but none of these features is any good unless you load Outlook 2000 first. Unfortunately, the time and trouble necessary to load Outlook 2000 may be just enough of an obstacle to keep you from using Outlook 2000 as often as you could.

To fix this problem and remove one less excuse for not organizing your time, your computer, and your information, you can make Microsoft Outlook 2000 load automatically, as soon as you turn on your computer.

To load Microsoft Outlook 2000 automatically, follow these steps:

1. **Click on the Start button on the Windows taskbar and then choose Settings⇨Taskbar.**

2. **Click on the Start Menu Programs tab.**

3. Click on <u>A</u>dd and then click on B<u>r</u>owse.

4. Double-click on Microsoft Outlook. (You may have to look inside the Program Files/Microsoft Office/Office folders first.)

5. Click on <u>N</u>ext and then double-click on the StartUp icon.

6. Click on Finish and then click on OK.

The next time you start (or restart) your computer, Outlook 2000 loads automatically.

You can have Windows load any program automatically if you click on that program name in Step 4 instead of clicking on Microsoft Outlook.

Any time you have Windows automatically load a program for you, the time Windows needs to boot up increases, so make sure that you load only those programs that you absolutely need when you turn on your computer.

In case you don't want Microsoft Outlook 2000 to load automatically any more (because doing so takes too much time), you can stop Outlook 2000 from loading by following these steps:

1. Click on the Start button on the Windows taskbar and then choose <u>S</u>ettings⇨<u>T</u>askbar.

2. Click on the Start Menu Programs tab.

3. Click on <u>R</u>emove.

4. Click on the plus sign to the left of the StartUp folder, then click on Outlook, and then click on <u>R</u>emove.

5. Click on Close and then click on OK.

Removing Outlook from the StartUp folder does not remove Outlook from your computer.

Organizing Files and Folders on Your Hard Disk

If you don't like using the Windows Explorer program to create new folders, copy or move files around, or delete files and folders, then you can use Microsoft Outlook 2000 to organize your hard disk instead.

To view all the files and folders stored on your computer using Microsoft Outlook 2000, follow these steps:

1. **Click on the Other Shortcuts button in the Outlook Bar.**

   If the Outlook Bar is not visible, then choose View⇨Outlook Bar.

2. **Click on the My Computer icon in the Outlook Bar.**

   Outlook displays all the drives in your computer.

3. **Choose View⇨Current View and then choose one of the following:**

   • **Icons:** Displays files and folders as icons, as shown in Figure 14-1

   • **Details:** Displays folders as tiny icons

   • **By Type:** Displays folders as text

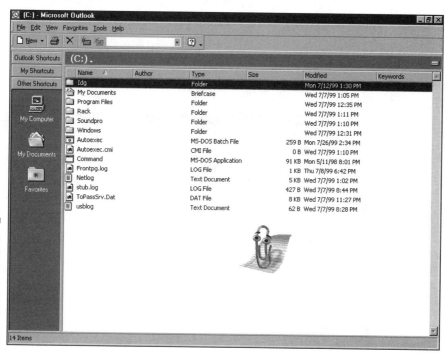

Figure 14-1:
Outlook 2000 displaying icons to represent files and folders.

Navigating within a folder

You can also use the Microsoft Outlook 2000 Outlook Bar to navigate through all your files.

To open (and close) any file or folder stored on your computer using Microsoft Outlook 2000 instead of Windows Explorer, follow these steps:

1. **Double-click on the folder on the left side of your computer screen.**

   Microsoft Outlook 2000 opens that folder and displays the folder's contents (which can be more folders or files).

2. **Continue clicking on folder icons to view the folders' contents.**

   Each time you click on a folder, Outlook 2000 displays a folder list on the right side of your computer screen, as shown in Figure 14-2.

3. **Click on the drive or folder that you want to view.**

Folder list

Folder

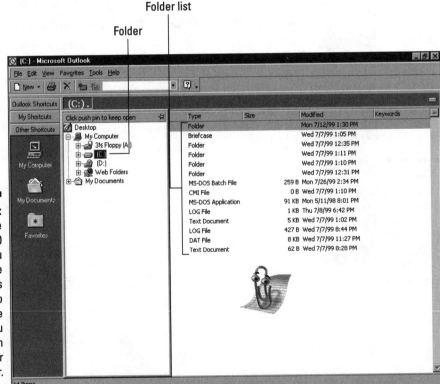

Figure 14-2:
You can use
Outlook 2000
as you
can use
Windows
Explorer to
view all the
files you
store on
your
computer.

In Step 2, you can keep the folder list open by clicking on the push-pin icon in the upper right-hand corner of the folder list window.

Rather than dig through multiple folders over and over again, you can display your most frequently used folders on the Outlook bar. To put a folder on the Outlook bar, move the mouse pointer over the folder, click the right mouse button, and then click on Add to Outlook bar.

Creating a new folder

If you want to create a new folder, follow these steps:

1. **Follow the instructions in the "Navigating within a folder" section.**

2. **Choose File⇨New⇨Folder.**

   A Create New Folder dialog box appears, as shown in Figure 14-3.

Figure 14-3:
The Create
New Folder
dialog box
for creating
a new folder
on your hard
disk or
floppy disk.

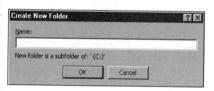

3. **Type a new name for your folder in the Name box and then click on OK.**

You can move a folder or file into a folder by dragging that folder or file to its destination folder.

Deleting and renaming a folder or file

Because Microsoft Outlook 2000 can mimic the Windows Explorer program, you'll be pleased to know that you can delete or rename a folder or file at any time.

To delete a folder or file, follow these steps:

1. **Follow the instructions in the "Navigating within a folder" section.**

2. **Move the mouse pointer over the folder or file that you want to delete and then click the right mouse button.**

3. **Choose Delete.**

   A dialog box appears, asking if you really want to delete your folder or file.

4. **Click on Yes.**

To rename a folder or file, follow these steps:

1. **Follow the instructions in the "Navigating within a folder" section.**

2. **Move the mouse pointer over the folder or file that you want to rename and then click the right mouse button.**

3. **Choose Rename.**

   A Rename dialog box appears.

4. **Type a new name for your folder or file in the New name box and then click on OK.**

Launching a file

Besides letting you edit, rename, or delete files, Microsoft Outlook 2000 also lets you launch the program that created a file (provided you have that program on your hard disk in the first place).

To load a file plus the program that created that file (such as clicking on an Excel worksheet file to launch Excel 2000), follow these steps:

1. **Follow the instructions in the "Navigating within a folder" section.**

2. **Double-click on the file that you want to edit.**

   Microsoft Outlook 2000 obediently loads the program that created the file and then displays your file contents.

3. **Choose File⇨Exit from the program menu that loaded in Step 1 (such as Excel 2000).**

   Microsoft Outlook 2000 cheerfully appears once more, ready to do your bidding again.

Chapter 15

Jotting Down a Journal and Notes

• •

In This Chapter

▶ Taking down notes

▶ Tracking time with a journal

▶ Printing a journal

• •

*M*icrosoft Outlook 2000 can organize your information so that you can be more productive (just as soon as you spend enough time figuring out how to use Outlook 2000 in the first place). To help achieve the noble goal of organization, Outlook 2000 provides two neat features that you probably won't find in any other personal information organizer: sticky notes and a journal.

Sticky notes let you jot down ideas as they occur to you. A journal lets you keep track of what you've done so that you can identify how you've been spending your time.

Jotting Down Notes

Usually when you come up with an idea, you have to scramble for a piece of paper. If you happen to be sitting in front of your computer when you have an idea, you can store your thoughts directly in Microsoft Outlook 2000 instead.

To ensure that Microsoft Outlook 2000 is available for writing notes, load Outlook 2000 and then minimize it. That way, when you want to jot down a note in Outlook 2000, you won't have to wait for Outlook 2000 to load (and risk forgetting what you wanted to jot down in the first place).

Creating a note within Microsoft Outlook 2000

When you want to create a note, follow these steps:

1. **Choose File⇨New⇨Note, or press Ctrl+Shift+N.**

   A blank note window appears, as shown in Figure 15-1.

2. **Type your ideas in the note window and then click on the close box of the note window when you're done.**

If you want to jot down notes in a single note window while using another program, such as Word 2000 or Excel 2000, load Outlook 2000 and press Ctrl+Shift+N to create a note. Now switch back to your other program. When you need to jot something in the note window, click on the note window button on the Windows taskbar, and the note window pops up. Then click on the other program button on the Windows taskbar to switch back to your other program.

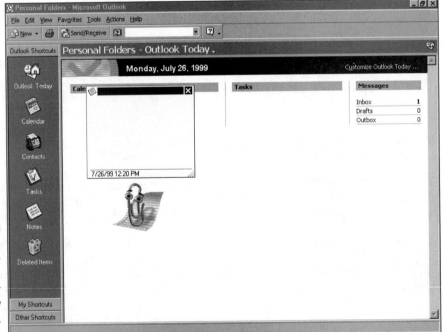

Figure 15-1:
A new
Notes
window for
typing new
ideas.

If you want to customize the way your notes look, then choose <u>T</u>ools⇨<u>O</u>ptions so that an Options dialog box appears. Click on the Preferences tab and then click on Note Options to choose a color, font, and size for your notes.

Editing your notes

In case you need to edit the contents of a note, follow these steps:

1. **Click on the Outlook Shortcuts button in the Outlook Bar.**

   If the Outlook Bar is not visible, then choose <u>V</u>iew⇨<u>O</u>utlook Bar.

2. **Click on the Notes icon in the Outlook Bar.**

   The Notes window appears, displaying all your previously created notes, as shown in Figure 15-2.

3. **Double-click on the note that you want to edit.**

   The note window appears.

4. **Click anywhere inside the note and then use the arrow keys, Backspace, or Delete keys to edit your note.**

5. **Click on the close box of the note window when you're done.**

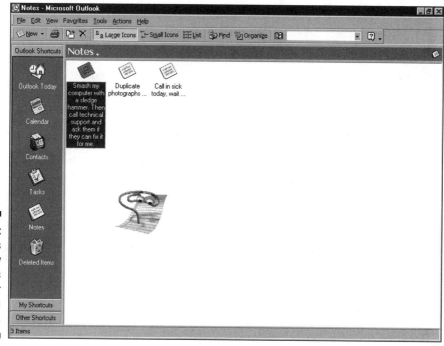

Figure 15-2: The Notes window displays all your available notes.

You can color code your notes by right-clicking on a note, then choosing Color, and then selecting the color that you want, such as Blue or Green.

You can change the way Microsoft Outlook 2000 displays your notes by choosing <u>V</u>iew⇨Current <u>V</u>iew and then selecting an option, such as Icon or By Color.

Printing your notes

A note may contain something important that you want to print, just in case you don't trust that your computer's hard disk saves your data indefinitely. To print a note, follow these steps:

1. **Click on the Outlook Shortcuts button in the Outlook Bar.**

   If the Outlook Bar is not visible, choose <u>V</u>iew⇨<u>O</u>utlook Bar.

2. **Click on the Notes icon in the Outlook Bar.**

   The Notes window appears, displaying all your previously created notes (refer to Figure 15-2).

3. **Click on the note that you want to print.**

4. **Choose <u>F</u>ile⇨<u>P</u>rint, or press Ctrl+P.**

   A Print dialog box appears.

5. **Click on OK.**

In Step 3, you can also double-click on the note that you want to print, then click on the control box of a note window, and then choose Print.

E-mailing your notes

If you write down a note that someone else may want to see, then you can e-mail your note to that person. To e-mail a note, follow these steps:

1. **Click on the Outlook Shortcuts button in the Outlook Bar.**

   If the Outlook Bar is not visible, then choose <u>V</u>iew⇨<u>O</u>utlook Bar.

2. **Click on the Notes icon in the Outlook Bar.**

   The Notes window appears, displaying all of your previously created notes (refer to Figure 15-2).

3. **Click on the note that you want to e-mail.**

4. **Choose <u>A</u>ctions⇨For<u>w</u>ard, or press Ctrl+F.**

   An e-mail window appears, as shown in Figure 15-3.

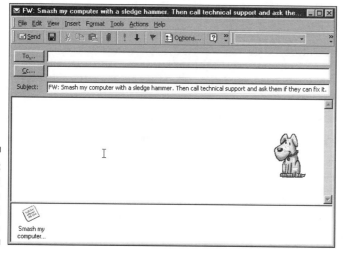

Figure 15-3:
E-mailing a
note to a
friend or an
enemy.

5. **Type an e-mail address, type any additional text that you want to send, and then click on Send.**

Deleting a note

Chances are good that you won't want to keep your notes around for the rest of your life (or even until next month). To delete a note, follow these steps:

1. **Click on the Outlook Shortcuts button in the Outlook Bar.**

   If the Outlook Bar is not visible, choose View➪Outlook Bar.

2. **Click on the Notes icon in the Outlook Bar.**

   The Notes window appears, displaying all of your previously created notes (refer to Figure 15-2).

3. **Click on the note that you want to delete.**

4. **Choose Edit➪Delete, then click the Delete icon on the toolbar, or press Ctrl+D.z**

If you delete a note by mistake, press Ctrl+Z to bring the note back again.

Tracking Time with a Journal

The Microsoft Outlook 2000 journal lets you track your activities so that you can see what you did in the past. By reviewing your journal, you can find out what day you made an important phone call or when you last sent e-mail to your parents.

Microsoft Outlook 2000 can record the following:

- ✔ When you access any Office 2000 file (such as Word 2000 or PowerPoint 2000)
- ✔ When you send e-mail and to whom
- ✔ When you request or cancel a meeting
- ✔ When you request or cancel a task

Automatically tracking activities with your journal

To tell Outlook 2000 what types of activities you want to record, follow these steps:

1. **Click on the My Shortcuts button in the Outlook Bar.**

   If the Outlook Bar is not visible, then choose View➪Outlook Bar.

2. **Click on the Journal icon in the Outlook Bar.**

   A dialog box appears, asking if you want to turn on the Journal to track Office 2000 documents.

3. **Click on Yes.**

   A Journal Options dialog box appears, as shown in Figure 15-4.

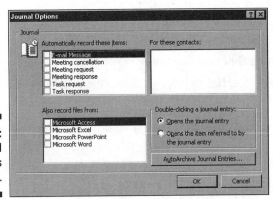

Figure 15-4:
The Journal
Options
dialog box.

4. **Click on the check boxes of all the activities that you want to record.**

5. **Click on OK.**

If you want to modify the activities that your Journal automatically tracks, then choose Tools⇨Options, and then click on Journal Options. The Journal Options dialog box appears so that you can make changes.

Manually tracking an activity with your journal

Rather than rely on Microsoft Outlook 2000 to automatically track activities, you can place an activity directly into your journal at any time by following these steps:

1. **Choose File⇨New⇨Journal Entry.**

2. **In the Subject box, type a description of the item that you want to record in your journal.**

3. **Click on the Entry type list box and then choose an entry type, such as Phone call or Task.**

4. **Click on the Start time or Duration list boxes.**

   If you want to time your activity, click on the Start Timer button.

5. **Type any text that you want to record.**

6. **Click on Save and then Close.**

Viewing your journal

Outlook organizes your journal entries by categories, such as phone calls that you've made, e-mail that you've sent, or Word 2000 files that you've accessed.

To take a look at your journal entries, follow these steps:

1. **Click on the My Shortcuts button in the Outlook Bar.**

   If the Outlook Bar is not visible, then choose View⇨Outlook Bar.

2. **Click on the Journal icon in the Outlook Bar.**

3. **Click on the plus sign of a journal entry to view all your entries organized by date and time, as shown in Figure 15-5.**

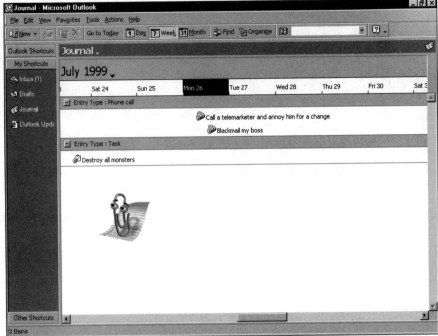

Figure 15-5:
Journal
entries
organized
by
categories.

Printing a journal entry

You may want to get a printed copy of a particular journal entry. That way you can show your boss (in black and white) just how much time you've been wasting attending his meetings that are designed to teach you how to spend your time more productively.

To print a journal entry, follow these steps:

1. **Click on the My Shortcuts button in the Outlook Bar.**

   If the Outlook Bar is not visible, then choose View➪Outlook Bar.

2. **Click on the Journal icon in the Outlook Bar.**

3. **Click on the plus sign of a journal entry to view all your entries organized by date and time.**

4. **Click on the journal entry that you want to print and then choose File➪Print, or press Ctrl+P.**

   A Print dialog box appears.

5. **Click on OK.**

Deleting a journal entry

You probably don't want to keep track of your journal entries forever. To delete a journal entry (and clear up a little bit of space on your hard disk), follow these steps:

1. **Click on the My Shortcuts button in the Outlook Bar.**

   If the Outlook Bar is not visible, then choose View⇨Outlook Bar.

2. **Click on the Journal icon in the Outlook Bar.**

3. **Click on the plus sign of a journal entry to view all your entries organized by date and time.**

4. **Click on the journal entry that you want to delete.**

5. **Choose Edit⇨Delete, then click the Delete icon on the toolbar, or press Ctrl+D.**

If you delete a journal entry by mistake, you can retrieve the entry right away by pressing Ctrl+Z.

To delete an entire journal category (such as Phone call or Task) along with any entries stored inside, follow these steps:

1. **Click on the My Shortcuts button in the Outlook Bar.**

   If the Outlook Bar is not visible, then choose View⇨Outlook Bar.

2. **Click on the Journal icon in the Outlook Bar.**

3. **Click on the journal entry type that you want to delete (such as Phone call).**

4. **Choose Edit⇨Delete, then click the Delete icon on the toolbar, or press Ctrl+D.**

   A dialog box appears, asking if you really want to delete the entire entry category.

5. **Click on OK.**

If you delete a journal category accidentally, don't panic. You can recover the category, plus all entries stored inside, by pressing Ctrl+Z right away.

Part V
Storing Stuff in Microsoft Access 2000

The 5th Wave — By Rich Tennant

"Don't worry, scarecrow — without the Access database there's no sense in taking your laptop to the Emerald City anyway."

In this part . . .

Microsoft Access 2000 is the most popular relational database program in the world, but if you don't have the slightest idea what a relational database is, don't worry. Just remember that Access 2000 can store and retrieve any type of information, such as names, addresses, part numbers, and inventory bar codes.

This part of the book shows you how to automate and customize Access 2000 for your own purposes. Need a specialized program for tracking information but don't feel like shelling out hundreds of dollars to buy one? Then learn to customize and program Access 2000 to make it obey your commands.

Who knows? With enough practice, you can find out enough about programming Access 2000 that you can start creating your own custom programs to sell or give away. And then you can get a better job, thanks to the power of Access 2000.

Chapter 16

Creating Databases from Scratch

· ·

In This Chapter

▶ Designing tables

▶ Creating new forms with a wizard

▶ Editing tables and forms

· ·

*M*icrosoft Access 2000 gives you two ways to create a database: Use an existing database design or create your own database from scratch. If you use an existing database design, you may find that the database needs modifying before you can use it. In many cases, modifying an existing database is always easier than creating a new database (just as copying somebody else's homework is often easier than thinking for yourself).

But, if you want absolute control over the design of your database, you should learn to create your own databases. While creating your own database can be more complicated and time-consuming than using an existing database design, database creation can be an art in itself. Creating your own database allows you to design custom databases for your job, business, or personal life in case you really find creating databases fun and enjoyable.

Creating a New Database

The two most important parts of a database are its tables and forms. The tables define the type of data you're storing (such as names, phone numbers, blood type, and so on). Unfortunately, tables display data in rows and columns, making them look as inviting to read as the stock exchange listing in *The Wall Street Journal*.

To make data entry and viewing easier, you also need forms. A form simply provides a user-interface for accessing your data. You don't need to use forms; forms exist solely to make viewing and editing your data as simple to use as Microsoft Windows itself (which may not be saying much, but at least you get the idea).

To create a new database, follow these steps:

1. **Choose File⇨New Database, or press Ctrl+N.**

   A New database window appears, as shown in Figure 16-1.

2. **Click on the General tab, then click on the Database icon, and then click on OK. (If you click on the Databases tab, then you can create a new database based on an existing database design.)**

   A File New Database dialog box appears.

3. **Type the name for your database, then click on the folder where you want to store your database, and then click on Create. A completely blank database window appears, daring you to do something useful.**

When you start Access 2000, a Microsoft Access dialog box appears on the screen immediately after Access 2000 loads. Just click on the Blank Database option button, click on OK, and then proceed with Steps 2 and 3.

Designing a database

Corporations pay fortunes to programmers who can design databases, so don't expect to become a database expert overnight. Essentially, designing a database means taking the time to understand what type of information you need to save for the future and how you want to organize your data to make access as simple as possible.

While designing a database may sound easy, doing so can get fairly complicated in a hurry if you're designing a database for a company that needs to track inventory, part numbers, customer addresses, shipping dates, and delivery dates.

Designing a database properly is like laying the foundation for a home. Do it right and the home can last for years. Do it wrong, and you'll probably have to rip out the entire foundation and start all over again, which is something that large corporations hate doing, especially if it means paying their programmers overtime.

So before rushing right into designing a database, take some time to design your database on paper first. That way you can erase, rewrite, and scribble all you want without wasting valuable time using your computer. To help you design your database correctly, ask yourself the following:

✔ **What information do I need to save and retrieve?** (This helps you determine what fields your database needs, where a field contains one type of data, such as a name or an address.)

✔ **Which information should I logically group together?** (This helps you decide how to organize fields into tables, such as storing customer information in one table and supplier information in another table.)

✔ **How do I want to display information for typing new data and for retrieving existing data?** (This helps you design your database forms for displaying data on the screen.)

Many Ph.D.s in computer science spend years studying optimum database designs, so don't feel bad if you have trouble designing a database the first time. Like any skill, database design can improve with practice, so feel free to practice at your job where you can get paid overtime to fix mistakes while learning at the same time.

Creating a database table

The simplest database can have just one table. For example, if you want to create a database just to store names and phone numbers, your database can consist of a single table that has just two fields, called NAME and PHONE.

A database table is nothing more than a container for your data.

To create a database table, make sure the database window appears and then follow these steps:

1. **Click on the Tables icon.**

   The Database window displays three options, as shown in Figure 16-2.

   • **Create table in Design view:** Displays a simple grid where you can define your fields along with their characteristics, such as the maximum length of characters a text field can contain.

- **Create table by using wizard:** Guides you step-by-step in defining the fields you need to store.

- **Create table by entering data:** Displays a spreadsheet-like grid for typing your fields.

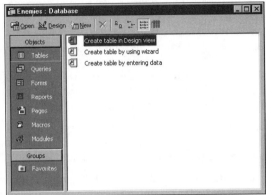

Figure 16-2:
The Database window displays three ways to create a new database table.

2. **Double-click on the Create table by using wizard icon.**

   A Table Wizard dialog box appears, as shown in Figure 16-3.

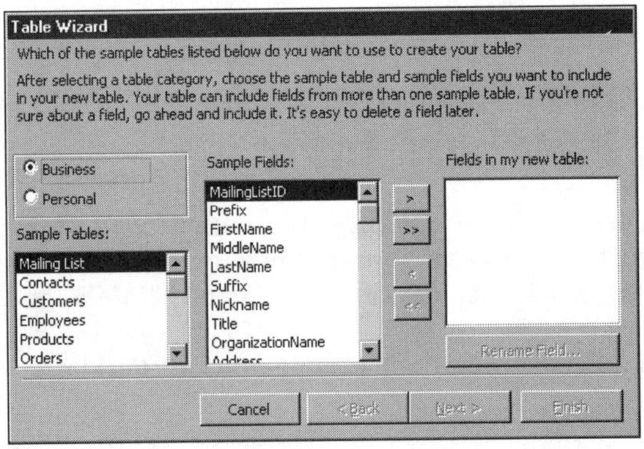

Figure 16-3:
The Table Wizard dialog box for helping you design a new table.

3. **Click on the Business or Personal option button and then click on a table in the Sample Tables list box that most closely resembles the type of data that you want to store in your own table, such as Mailing List or Contacts.**

4. **Click on a field in the Sample Fields list box and then choose the field that most closely resembles the field that you want to use in your own table, such as FirstName.**

5. **Click on the > button. Repeat Steps 3, 4, and 5 for each field that you want to add to your table.**

6. **Click on Next.**

   Another Table Wizard dialog box appears, asking what name you want to give to your table.

7. **Type a name for your table and then click on Next.**

   A final Table Wizard dialog box appears, asking what to do after creating a table.

8. **Click on the Enter data into the table using a form the wizard creates for me option button and then click on Finish.**

   Microsoft Access 2000 displays a form for you to start typing in your data.

If you click on the Create table in Design view or Create table by entering data icon in Step 2, then you have more control over designing your database table, but creating your database table will take you longer.

If you prefer entering data using a table, then click on the Enter data into the table option button in Step 8.

Creating a form

A form provides a window that displays information from your database. Although you don't have to use a form for your database, using a form can make viewing and editing your data much easier than trying to hunt for data in the row-and-column format of a database table.

A record contains one or more related fields that represent a single item, such as a person's name, phone number, and address.

The two common ways to enter information in a database table are through the use of a form (which displays a single record at a time) or a table (which displays all your records in a grid at the same time). Because a form more closely resembles a paper form, many people find forms easier for viewing, editing, and typing data.

To create a form to display information trapped inside a table, make sure that the database window appears and then follow these steps:

1. **Click on the Forms icon and then click on New.**

   The Database window displays two options, as shown in Figure 16-4.

- **Create form in Design view:** Displays a blank form in which you can draw your fields to display.

- **Create form by using wizard:** Guides you step-by-step in defining the fields to appear on the form.

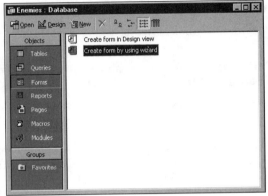

Figure 16-4:
The Database window displays two ways to create a new form.

2. **Double-click on the Create form by using wizard icon.**

A Form Wizard dialog box appears, as shown in Figure 16-5.

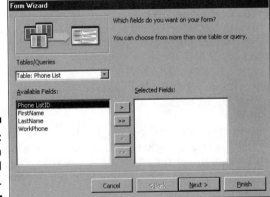

Figure 16-5:
The Form Wizard dialog box.

3. **Click on a field (as shown in the Available Fields list box) that you want to display on your form and then click on the > button.**

4. **Repeat Step 3 for each field that you want to add to your form. Then click on Next.**

Another form Wizard dialog box appears and asks you to choose a layout, as shown in Figure 16-6.

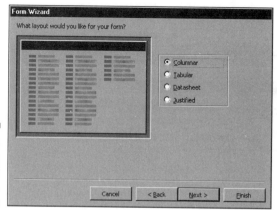

Figure 16-6:
Choosing
the layout of
your form.

5. **Click on an option button (such as Columnar or Tabular) and then click on Next.**

Still another Form Wizard dialog box appears and asks for a form style to use, as shown in Figure 16-7.

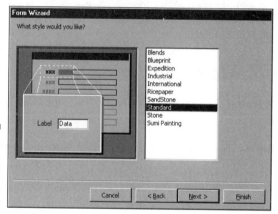

Figure 16-7:
Choosing
the style of
your form.

6. **Click on a pattern that you want to use (such as International or Standard) and then click on Next.**

Yet another annoying Form Wizard dialog box appears, bugging you for a name to give your form.

7. **Type a name for your form and then click on Finish.**

Microsoft Access 2000 displays your form, ready for you to start typing data, as shown in Figure 16-8.

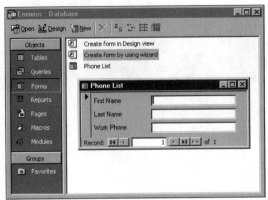

Figure 16-8:
A typical
form
created for
you by
the Form
Wizard.

Editing a Table

No matter how carefully you design your tables ahead of time, you may need to edit the tables at a later date. Editing a table can be as simple as correcting a spelling mistake for a field (such as typing NMAE instead of NAME) or as drastic as deleting existing fields or adding entirely new ones.

Modifying fields within a table

To edit the fields of a table, make sure that the database window appears and then follow these steps:

1. **Click on the Tables icon, then click on the table that you want to edit, and then click on Design.**

   Microsoft Access 2000 displays the fields that make up your table.

2. **Click on the field that you want to edit.**

   Microsoft Access 2000 displays the properties of your chosen field at the bottom of the screen, as shown in Figure 16-9.

3. **Click on the Data Type column and then click on the downward-pointing arrow to choose a data type to store in your chosen field (such as Text or Date/Time).**

4. **Click on the field property that you want to modify (such as the Caption) and then type or click on an option.**

5. **Repeat Step 4 for each field that you want to edit.**

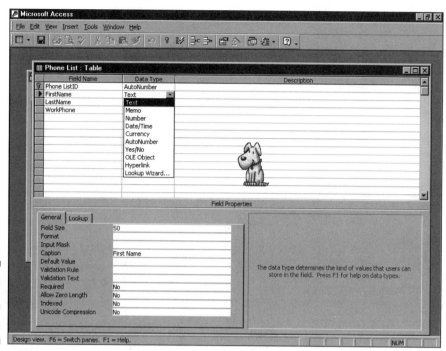

Figure 16-9:
Modifying
the fields of
a table.

6. **Click on the close box of the Table window when you're done.**

   A dialog box appears, asking if you want to save any changes you made to the table.

7. **Click on Yes or No.**

Deleting a field

If you delete a field, then you also delete any information stored in that field. So only delete a field if you can afford to lose all the data stored in that field as well.

To delete a field, make sure that the Database window appears and then follow these steps:

1. **Click on the Tables icon, then click on the table that you want to edit, and then click on Design.**

   Microsoft Access 2000 displays the fields that make up your table (refer to Figure 16-9).

2. **Click to the left of the field that you want to delete.**

   Microsoft Access 2000 highlights the entire row.

3. **Choose Edit⇨Delete.**

   A dialog box appears, warning that you are about to permanently delete your field and the data stored inside that field.

4. **Click on Yes (or No if you decide to save your field at the last minute).**

   Another dialog box appears, warning that you are about to permanently delete one or more indexes.

5. **Click on Yes (or No if you decide to save your field at the last minute).**

If you delete a field by mistake, then press Ctrl+Z to bring it back again.

Adding a new field

After you've finished designing your database and had a chance to use it, you may suddenly realize that your database needs to store additional information. Rather than toss out your entire database, you can just add a new field to a table.

When you add a new field to a table, the field won't contain any data. So if your database consists of one million names and addresses and you suddenly add a new field to store Social Security numbers, then the Social Security field will be blank for all one million existing names and addresses. Have fun typing.

To add a new field to a table, make sure that the Database window appears and then follow these steps:

1. **Click on the Tables icon, then click on the table that you want to edit, and then click on Design.**

   Microsoft Access 2000 displays the fields that make up your table (refer to Figure 16-9).

2. **Click on a blank row at the bottom of the existing field names. (As another alternative, click on any field and then choose Insert⇨Rows to sandwich in a new row between two existing fields.)**

3. **Click on the Field Name column, then type a name for your field, and then press Tab.**

4. **Click on the Data Type list box and then choose a data type (such as Text or Currency).**

5. **Click on any field properties at the bottom of the window that you want to modify, such as Field Size.**

6. **Click on the close box of the Table window.**

   A dialog box appears, asking if you want to save your changes.

7. **Click on Yes.**

Depending on the data type that you choose (such as Date or Currency), you may need to define additional field properties in Step 5, such as format, field size, and default value.

Editing a Form

A form can display one or more fields on the screen so that you can view and edit the data easily. Because a form acts as the user interface to your data, you may want to move fields around, add pictures to your form, or resize fields.

Just remember that any changes you make to a form are purely decorative. Design a form properly and people may find using your database fun and easy. Design a poorly organized and hideously colored form and people may not be able to use your database at all, even though you may have done nothing more than change the colors of the form to an eye-popping fluorescent orange.

To make editing your form easier, you may want to click on the Maximize button of the form window.

Moving or resizing a field

Sometimes a field may be too small or located in the wrong place on the screen. To fix such problems, you can move or resize a field to make it smaller or larger.

A field label contains descriptive text, such as First Name. A field is an empty box that displays actual data, such as Mary or Joe.

To move a field, make sure that the Database window appears and then follow these steps:

1. **Click on the Forms icon, then click on the form that you want to edit, and then click on Design.**

   Microsoft Access 2000 displays your chosen form along with the Access 2000 Toolbox, as shown in Figure 16-10.

Field labels   Fields

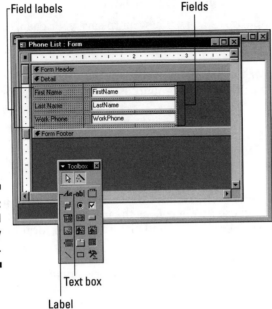

Figure 16-10:
A typical
form ready
for editing.

Text box

Label

2. **Move the mouse pointer over the gray field that you want to move.**

3. **Hold down the left mouse button and drag the mouse.**

   Microsoft Access 2000 displays handles around your chosen field and field label and turns the mouse pointer into a black hand.

4. **Release the left mouse button when the field is in a new location that you can live with.**

If you want to move a field label without moving a field (or vice versa), follow these steps:

1. **Click on the Forms icon, click on the form that you want to edit, and then click on Design.**

   Microsoft Access 2000 displays your chosen form along with the Access 2000 Toolbox (refer to Figure 16-10).

2. **Move the mouse pointer to the upper left-hand-corner handle over the field label (or field) that you want to move.**

   The mouse pointer turns into a black hand with one finger (not that finger) pointing straight up.

3. **Hold down the left mouse button and drag the mouse.**

4. **Release the left mouse button when you're happy with the new location of the field label or field.**

To resize a field or field label, follow these steps:

1. **Click on the Forms icon, then click on the form that you want to edit, and then click on Design.**

   Microsoft Access 2000 displays your chosen form along with the Access 2000 Toolbox (refer to Figure 16-10).

2. **Move the mouse pointer over the field (or field label) that you want to resize and click the left mouse button.**

   Gray handles appear around your chosen field and field label.

3. **Move the mouse pointer over a gray handle until the mouse pointer turns into a double-pointing arrow.**

4. **Hold down the left mouse button and drag the mouse to change the size of the field (or field label).**

5. **Release the left mouse button when you're happy with the new size of your field (or field label).**

Deleting a field

If you don't want a form to display certain information, then just delete that field from your form.

Deleting a field from a form simply changes the way your form displays data on the screen; deleting a field does not delete any data stored in the database itself.

To delete a field from a form, follow these steps:

1. **Click on the Forms icon, then click on the form that you want to edit, and then click on Design.**

   Microsoft Access 2000 displays your chosen form along with the Access 2000 Toolbox (refer to Figure 16-10).

2. **Click on the field that you want to delete.**

3. **Choose Edit⇨Delete, or press Delete.**

   Microsoft Access 2000 meekly deletes both your field label and its accompanying field at the same time.

If you delete a field and its field label by mistake, then press Ctrl+Z right away to retrieve them.

Editing a field label on a form

If you want to be creative, you can also edit the text that appears inside each field label.

To edit the text in a field label, follow these steps:

1. **Click on the Forms icon, then click on the form that you want to edit, and then click on <u>D</u>esign.**

   Microsoft Access 2000 displays your chosen form along with the Access 2000 Toolbox (refer to Figure 16-10).

2. **Double-click on the field label that you want to change.**

   A Property window appears, as shown in Figure 16-11.

3. **Click on the Caption box and then type or edit a new caption.**

4. **Click on the close box of the Property window to make the window go away.**

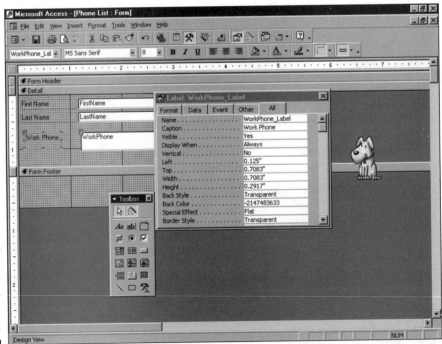

Figure 16-11:
A Property window for modifying a field label.

Adding a new field on a form

If you add a new field to a table, chances are good that you need to display this new field data on a form as well.

To add a new field to a form, follow these steps:

1. **Click on the Forms icon, then click on the form that you want to edit, and then click on <u>D</u>esign.**

   Microsoft Access 2000 displays your chosen form along with the Access 2000 Toolbox (refer to Figure 16-10).

2. **Click on the Text Box icon on the Toolbox.**

3. **Move the mouse pointer over the form.**

   The mouse pointer turns into a crosshair with a miniature text box underneath.

4. **Hold down the left mouse button, drag the mouse, and release the left mouse button.**

   Your newly drawn field appears, as shown in Figure 16-12.

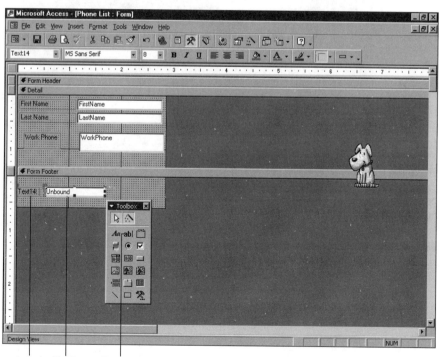

Figure 16-12:
A new field.

Label   Fields   Text box

5. **Double-click on the field label of your newly created field.**

   A Property window appears (refer to Figure 16-11).

6. **Click on the Caption box and then type a label for your field (such as Name or E-mail address).**

7. **Double-click on your newly created field.**

   A Property window appears for your field.

8. **Click on the Control Source list box and then choose a table, as shown in Figure 16-13.**

9. **Click on the close box of the Property window.**

You may need to resize or move your newly created field so that you can display all the data on the screen at once.

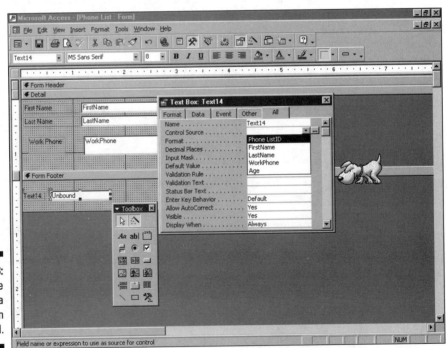

Figure 16-13:
Defining the type of data to display in a field.

Adding a label to a form

Think of labels as descriptive text. Every field should have a label to identify the type of data being displayed, but you can add additional labels at any time for purely decorative purposes as well.

To add a label to a form, follow these steps:

1. **Click on the Forms icon, then click on the form that you want to edit, and then click on Design.**

   Microsoft Access 2000 displays your chosen form along with the Access 2000 Toolbox (refer to Figure 16-10).

3. **Click on the Label icon on the Toolbox.**

4. **Move the mouse pointer over the form, hold down the left mouse button, and drag the mouse.**

5. **Release the left mouse button when you're happy with the size of the label.**

   Microsoft Access 2000 displays your blank label on the form.

6. **Type the text that you want your label to display and then click anywhere outside the label when you're done.**

If you double-click on a label, then you can choose colors to make your label more interesting.

Saving your changes to a form

While you're modifying your form, you can choose File⇨Save, or click on the Save icon on the toolbar to save your form. When you're done designing your form, click on the close box of the form window to close the form window. If you haven't saved your changes, a dialog box reminds you to click on either Yes (to save your changes) or No (to ignore your changes).

When you save changes to a form, you're not changing any actual data in your database.

Chapter 17

Automating Microsoft Access 2000

. . . .

In This Chapter

▶ Creating macros to carry out boring or repetitive tasks

▶ Using command buttons to make Access perform tasks

▶ Programming Visual Basic to automate Access

▶ Converting Access databases into Web pages

. . . .

*W*hy should you work any harder than you have to when you have a personal computer (or a summer intern willing to work for minimum wage) ready to do your work for you? Computers are supposed to make our lives easier, so you'll be happy to know that you can automate Microsoft Access 2000 so that you can focus on important work and let Access worry about trivial details, such as typing state abbreviations and parts-number codes.

Depending on how much freedom you want to give Microsoft Access 2000, you can automate Access 2000 the following ways:

✔ You can create macros to help you reduce the number of keystrokes that you use or limit the number of menu commands you have to choose.

✔ You can use the Command Button Wizard to create and personalize commands and automate your database.

✔ If you want to go even further in personalizing your database, you can use a real-life programming language, Visual Basic, which can not only create command buttons but can also create instructions to make Microsoft Access 2000 follow your every wish and command perfectly.

Which feature should you choose? If you want to automate Microsoft Access 2000 for your personal benefit, you can create a macro or a command button. If you plan to automate Microsoft Access 2000 for others, you can use a command button or Visual Basic. If you really need to create something complicated that requires writing your own program, then use Visual Basic.

Making Macros

A macro acts like a tape recorder. First you record your keystrokes on disk. Then you can "play back" those same keystrokes at the touch of a button. Macros let you perform a repetitive or complicated task one time and then tell Microsoft Access 2000, "Remember that really long series of keystrokes that I asked you to record three months ago? Well, I want you to perform those keystrokes all over again while I go out to lunch."

Creating a macro

At its simplest level, a macro can automatically type text for you, such as *Massachusetts,* or perform an action, such as opening and printing a form. Microsoft Access 2000 lets you create macros that can perform all types of tasks. Here are just two of the more common macro uses:

✔ Simulate someone's typing at the keyboard

✔ Choose a command from the Microsoft Access 2000 pull-down menus

Simulating someone's typing at the keyboard

Macros that simulate someone's typing at a keyboard are most useful for getting Microsoft Access 2000 to type long, repetitive text for you so that you don't have to type the text yourself. For example, if you have to type a long-winded name, such as *The American Corporation for the Creation of Political Dishonesty,* over and over again, you'll probably slowly go mad.

While you could save yourself time and effort by typing a shortened version of the above phrase (such as substituting "The American Corporation for the Creation of Political Dishonesty" with "Congress"), you may find that using a macro simplifies the task even more. Such a task is perfectly suited for your computer because your computer is perfectly happy performing dull, monotonous, mindless, repetitive tasks, over and over again until you tell it to stop.

To create a macro that simulates typing at the keyboard, follow these steps:

1. **First open the database window, then click on the Macro icon, and then click on New.**

   A Macro window appears.

2. **Click on the gray downward-pointing arrow in the Action list box and then choose SendKeys, as shown in Figure 17-1.**

   An Action Arguments box appears at the bottom of the Macro window.

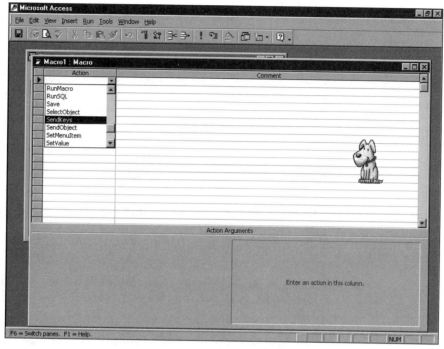

Figure 17-1:
The macro
window in
which you
can create
your own
macro.

3. **Click on the Keystrokes box and then type the text that you want the macro to type for you. (You can type as many as 256 characters.)**

4. **Click on the Wait list box and then choose Yes or No.**

   Choose Yes only if your macro types text too rapidly for your database to handle.

5. **Click on the close box in the Macro window.**

   A dialog box appears, asking if you want to save your macro.

6. **Click on Yes.**

   A Save As dialog box appears, asking you to name your macro.

7. **Type a name in the Macro Name box and then click on OK.**

You can always rename a macro from within the Database window by right-clicking the mouse button over the macro, choosing Rename, and then typing a new name.

Choosing a Microsoft Access menu command

Sometimes you may need a macro that can choose one or more Access menu commands for you so that you don't have to waste time choosing them yourself. For example, if you want to transfer your Access data to an Excel worksheet, then you have to choose Tools➪OfficeLinks➪Analyze It With MS Excel. Clumsy? Yes. So instead let an Access macro do your work for you.

To create a macro that chooses menu commands, follow these steps:

1. **Open the database window, click on the Macro icon, and then click on New.**

   A Macro window appears (refer to Figure 17-1).

2. **Click on the gray downward-pointing arrow in the Action list box and then choose RunCommand.**

   Microsoft Access 2000 displays a Command list box at the bottom of the Macro window.

3. **Click on the Command list box and then choose the command that you want to run, such as Undo, Save As, or Find.**

4. **Click on the close box in the Macro window.**

   A dialog box appears, asking if you want to save your macro.

5. **Click on Yes.**

   A Save As dialog box appears, asking you to name your macro.

6. **Type a name in the Macro Name box and then click on OK.**

Running a macro

Macros are no good unless you plan to use them once in a while. To give you as much flexibility as possible when you run a macro, Microsoft Access 2000 lets you choose to run a macro by name or by assigning the macro to a specific keystroke (such as Ctrl+3) and then pressing that keystroke when you want the macro to run.

Some macros, such as those that simulate someone's typing at the keyboard, require the cursor to be in a specific location before you run the macros. If you run a macro with the cursor in the wrong location, then that macro may run blissfully unaware that data is possibly being typed in the wrong place.

Choosing a macro to run by name

When you want to run a macro, Access has no idea which macro you want to run. You have to use the Access menus to tell Access, "Hey, stupid! Run the macro named XXX right now."

To run a macro by name, follow these steps:

1. **Choose Tools⇨Macro⇨Run Macro.**

   The Run Macro dialog box appears, as shown in Figure 17-2.

2. **Click on the Macro Name list box and then choose the macro that you want to run.**

3. **Click on OK.**

Figure 17-2:
The Run
Macro
dialog box.

Running a macro from a keystroke combination

Although you can always run a macro by its name, assigning a keystroke combination to the macro first may be more convenient. All you have to do then is quickly type the keystroke combination (such as Ctrl+2), and the macro runs right away.

The main drawback to running a macro by using a keystroke combination is that you have to remember which keystroke combination you assigned to your macro. Table 17-1 lists some of the more common types of keystrokes that you can assign to a macro.

Table 17-1	Common Types of Keystrokes Assigned to Macros	
Keystroke Combination	**Example**	**How Access Interprets the Keystroke**
Ctrl+Letter key	Ctrl+Q	^Q
Ctrl+Number key	Ctrl+5	^5
Any function key	F11	{F11}
Ctrl+Any function key	Ctrl+F12	^{F12}
Shift+Any function key	Shift+F4	+{F4}

Any keystrokes that you assign to a macro in Microsoft Access 2000 do not affect any keystrokes that you may have assigned to macros in other Office 2000 programs, such as Microsoft Excel 2000.

To assign a keystroke combination to a new macro, follow these steps:

1. **Open the database window, click on the Macro icon, and then click on New.**

   The Macro window appears.

2. **Click on the Macro Names icon in the toolbar.**

   The Macro Name column magically appears, as shown in Figure 17-3.

3. **Click on the Macro Name column and then type the keystroke combination that you want to assign, such as ^4 for Ctrl+4 or +{F3} for Shift+F3.**

4. **Click on the Action column and then click on the downward-pointing arrow to choose an action (such as SendKeys).**

   You may need to type additional information in the Action Arguments part of the Macro window to define what your macro actually does.

5. **Click on the close box in the Macro window.**

   A dialog box appears, asking whether you want to save your macro.

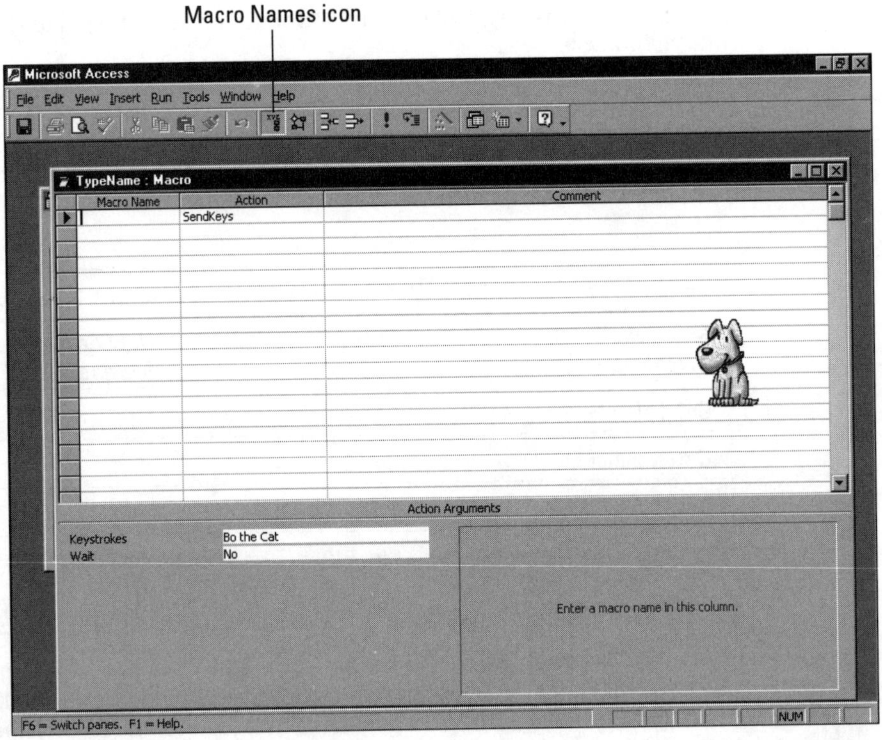

Figure 17-3:
The Macro
window.

6. Type AutoKeys in the Macro Name and then click on Yes.

A Save As dialog box appears. Your macro is ready to use.

If you want to assign keystroke combinations to additional macros, click on the AutoKeys macro and then click on Design. Then type each macro on a separate line in the AutoKeys Macro window.

Running a macro automatically

Rather than choosing a macro by name or pressing a macro's unique keystroke combination, you have the option with Microsoft Access 2000 to make a macro run after you update data in a field or the moment that you click on a field. By having a macro run automatically, you won't have to waste a precious second or two giving the command yourself to run the macro.

To make a macro run automatically, you need to define

✔ The macro that you want to run

✔ The event that causes the macro to run

An *event* is a special term used to describe an action whenever a user does something to a Microsoft Access 2000 field, such as updating data, clicking the mouse on the field, or moving the cursor out of the field.

To run a macro automatically, follow these steps:

1. Open the database window and then click on the Forms icon.

2. Click on the form that you want to use and then click on Design.

3. Double-click on the field to control the macro.

A Properties window appears.

4. Click on the Event tab, as shown in Figure 17-4.

Figure 17-4:
The Event
tab in the
Properties
window.

Text Box: FirstName
Format	Data	Event	Other	All
Before Update . . . .
After Update . . . .
On Change . . . .
On Enter . . . .
On Exit . . . .
On Got Focus . . . .
On Lost Focus . . . .
On Click . . . .
On Dbl Click . . . .
On Mouse Down . . . .
On Mouse Move . . . .
On Mouse Up . . . .
On Key Down . . . .

5. **Click on an event box (such as On Mouse Down, On Click, or On Enter) and then click on the downward-pointing arrow.**

   A list of macro names appears.

6. **Click on the macro that you want to run when your chosen event occurs.**

7. **Click on the close box of the Properties window.**

8. **Click on the close box of the Form window.**

   A dialog box appears, asking if you want to save your changes.

9. **Click on Yes.**

The next time anyone uses the form chosen in Step 2 and creates the event that you chose in Step 5, then the macro you chose in Step 6 runs.

Deleting a macro

No matter how useful a macro may be, the time comes when you want to delete it. To delete a macro, follow these steps:

1. **Open the database window, click the Macro icon, and then click on the macro that you want to delete.**

2. **Choose Edit⇨Delete, press Delete, or click on the Delete icon.**

   A dialog box appears, asking whether you really want to delete your macro.

3. **Click on Yes.**

If you delete a macro by mistake, immediately press Ctrl+Z to make Microsoft Access 2000 recover the macro for you.

Using Command Buttons

The main purpose of a form is to make your database easier to use. A form simply displays data in a window. So to make your forms even easier for someone to use (especially a computer novice), you can add command buttons to your forms as well.

A command button provides users with a convenient button that they can click on to perform an action, such as displaying the next record in your database or printing the current record. If a form didn't offer command buttons for performing these actions, then users would be forced to wade through Microsoft Access 2000's pull-down menus to find the proper commands to use, which can be intimidating and confusing.

You can create command buttons in Microsoft Access 2000 two ways:

✔ Use the Command Button Wizard.

✔ Use Visual Basic for Application (abbreviated as VBA). For more information on creating command buttons using VBA, see the section "Using VBA to Automate Your Databases," later in this chapter.

The Command Button Wizard is meant to guide you, step-by-step, in creating a command button. Functionally, no difference exists between a command button created using Visual Basic and a command button created using the Command Button Wizard.

Although you can clutter a form with as many command buttons as you want, using them sparingly and arranging them neatly can make finding and using command buttons easier.

Using the Command Button Wizard

The main purpose of the Command Button Wizard is to help you create a command button and choose a common action for that command button to follow.

To create a command button using the Microsoft Access 2000 Command Button Wizard, you must be in Form design view. To create a command button using the Command Button Wizard, follow these steps:

1. **Open the database window and then click on the Forms icon.**

2. **Click on the form that you want to use and then click on <u>D</u>esign.**

3. **Click on the Control Wizard icon on the Toolbox.**

   The Control Wizard icon should appear "pressed in" on the Toolbox. If the Control Wizard already appears "pressed in," you can skip Step 3.

4. **Click on the Command Button icon on the Toolbox.**

5. **Move the mouse pointer to the location on the form where you want to place your command button. Then hold down the left mouse button, drag the mouse to draw your command button, and then release the mouse button.**

   Access draws your command button and displays the Command Button Wizard dialog box, as shown in Figure 17-5.

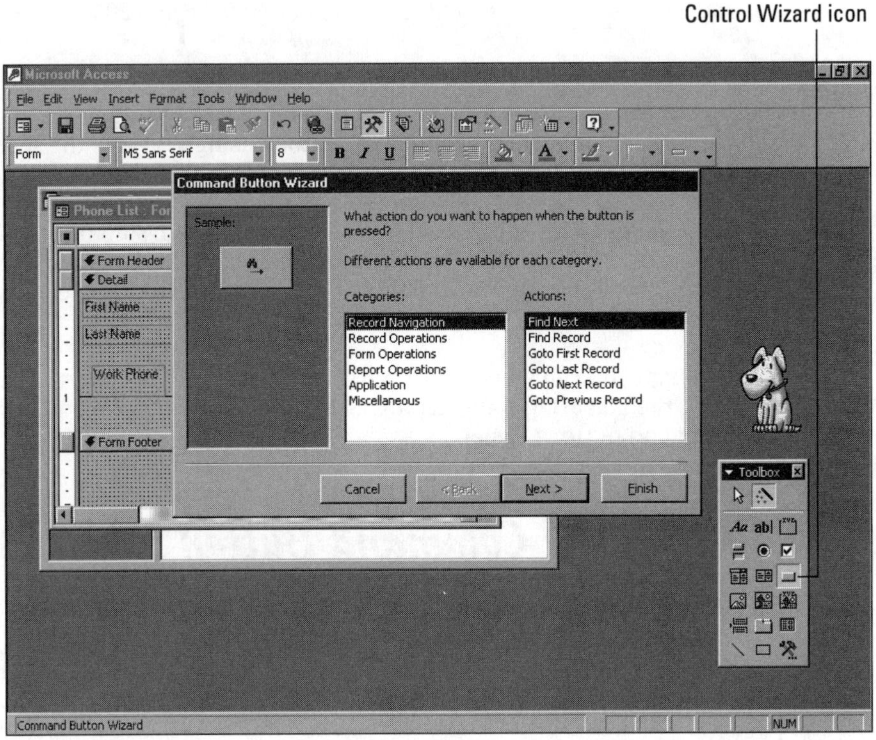

Control Wizard icon

Figure 17-5:
The
Command
Button
Wizard
dialog box.

6. **Click on a category (such as Miscellaneous if you want to run a macro from a command button) in the Categories list box.**

7. **Click on an action (such as Run Macro) in the Actions list box.**

8. **Click on Next.**

   Another Command Button Wizard dialog box appears, asking you to choose an option based on your choices in Steps 5 and 6.

9. **Choose the options that you want and then click on Next.**

10. **Repeat Step 8 until the Command Button Wizard asks for a name to give to your command button.**

11. **Type a name and then click on Finish.**

    Access displays the command button on your form.

12. **Click on the close box in the Form design window.**

    A dialog box appears, asking whether you want to save your changes.

13. **Click on Yes.**

    Your command button is now ready to use.

Deleting a command button

Because you can always add a command button to a form, you shouldn't be surprised that you can also delete a command button at any time.

To delete a command button, follow these steps:

1. **Open the database window and then click on the Forms icon.**

2. **Click on the form that contains the command button that you want to delete and then click on Design.**

3. **Click on the command button that you want to delete.**

   Access displays gray handles around the command button.

4. **Choose Edit⇨Delete, then click on the Delete icon, or press Delete.**

   The command button disappears.

5. **Click on the close box in the Form design window.**

   A dialog box appears, asking whether you want to save your changes.

6. **Click on Yes.**

If you delete a command button by mistake, then press Ctrl+Z right away to bring the command button back again.

The two faces of Visual Basic

Microsoft sells a separate language compiler called Visual Basic, which lets you write general-purpose programs, such as games, utilities, or even databases. If you want to write different types of programs, then you have to buy a copy of Visual Basic.

If you only need to write custom databases, then use the version of Visual Basic that Microsoft includes with Access 2000, which is called Visual Basic for Applications (VBA).

So, when someone mentions "Visual Basic," he or she may be talking about Visual Basic (the language compiler that you have to buy separately) or Visual Basic for Applications, which is the programming language that comes free inside Microsoft Office 2000.

When I use the term *Visual Basic* in this book, I'm referring to VBA, the version of Visual Basic that comes inside Microsoft Office 2000.

Using VBA to Automate Your Databases

Microsoft Office 2000 includes a special programming language called Visual Basic for Applications (VBA). VBA lets you write miniature programs that automate your Microsoft Office 2000 programs, such as Access 2000.

Although you can create supercomplicated programs using VBA, most VBA programs consist of two parts:

✔ Command buttons, which allow you to use your database without using a single Access menu command. Figure 17-6 shows command buttons that let a user perform various tasks at the click of a button.

✔ Event procedures, which are the instructions that tell each command button what task to perform when clicked on by a user. Without an event procedure, a command button looks nice but doesn't do anything useful (much like the Vice President of the United States).

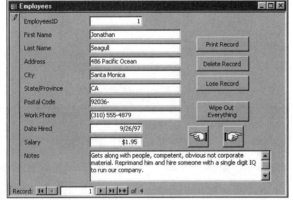

Figure 17-6:
Typical command buttons on a form.

When you create command buttons using the Command Button Wizard, the Command Button Wizard shields you from having to write specific VBA instructions.

Creating a command button using VBA

The Command Button Wizard can help you create command buttons that perform common actions, such as displaying the first record of a database or deleting a record. But if you want to create a command button that does something more complicated or unique to your specific database (such as displaying a list of all your best customers and printing out the entire list), then you may need to use the Visual Basic for Applications programming language.

Using Visual Basic for Applications with a command button involves two steps:

- ✔ Creating a command button
- ✔ Writing Visual Basic for Applications instructions to make the command button do something useful

To create a command button so that you can write VBA instructions, follow these steps:

1. **Open the database window and then click on the Forms icon.**

2. **Click on the form that you want to use and then click on <u>D</u>esign.**

3. **Click on the Control Wizard icon on the Toolbox so that the icon is not pressed in, as shown in Figure 17-7.**

   If the Control Wizard icon does not appear pressed in, skip this step.

   The Command Button Wizard will get in your way if you want to write a VBA instruction to control your command button.

Control Wizard icon

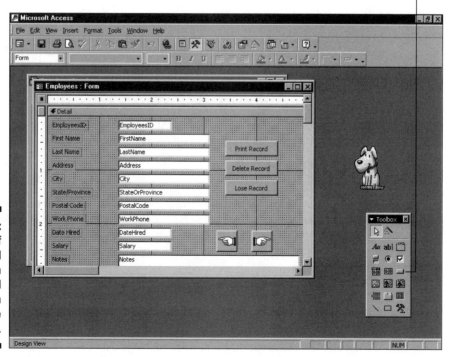

Figure 17-7: Turning off the Control Wizard with the Control Wizard icon on the Toolbox.

4. **Click on the Command Button icon on the Toolbox.**

5. **Move the mouse to the location where you want to place your command button. Hold down the left mouse button, drag the mouse to draw your command button, and then release the mouse button.**

Microsoft Access 2000 draws your command button. At this point, you're ready to start writing your Visual Basic for Applications instructions by following the steps listed in the "Writing an event procedure" section later in this chapter.

All about event procedures

After you've drawn one or more command buttons on a form, the command buttons won't do anything until you write instructions that tell the command buttons what to do if someone clicks on them. Some of the more common types of Visual Basic for Applications commands let you perform these tasks:

- ✔ Assign another object, such as a text box, a string, or a value
- ✔ Display a message box
- ✔ Perform a calculation

Assigning another object a string or value

If you want to change the contents of a field (also known as an *object*), you can use Visual Basic to stuff a text string or number into that field. To change a field's contents, you have to know the name of the field and the text or number that you want to stuff into the field, such as:

```
Private Sub cmdZip_Click()
PostalCode = "91702"
End Sub
```

If you have a command button named cmdZip and you click on the button, then Microsoft Access 2000 looks for an object (such as a field) called PostalCode and replaces the field's contents with the text string 91702.

Displaying a message box

You can also program Microsoft Access 2000 to display a message box whenever a user clicks on a command button. To create a message box, you have to specify the message that you want displayed and the title of the message box. Figure 17-8 shows the message box that the following VBA code creates:

```
Private Sub cmdZip_Click()
MsgBox "Delete everything?", , "Warning!!!"
End Sub
```

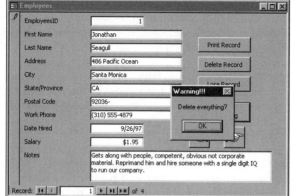

Figure 17-8:
The
Warning
dialog box
created by
actual
Visual Basic
code.

Performing a calculation

Visual Basic can perform simple addition, subtraction, multiplication, or division by using numbers stored in one or more objects. Table 17-2 shows typical commands for performing a calculation.

Table 17-2	Common Visual Basic Mathematical Operators	
Operation	*Operator*	*Real-Life Visual Basic Example*
Addition	+	Total = SalesTax + ProductCost
Subtraction	–	TakeHomePay = Salary – IncomeTax
Multiplication	*	Rabbits = Parents * Days
Division	/	Government = Conservatives /Liberals

The joy of Visual Basic for Applications programming

Visual Basic for Applications includes all sorts of commands that let you create arrays, perform conditional execution by using If/Then statements, and manipulate the information stored in your Microsoft Access 2000 database. If you have no idea what these terms mean and you don't care, then you probably will never need to learn more about Visual Basic.

What can Visual Basic do for you, and why should you bother learning how to use Visual Basic? Access is great for storing information, but unless you know the right commands to choose from the pull-down menus in Access, the information just sits there.

By using Visual Basic, you can create your own programs to store and retrieve information, such as a mail-order-management program, an inventory-tracking program, a church-management program, a political-contribution-tracking program, or any other type of program that requires storing lots of different information.

Visual Basic essentially lets you turn your Microsoft Access 2000 databases into custom programs. If you ever have wished that you had a special program to help you store, track, and organize information, then writing your own Visual Basic program in Microsoft Access 2000 may be just what you need.

Writing an event procedure

To write an event procedure for a command button that you've already created, follow these steps:

1. **Right-click on the command button for which you want to write an event procedure.**

   A pop-up menu appears.

2. **Click on Build Event.**

   The Choose Builder window appears, as shown in Figure 17-9.

Figure 17-9:
The Choose
Builder
window for
picking a
way to pro-
gram your
command
button.

3. **Click on Code Builder and then click on OK.**

4. **The Visual Basic code editor appears, as shown in Figure 17-10.**

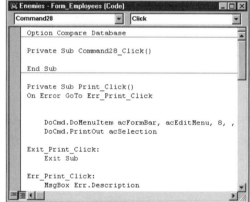

Figure 17-10:
The Visual
Basic code
editor where
you can type
Visual Basic
commands.

5. **Type your Visual Basic code to perform a task, such as assigning the contents of a field with a string or number or displaying a message box.**

6. **Choose File⇨Close and Return to Microsoft Access, or press Alt+Q.**

7. **Click on the close box of the Form window.**

   A dialog box appears, asking if you want to save your changes.

8. **Click on Yes.**

Obviously, this brief introduction to the Visual Basic for Applications programming language barely scratches the surface of how to program Microsoft Access 2000. If you're intrigued and want to learn more about Visual Basic programming, pick up a copy of *Access Programming For Dummies* by Rob Krumm (published by IDG Books Worldwide).

Part VI

Printing Stuff with Microsoft Publisher 2000

The 5th Wave   By Rich Tennant

MY GOD! IT'S WORKING! I'M GETTING ITALICS!

In this part . . .

Using Microsoft Publisher 2000, you can create flyers, brochures, pamphlets, and letterhead to make your business look as important and professional as multinational corporations. So to help you create, design, and ultimately print out professional publications, this part of the book explains how to use colors, calendars, special paper, and layout guides for precisely aligning objects on a page.

Remember that the first impression your publications make may be the only chance you'll get to impress an important business client or customer, so take time to learn the best ways to keep your Microsoft Publisher 2000 publications looking as sharp as possible.

Chapter 18

Prettying Up Microsoft Publisher 2000 Publications

● ●

In This Chapter

▶ Using Design Gallery objects

▶ Using color schemes

▶ Playing with special paper

● ●

*T*he main purpose of Microsoft Publisher 2000 is to help you print fancy-looking publications as quickly as possible without going nuts in the process. To make your publications look as professional as possible, Publisher comes with loads of special Design Gallery objects, which are pre-drawn borders, coupons, logos, and even complete forms that you can paste into your publication.

Once you've added a Design Gallery object, you can change the colors and print your publication on special paper to make your publication look extra special for making greeting cards, brochures, or just a friendly two-week notice telling your boss what to do with your old job after you leave.

Using Design Gallery Objects

Most people aren't very good at drawing, so Publisher provides some handy drawings stored in a Design Gallery. The Design Gallery lets you browse through various objects, such as banners, borders, and mastheads, that you can add to your publication and modify later.

Inserting a Design Gallery object

The Design Gallery stores various objects that you can pick and add to your publication. To insert an object from the Design Gallery into your publication, follow these steps:

1. **Choose Insert➪Design Gallery Object.**

   The Design Gallery dialog box appears, as shown in Figure 18-1.

2. **Click on an object type listed under the Categories group, such as Calendars, Boxes, or Mastheads.**

   The Design Gallery dialog box displays variations of your chosen object type.

3. **Click on the pretty design that you want to insert in your publication and click on Insert Object.**

   Publisher draws your chosen object on your publication. You may have to move or resize the object.

If you click on the Objects by Design tab after Step 1, the Design Gallery dialog box displays objects that share a common graphic design appearance, as shown in Figure 18-2.

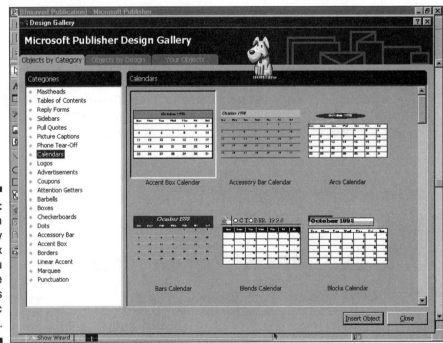

Figure 18-1:
The Design Gallery dialog box lets you browse through its graphic objects.

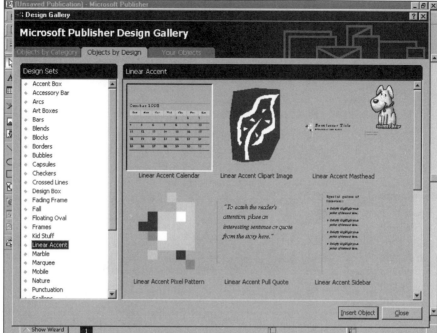

Figure 18-2:
The Design
Gallery
dialog box
organizes
objects by
common
graphic
layout
appearance.

Changing the appearance of a Design Gallery object

After you've inserted a Design Gallery object in your publication, you may want to modify the object by changing its graphic appearance. To change a Design Gallery object's appearance, follow these steps:

1. **Click on the Design Gallery object that you want to change.**

   Black handles appear around the entire Design Gallery object, and a Wizard button appears underneath, as shown in Figure 18-3.

2. **Click on the Wizard button.**

   A Wizard window appears, as shown in Figure 18-4.

3. **Click on the option(s) that you want to change.**

   Depending on the Design Gallery object you choose, the Wizard window may display different options that you can change.

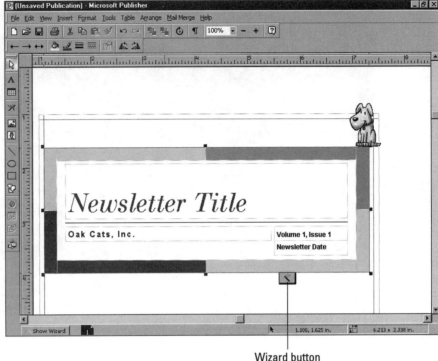

Figure 18-3:
The Wizard
button pops
up to help
you edit
your Design
Gallery
object.

Wizard button

4. **Click on the close box of the Wizard window to make the window go away.**

If you decide you don't like the new appearance of your object, then press Ctrl+Z to return to the previous graphic design.

Editing text in a Design Gallery object

Some (but not all) Design Gallery objects display text in separate text boxes. If you want to edit this text, follow these steps:

1. **Click on the text box portion of the Design Gallery object that you want to edit.**

   Publisher displays a border around your chosen text box with a blinking cursor inside that text box.

2. **Edit or type any new text.**

   You can press Ctrl+A to select all the text in a single text box.

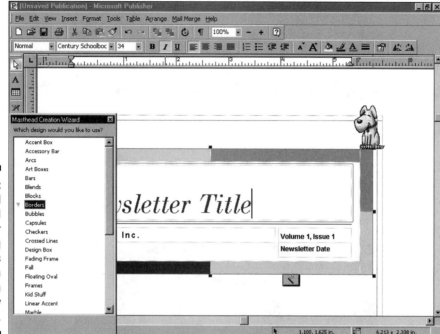

Figure 18-4:
A typical
Wizard
window for
modifying
the colors
and design
of a Design
Gallery
object.

Deleting a Design Gallery object

In case you want to get rid of a Design Gallery object, you can by following these steps:

1. **Click on the Design Gallery object that you want to delete.**

   Publisher displays a border around your chosen text box with a blinking cursor inside that text box.

2. **Press Delete or choose Edit⇨Cut.**

If you delete a Design Gallery object by mistake, then press Ctrl+Z right away to bring the object back again.

Using Color Schemes

A color scheme consists of several different colors used for different parts of your publication, such as one color for a background and another color for text. Microsoft Publisher 2000 provides dozens of different color schemes (with names like Heather or Mist), which can define the colors used in all your Design Gallery objects. So, if you like a particular Design Gallery object but don't like its color, you can choose a different color scheme or make up one of your own.

Applying an existing color scheme

To change the color scheme used to color your Design Graphic objects, follow these steps:

1. **Draw one or more Design Gallery objects on your publication.**

2. **Choose Format⇨Color Scheme.**

    A Color Scheme dialog box appears, as shown in Figure 18-5.

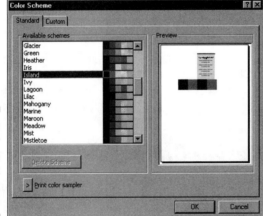

Figure 18-5:
The Color Scheme dialog box for choosing new colors.

3. **Click on a color scheme (such as Mistletoe or Iris) that you want to use for all your Design Gallery objects.**

    Each time you click on a different color scheme, Publisher shows you how your chosen color scheme affects your Design Gallery objects.

    Note: All Design Gallery objects in the same publication must share a single color scheme. So if you change the color scheme for one Design Gallery object, Microsoft Publisher 2000 automatically changes the color scheme for all the other Design Gallery objects in your publication as well.

4. **Click on OK.**

Making your own color scheme

For those who don't like any of the existing color schemes that Microsoft has generously provided for you, take some time to design your own color schemes.

To define your own color scheme, follow these steps:

1. **Choose Format⇨Color Scheme.**

2. **Click on the Custom tab.**

   A Custom tab appears in the Color Scheme dialog box, as shown in Figure 18-6.

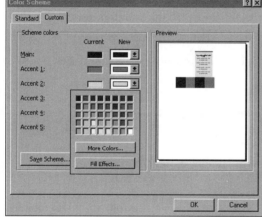

Figure 18-6:
The Custom tab allows you to design your own color schemes.

3. **Click on the New list box for each color scheme that you want to modify, such as Main or Accent 2.**

   The Color Scheme dialog box shows you the effect of your newly chosen color on the Design Gallery objects in your publication.

4. **Click on the Save Scheme button.**

   A dialog box appears, asking for a name.

5. **Type a name for your color scheme and then click on OK.**

6. **Click on OK.**

Playing with Special Paper

Although Microsoft Publisher 2000 can help you create pretty brochures and flyers using nothing more than an ordinary piece of paper and a halfway decent printer, you may want to go an extra step further and buy special paper to print on as well.

Special paper has two uses:

✔ To print your publication on paper that already provides a background design, such as a certificate or postcard.

✔ To print on special-size paper, such as business cards or postcards, that contains perforations to make the paper easier to separate.

You need to order special paper through a mail-order catalog that specializes in different paper or through a retail store that offers special types of paper.

To tell Microsoft Publisher 2000 to print on special paper, follow these steps:

1. **Choose <u>V</u>iew⇨<u>S</u>pecial Paper.**

   A Special Paper dialog box appears. This dialog box specifies the exact type of special paper that you need to buy, such as Blue Certificate — Paper Direct CT1051.

2. **Click on the type of special paper that you want to use.**

3. **Click on OK.**

   Publisher 2000 shows you what your publication will look like when printed on the special paper that you chose in Step 2.

Publisher 2000 can show you what your publication will look like when printed on special paper, but you must buy that specific special paper if you want your printed publication to look exactly the same as it appears on your screen.

Chapter 19

Arranging Objects on a Page

. . . .

. . . .

A typical Microsoft Publisher 2000 publication consists of text and graphics that you can move around on a page. Whereas just slapping a text box or graphic anywhere on a page may be fine for creating a simple flyer or sign, you may want to take a little more care with the placement of your text and graphic when you're designing a more important publication, such as a business brochure or poster.

To help you precisely align your objects on a page, Microsoft Publisher 2000 comes loaded with various features for making sure that your objects appear exactly where you want them.

Playing with Layout and Ruler Guides

Try drawing a perfect square on a blank sheet of paper with a pencil. Not easy, is it? Now try drawing that same square on a sheet of graph paper that has both vertical and horizontal lines drawn across it. Obviously, drawing a square on a sheet of graph paper is easier, because the graph paper provides lines to guide you into drawing straight lines.

Because the lines on a sheet of graph paper can be so useful in helping people draw objects and then accurately place them, Microsoft Publisher 2000 offers a similar feature called *guides*.

A guide does nothing more than display a line on your page so that you can draw or place objects on that page. These guides don't appear when you print; the guides exist only to provide a visual tool for aligning objects on a page.

Microsoft Publisher 2000 provides two types of guides:

✔ Layout guides for designing the layout of an entire page (layout guides appear on a page as pink and blue lines)

✔ Ruler guides for drawing a single line based off the vertical or horizontal rulers (ruler guides appear on a page as green lines)

Use layout guides to design the overall structure of an entire page. For example, if you want to create a newsletter divided into two vertical columns, you use a layout guide.

Use ruler guides when you need to align objects at a specific location. For example, if you want to place three text boxes so that their left sides all appear exactly 1.35 inches from the left margin, you use a ruler guide.

Layout guides affect every page in your publication. Ruler guides only appear on a single page.

To temporarily hide all guides from view, choose View⇨Hide Boundaries and Guides (or press Ctrl+Shift+O). To show all guides again, choose View⇨ Show Boundaries and Guides (or press Ctrl+Shift+O).

Designing a layout guide

A layout guide divides an entire page into symmetric parts, such as dividing a page into two columns and three rows. A layout guide consists of two parts:

✔ Page margins define the top, bottom, left, and right margins of a page (page margins appear as pink lines).

✔ Grid guides divide a page into rows and columns (grid guides appear on a page as blue lines).

To design a layout guide for a page, follow these steps:

1. **Choose Arrange⇨Layout Guides.**

   A Layout Guides dialog box appears, as shown in Figure 19-1.

2. **Click on the up/down arrow (or type a specific number) in the Margin Guides (Left, Right, Top, or Bottom) to define your page margins.**

   For example, if you want a left page margin of 1.83 inches, type 1.83 in the Left margin guide box.

3. **Click on the up/down arrows in the Columns or Rows boxes to define the number of columns and rows that you want.**

The Layout Guides dialog box showing your layout guides appears.

4. **Click on OK.**

Your new layout guides will now appear on every page of your current publication.

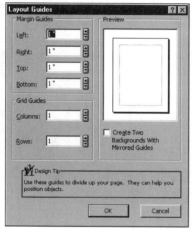

Figure 19-1:
The Layout Guides dialog box for designing a layout for every page in your publication.

Placing a ruler guide

Ruler guides (which appear as green lines) can come in handy for aligning objects on a single page. To draw a ruler guide on a page, follow these steps:

1. **Move the mouse pointer over the horizontal or vertical ruler.**

If the horizontal or vertical rulers are not visible, then choose View➪Rulers.

2. **Move the mouse pointer over the horizontal or vertical ruler.**

3. **Hold down the left mouse button and drag the mouse over your page.**

The mouse pointer turns into a special Adjust icon, and the ruler guide appears as a green line, as shown in Figure 19-2. (Because Figure 19-2 appears in black and white, the green ruler guide line appears black.)

4. **Release the left mouse button when you're happy with the location of your ruler guide.**

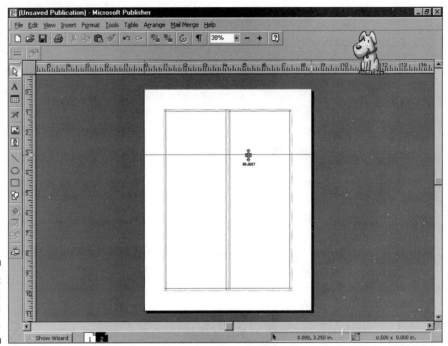

Figure 19-2:
Drawing a
ruler guide
on a page.

Moving a ruler guide

In case you don't like the location of your ruler guide, you can move the ruler guide at any time by following these steps:

1. **Hold down the Shift key.**

2. **Move the mouse pointer over the ruler guide until the mouse pointer turns into an Adjust icon.**

3. **Drag the mouse (while still holding down the left mouse button) to move the ruler guide to a new location.**

4. **Release the left mouse button when you're happy with the new location of the ruler guide.**

Deleting a ruler guide

You may draw a ruler guide on a page and then decide you don't need it any more. So to remove a ruler guide, follow these steps:

1. **Hold down the Shift key.**

2. **Move the mouse pointer over the ruler guide until the mouse pointer turns into an Adjust icon.**

3. **Drag the mouse (while still holding down the left mouse button) to move the ruler guide off your page.**

4. **Release the left mouse button.**

To get rid of all ruler guides on a single page at once, choose Arrange⇨ Ruler Guides⇨Clear All Ruler Guides.

Aligning Objects with the Snap To Feature

Both layout and ruler guides allow you to place an object (such as a text box or graphic image) more precisely on a page. For additional help, you may want to use Microsoft Publisher 2000's Snap To feature.

The Snap To feature helps you to align objects more precisely with

- ✔ A layout or ruler guide
- ✔ A ruler mark (this is independent of any ruler guides you may have placed)
- ✔ Another object

The moment you move an object to a guide, ruler mark (such as the $\frac{1}{16}$-inch mark on a ruler), or another object, the Snap To feature automatically aligns your object. That way you don't have to painstakingly align your objects yourself.

Turning on the Snap To feature

Before you can use the Snap To feature, you have to turn it on. To turn on the Snap To feature, first go to Tools and then choose one of the following:

- ✔ Snap to Ruler Marks
- ✔ Snap to Guides
- ✔ Snap to Objects

Microsoft Publisher 2000 displays a check mark next to your chosen option. You can choose all three options if you want.

The Snap To feature only works when you drag (move) an object. The Snap To feature doesn't affect the placement of any objects that you do not move.

Moving multiple objects at once

If you want to move two or more objects at once, follow these steps:

1. **Click on the first object that you want to move.**

   Black handles appear around your chosen object.

2. **Hold down the Shift or Ctrl button and then click on the next object that you want to move.**

3. **Repeat Step 2 for each object that you want to move.**

   Publisher highlights each object with gray handles and draws a box that encloses all your objects.

4. **Release the Shift or Ctrl button (whichever button you pressed in Step 2) and move the mouse pointer over one of your selected objects until the mouse pointer turns into a Move icon.**

5. **Drag the mouse to move your chosen objects.**

   If you have the Snap To feature turned on, Publisher aligns your group of objects according to the left, right, top, or bottom side of the entire box that encloses your group of objects. The sides of this box correspond to the location of the objects that you choose. For example, the left side of the box is defined by the object (such as a text box) that appears farthest to the left of the screen, and the right side of the box is defined by the object (such as a picture box) that appears farthest to the right of the screen, and so on.

Moving objects in a straight line

Sometimes you may want to move an object up/down or right/left in a straight line. Unless you have good eye-hand coordination, such a task may seem cumbersome unless you follow these steps:

1. **Click on the object that you want to move.**

   If you want to move two or more objects, select all the objects that you want to move according to the steps in the previous section, "Moving multiple objects at once."

2. **Hold down the Shift button.**

3. **Move the mouse pointer over your selected object until the mouse pointer turns into a Move icon.**

4. **Hold down the left mouse button and drag the mouse to move your object to a new location.**

   Note that Microsoft Publisher 2000 only allows you to move the object in a straight line.

5. **Release the left mouse button and the Shift key when your object is in its new location.**

Checking Your Design

You can create really great or really awful-looking publications using Microsoft Publisher 2000; the choice is yours. Although Publisher 2000 can't help you with the aesthetic appearance of your publications, Publisher 2000 can help prevent common problems in creating a publication.

Some of the common problems that Publisher 2000 can catch for you include:

- ✔ Empty frames, such as text boxes without any text in them
- ✔ Covered objects, where one object overlaps another and partially blocks one of the objects
- ✔ Text in overflow area, which occurs when a text box isn't large enough to display all the text stored inside of it
- ✔ Objects in nonprinting region, such as a graphic that appears outside the page margin
- ✔ Disproportional pictures, making sure that your graphic images aren't too small or too large
- ✔ Spacing between sentences, checking for two spaces after each period

Customizing the Design Checker

Microsoft Publisher 2000 comes with a special Design Checker, which acts like a graphic design teacher who can examine your publication before you print it out. Because the Design Checker may flag errors that you created on purpose for artistic effects, you may want to take some time to modify the problems that the Design Checker looks for.

To customize the Design Checker, follow these steps:

1. **Choose Tools⇨Design Checker.**

   The Design Checker dialog box appears, as shown in Figure 19-3.

2. **Choose Format⇨Color Scheme.**

3. **Click on Options.**

   An Options dialog box appears, as shown in Figure 19-4.

Figure 19-3:
The Design
Checker
dialog box
can check
your
publication
for common
errors.

Figure 19-4:
The Options
dialog
box for
customizing
the Design
Checker.

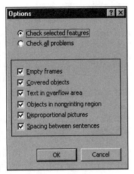

4. **Click on the options that you want. (Clearing a check mark in an option turns that option off.)**

5. **Click on OK.**

   The Design Checker dialog box appears again (refer to Figure 19-3).

6. **Click on Cancel.**

Running the Design Checker

Before you take that all-important step and start printing your publication, you should run the Design Checker to catch any problems in your publication. That way you can fix the problems before you print 1,000 copies of a flyer that doesn't correctly display your company's name.

To run the Design Checker, follow these steps:

1. **Choose Tools⇨Design Checker.**

   The Design Checker dialog box appears (refer to Figure 19-3).

2. **Click on the <u>A</u>ll or <u>P</u>ages option button.**

    If you click on the Pages option button, then you have to specify the pages that you want to check, such as pages 4 through 92.

3. **Click on OK.**

    Each time the Design Checker finds a possible problem with your publication, it displays a dialog box that tells you of the possible problem and gives you a chance to fix the problem, as shown in Figure 19-5.

4. **Click on an option (such as <u>I</u>gnore to ignore the problem, <u>E</u>xplain to get more information about the problem, or Change to accept the Design Checker's recommended solution for fixing the problem).**

    When the Design Checker is done, it displays a dialog box to inform you of this wonderful fact.

5. **Click on OK.**

Part VII
Playing with Microsoft FrontPage and PhotoDraw 2000

In this part . . .

*B*ig businesses, individuals, and even children are
posting Web pages on the Internet, so why not you?
With the dynamic duo of Microsoft FrontPage 2000 and
Microsoft PhotoDraw 2000, you can design your own Web
pages and include drawings, scanned images, or touched-
up photographs.

This part of the book explains how to use some of Microsoft
FrontPage 2000's special effects, such as creating a form on
a Web page and displaying animated graphics.

With the help of Microsoft PhotoDraw 2000, you can
create your own drawings or (more likely) edit existing
images. Put a dog's head on your cat's body. Draw a mus-
tache on your boss's face. Put your imagination to work,
and you can draw practically anything with the help of
Microsoft PhotoDraw 2000.

Chapter 20

Adding Cool Special Effects to Web Pages

· ·

In This Chapter

▶ Displaying stuff in a form

▶ Modifying form components

▶ Animating your Web pages

· ·

*E*veryone seems to be slapping together Web pages these days, which isn't difficult considering that practically every program can create Web pages. However, there's a big difference between a functional Web page and a really cool one.

While there's nothing wrong with plain-text Web pages with a few simple graphics thrown in, these types of Web pages can look as antiquated as a type-written letter complete with blobs of White-Out painted over misspellings. To make your Web pages appear just a bit more professional-looking, add some spice to your Web pages by using some special effects.

Not all browsers can display forms and other Microsoft FrontPage 2000 spe-cial effects, such as a marquee. So be aware that not everyone in the world is able to view Web pages that use the special effects described in this chapter.

Displaying Stuff in a Form

Forms are a special feature that allow your Web pages to display buttons, check boxes, and text boxes — just like many computer programs, such as a database. By using forms, your Web page can get data from the user. Some pop-ular uses for forms include order forms, surveys, and asking for passwords.

FrontPage provides two ways to create a form:

- ✔ **From scratch:** You do all the hard work in designing and laying out the form, text boxes, command buttons, or check boxes that you need.

- ✔ **Using the Form Page Wizard:** FrontPage automatically creates a form for you, and you just have to modify the form later.

Obviously, creating a form from scratch takes longer and can be more frustrating, but doing so provides the most control over the design of your form. For those who like taking the easy way out, the Form Page Wizard can be faster, but you may have to spend time editing the form that Form Page Wizard creates.

Microsoft FrontPage 2000 can help you make a form, but you still need to use a scripting language (such as Perl) to make the form actually do something useful with the data that the form receives from a user.

Making a form with the Form Page Wizard

To make a form quickly with the Form Page Wizard, follow these steps:

1. **Choose File⇨New⇨Page, or press Ctrl+N.**

   A New dialog box appears, as shown in Figure 20-1.

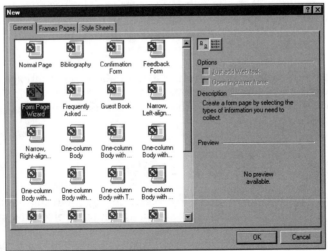

Figure 20-1: The New dialog box provides options for creating a new Web page.

2. **Click on the Form Page Wizard icon and then click on OK.**

   A Form Page Wizard dialog box appears.

3. **Click on Next.**

   Another Form Page Wizard dialog box appears, asking if you want to add any questions to your form.

4. **Click on Add.**

   The Form Page Wizard asks what type of questions you want to ask, as shown in Figure 20-2.

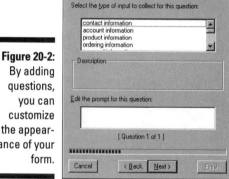

Figure 20-2:
By adding questions, you can customize the appearance of your form.

5. **Click on the type of information that you want your form to ask (such as account information or ordering information).**

   The Form Page Wizard displays a prompt at the bottom of the Form Page Wizard dialog box.

6. **Edit the text inside the prompt for the question text box and then click on Next.**

   The Form Page Wizard displays the type of information that the form asks the user, as shown in Figure 20-3.

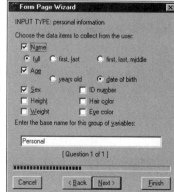

Figure 20-3:
A typical list of information that your form can ask.

7. **Click on the check boxes or option buttons of the data that you want to include on your form and then click on _N_ext.**

   The Form Page Wizard gives you another chance to choose more information for the form to ask.

8. **Repeat Steps 4 through 7 for each additional group of questions that you want your form to ask the user to fill out. Click on _N_ext when you're ready to continue.**

   The Form Page Wizard gives you a choice about how to ask its various questions, such as by displaying them as a numbered list or as a bulleted list, as shown in Figure 20-4.

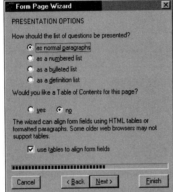

Figure 20-4:
Picking a
way to
display your
form's
questions.

9. **Click on the option button to choose the way that you want your questions displayed and then click on _N_ext.**

   The Form Page Wizard asks for the method that you want to use for outputting your form's data, as shown in Figure 20-5.

10. **Click on an option button (such as save results to a _W_eb page) and then click on _N_ext.**

11. **Click on _F_inish.**

    FrontPage 2000 displays your automatically created form, as shown in Figure 20-6.

Figure 20-5:
Picking a way to display your form's questions.

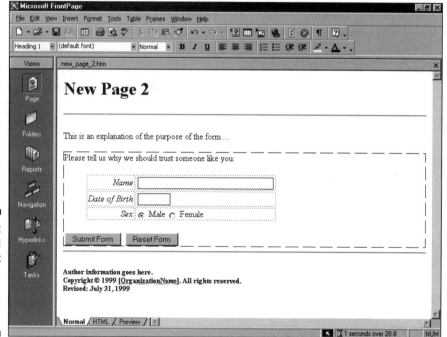

Figure 20-6:
A typical form that FrontPage 2000 cheerfully creates for you.

Making a form from scratch

The Form Page Wizard can help you create a form quickly so that you just have to edit the text and modify the appearance later. However, you may want to create your own forms by yourself. To create a form from scratch, follow these steps:

1. **Click on the location on your Web page where you want to add a form.**

2. **Choose Insert➪Form.**

   FrontPage 2000 displays a pop-up menu, listing all the form items you can add, such as an option button or check box, as shown in Figure 20-7.

   The rest of the civilized world calls these buttons "option" buttons, but Microsoft FrontPage calls them "radio" buttons. They are one and the same.

3. **Choose a form item, such as Check Box or Scrolling Text Box.**

   FrontPage 2000 draws your chosen form component. You have to edit the form component to make it actually do something.

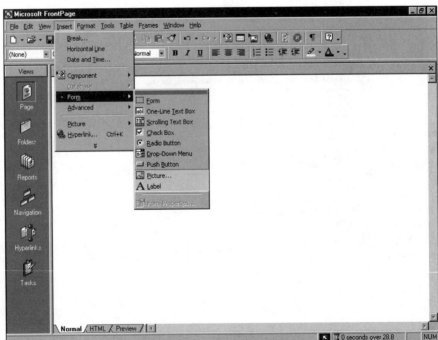

Figure 20-7:
Picking a
form
component
to add to
your Web
page.

Editing a Form

Once you've created a form (either by using the Form Page Wizard or by making a form by yourself), you may need to edit the form components to change the displayed text or to modify the size or color.

Changing the appearance of a form component

To make your form pretty (or just wildly chaotic), try changing your form component's fonts, colors, and border style. To change the appearance of any form component, follow these steps:

1. **Right-click on the form component (such as a check box) that you want to modify.**

   A pop-up menu appears.

2. **Click on Form Field Properties.**

   A Properties dialog box appears.

3. **Click on the Style button.**

   A Modify Style dialog box appears.

4. **Click on the Format button.**

   A pop-up menu appears, as shown in Figure 20-8.

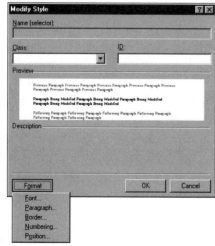

Figure 20-8:
All the different attributes that you can change on a form component.

5. **Click on the menu choice that you want to modify (such as Font or Paragraph).**

   The appropriate dialog box appears.

6. **Click on the options that you want and then click on OK when you're done.**

   You may need to click on OK a few times to clear all dialog boxes and view your Web pages once more.

After you change the appearance of a form component, you may need to click on the Preview tab at the bottom of the Web page to see how your changes look.

Editing a text box

FrontPage 2000 offers two types of text boxes to paste in your form:

- ✔ **One-line text box:** For accepting short data, such as a string of characters (like a name or a number)
- ✔ **Scrolling text box:** For displaying chunks of text that may require two or more lines

Modifying a one-line text box

Three items that you may want to modify in a one-line text box are

- ✔ **Width:** Defines the maximum number of characters that the text box can display.
- ✔ **Initial value:** Defines any text that you want to appear in the text box.
- ✔ **Password field:** Defines whether the text box disguises any text as a series of asterisks.

To modify a one-line text box, follow these steps:

1. **Right-click on the one-line text box that you want to modify and then click on Form Field Properties.**

   A Text Box Properties dialog box appears, as shown in Figure 20-9.

2. **Choose the options that you want for your one-line text box.**

   For example, type some text in the Initial value text box.

3. **Click on OK.**

Figure 20-9:
A Text Box
Properties
dialog box
for
modifying a
one-line text
box.

Modifying a scrolling text box

Three items that you may want to modify in a scrolling text box are

- ✔ **Width:** Defines the maximum number of characters the text box can display.
- ✔ **Initial value:** Defines any text that you want to appear in the text box.
- ✔ **Number of lines:** Defines how many lines of text to display.

To modify a scrolling text box, follow these steps:

1. **Right-click on the scrolling text box that you want to modify and then click on Form Field Properties.**

   A Scrolling Text Box Properties dialog box appears, as shown in Figure 20-10.

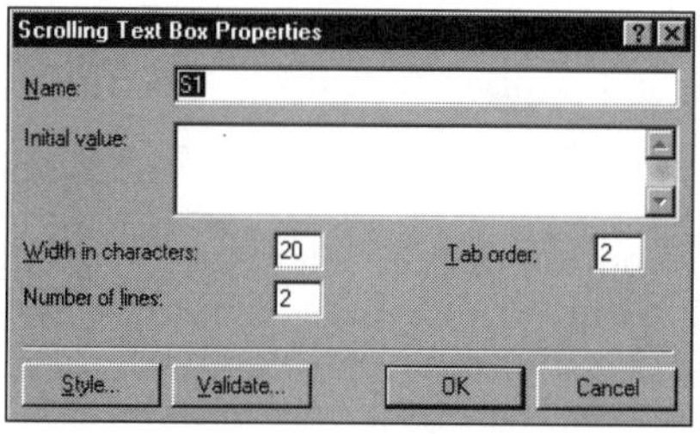

Figure 20-10:
A Scrolling
Text Box
Properties
dialog box.

2. **Choose the options that you want for your scrolling text box.**

   For example, type some text in the Initial value text box.

3. **Click on OK.**

Modifying a check box or option button

Check boxes and option buttons usually appear in groups of two or more and give the user a list of choices from which to choose. Only one option button can be chosen in a group. Unlike option buttons, two or more check boxes can be chosen at the same time.

Two items that you may want to modify in a check box or option button are

- ✓ **Initial state:** Defines whether the check box (or option button) appears selected or not.
- ✓ **Value:** Defines the information that the check box or option button stores if the user selects it.

To modify a check box or option button, follow these steps:

1. **Right-click on the check box or option button that you want to modify and then click on Form Field Properties.**

   A Properties dialog box appears, as shown in Figure 20-11.

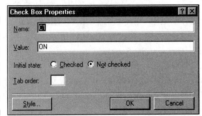

Figure 20-11:
The Check
Box
Properties
dialog box.

2. **Choose the options that you want for your one-line text box.**

   For example, click on Checked or Not checked (for a check box) or Selected or Not selected (for an option button).

3. **Click on OK.**

When you create a check box or option button, Microsoft FrontPage 2000 creates a single check box or option button all by itself without any descriptive text to identify what that check box or option button represents. To add a label to a check box or option button, follow these steps:

1. **Click next to the check box or option button where you want to insert a label.**

2. **Type the text that you want to appear next to your check box or option button.**

3. **Highlight both your check box or option button and the text that you typed in Step 2.**

4. **Choose Insert➪Form➪Label.**

FrontPage 2000 draws a dotted line around your label. From this point, you can select your check box or option button by clicking on the check box or on the label.

Modifying a drop-down menu

Drop-down menus provide a list of items that the user can choose. Drop-down menus can be more convenient to use than a group of check boxes or option buttons, because a drop-down menu takes up less space.

Three items that you may want to modify in a drop-down menu are

- ✔ **Height:** Defines how many lines of text the drop-down menu displays.
- ✔ **Allow multiple selections:** Allows the user to make one or more choices from the drop-down menu.
- ✔ **Choices:** Displays all the items that the user can select.

To modify a drop-down menu, follow these steps:

1. **Right-click on the drop-down menu that you want to modify and then click on Form Field Properties.**

   A Drop-Down Menu Properties dialog box appears, as shown in Figure 20-12.

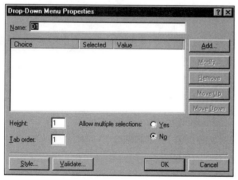

Figure 20-12:
A Drop-Down Menu Properties dialog box.

2. **Click on Add.**

   An Add Choice dialog box appears, as shown in Figure 20-13.

3. **Type an item in the Choice text box and then click on OK.**

   If you want the item to appear highlighted in the drop-down menu, then click on the Selected option button before clicking on OK.

4. **Repeat Steps 2 and 3 for each item that you want to display.**

5. **Choose any additional options that you want, such as typing a value in the Height box.**

6. **Click on OK.**

   Figure 20-14 shows what a typical drop-down menu looks like when complete.

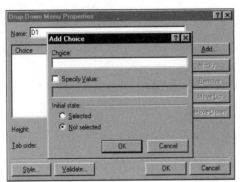

Figure 20-13:
An Add Choice dialog box for creating items to display in a drop-down menu.

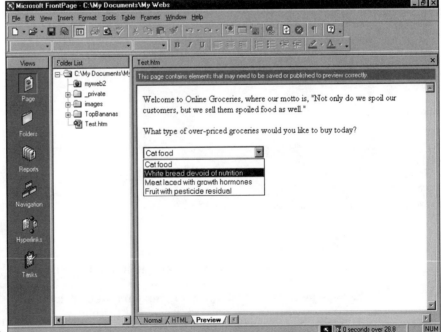

Figure 20-14:
The appearance of a typical drop-down menu.

Modifying a push button

Push buttons typically give a command to the form, such as telling the form to submit the data it receives or to reset the form. Two items that you may want to modify in a scrolling text box are

✔ **Value/label:** Defines what type of information is submitted when the user clicks on the push button and also displays the text on the push button itself.

✔ **Button type:** Allows you to select a standard Submit or Reset button, or choose the Button option for creating your own push buttons.

To modify a push button, follow these steps:

1. **Right-click on the push button that you want to modify and then click on Form Field Properties.**

   A Push Button Properties dialog box appears, as shown in Figure 20-15.

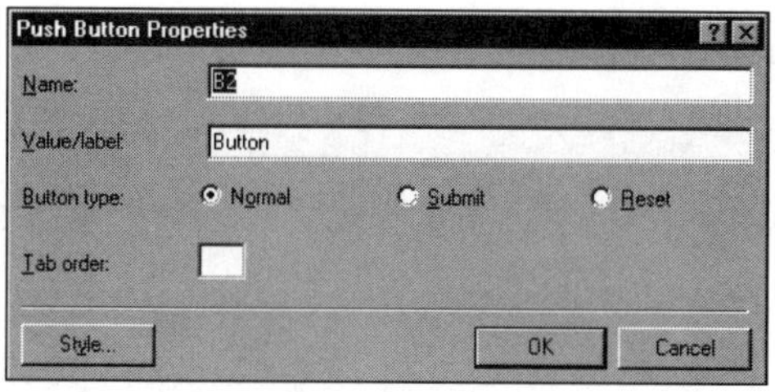

Figure 20-15: A Push Button Properties dialog box.

2. **Click on an option button in the Button type group, such as Normal, Submit, or Reset.**

   If you want to type your own caption for a push button, then click on the Normal option button.

3. **If you clicked on the Normal option button in Step 2, then type any text that you want to appear on your push button in the Value/label text box.**

4. **Click on OK.**

Animating Your Web Pages

In case form components aren't enough to make your Web pages look special, Microsoft FrontPage 2000 also lets you add animated components as well, such as:

✔ **Hover buttons:** Create special buttons that change appearance and color when you move (not click) the mouse pointer over them.

✔ **Marquees:** Scroll text across your Web page from side to side.

✔ **Banner ads:** Typically display advertisements that change periodically.

Not all browsers or Web page hosting companies support all these animation effects. To take full advantage of all Microsoft FrontPage 2000 features, users should be using the latest version of Internet Explorer, and your Web page hosting company should offer FrontPage extensions.

Making a hover button

Hover buttons act like ordinary buttons except they change their appearance as soon as the user moves the mouse pointer over them. Hover buttons can be useful to emphasize the location of hyperlink buttons, as shown in Figure 20-16.

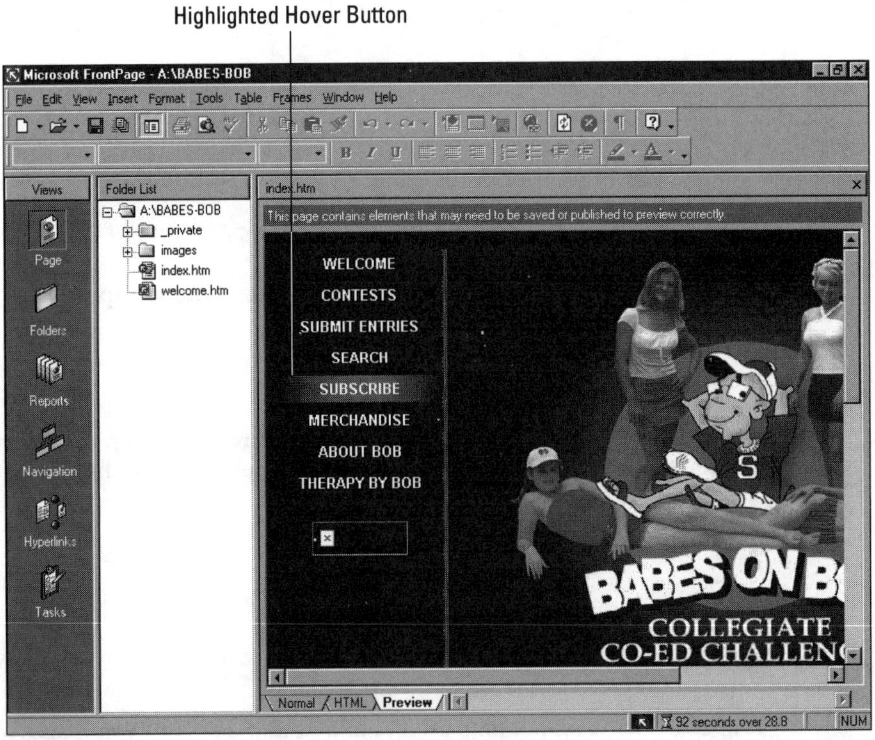

Highlighted Hover Button

Figure 20-16:
Use hover buttons to highlight your hyperlinks.

To create a hover button, follow these steps:

1. **Click on your Web page where you want to add the hover button.**

2. **Choose Insert⇨Component⇨Hover Button.**

   A Hover Button Properties dialog box appears, as shown in Figure 20-17.

3. **Click on the Button text box and then type the label that you want to appear on your button.**

4. **Click on Browse.**

   A Select Hover Button Hyperlink dialog box appears.

5. **Type a Web page address (such as** www.dummies.com**) in the URL text box, or click on a Web page. Click on OK when you're done.**

6. **Choose the colors and the effect that you want the hover button to display in the following list boxes:**

   • **Button color:** Displays the initial color of the hover button.

   • **Effect color:** Defines the color that appears when the mouse pointer moves over the hover button.

   • **Effect:** Defines how the hover button changes its appearance when the mouse pointer appears over a particular button.

7. **Click on OK.**

Attracting attention with a marquee

Displaying text on a Web page is fine if you want to offer large chunks of information. But if you want to catch someone's eye with a short message, use a marquee instead. A marquee scrolls text across the screen slowly (or quickly).

To create a marquee, follow these steps:

1. **Click on the Web page where you want to add the marquee.**

2. **Choose Insert⇨Component⇨Marquee.**

   A Marquee Properties dialog box appears, as shown in Figure 20-18.

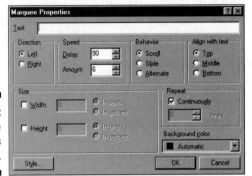

Figure 20-18:
A Marquee
Properties
dialog box.

3. **Type the text that you want to display in the marquee in the Text box.**

4. **Click on the other list boxes to define how your marquee works, such as clicking on the Left or Right option button to choose a direction or clicking on the Background color list box to choose a color.**

5. **Click on OK.**

Adding banner ads

Like television and radio, many Web sites provide free information or services in exchange for forcing you to view display ads. In case you want an ad on your Web page, you can insert a banner ad.

To place a banner ad, follow these steps:

1. **Click on the Web page where you want to insert the banner ad.**

2. **Choose Insert⇨Component⇨Banner Ad Manager.**

   A Banner Ad Manager Properties dialog box appears, as shown in Figure 20-19.

3. **Click on Browse.**

   A Select Banner Ad Hyperlink dialog box appears.

4. **Type a URL address in the URL box, or click on a Web page and then click on OK.**

5. **Click on Add.**

   An Add Picture for Banner Ad dialog box appears.

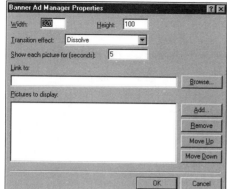

6. **Click on the picture that you want to display in your banner ad and then click on OK.**

7. **Repeat Steps 5 and 6 for each picture that you want to display in your banner ad.**

8. **Click on the Transition effect or Show each picture for (seconds) boxes if you want to change the way the banner ad displays pictures.**

9. **Click on OK.**

Chapter 21

Managing Your Web Pages

- -

In This Chapter

▶ Reporting on your Web pages

▶ Checking your hyperlinks

▶ Defining tasks

- -

*N*ot only can Microsoft FrontPage 2000 help you design Web pages, but it can also help you organize Web pages at the same time. So if you're creating a big Web site, then you won't have to worry should you forget to link one Web page to the rest of them.

To help you manage your Web pages, Microsoft FrontPage 2000 can display reports (showing you statistics about individual Web pages), hyperlinks (showing you how each Web page links to the others), and tasks (showing you tasks to finish before posting your Web pages for viewing).

Reporting on Your Web Pages

A FrontPage report lists information about your Web pages so that you don't have to examine each Web page individually. Some of the different types of reports that you can view include

- **Site Summary:** Displays a condensed version of the information provided by all the other types of reports.

- **All Files:** Lists every file that makes up your Web pages, including graphics and HTML files.

- **Recently Added Files:** Lists all files added to your Web site based on a criterion, such as all files added in the past 0 to 365 days. (You decide the criterion, such as only displaying files added in the past 30 days.)

- **Recently Changed Files:** Lists all files modified in the past 0 to 365 days. (You decide the criterion, such as only displaying files changed in the past 5 days.)

✔ **Older Files:** Lists all files not changed in the past 0 to 365 days. (You decide the criterion, such as only displaying files added in the past 60 days.)

✔ **Unlinked Files:** Lists all files with no hyperlink pointing to them.

✔ **Slow Pages:** Lists all files estimated to download at 28.8 baud from 0 to 600 seconds. (You decide the criterion, such as only displaying files that take 90 seconds or longer to download.)

✔ **Broken Hyperlinks:** Lists hyperlinks that point to nonexistent Web pages or that point to external links that FrontPage can't test for validity, such as www.dummies.com.

✔ **Component Errors:** Lists all components that may contain a broken hyperlink or other error to keep them from working, such as a table of contents component that points to a deleted Web page.

Reports can show you what may be wrong with your Web pages, but you still have to do the work to correct the problems.

FrontPage can only display a report for a collection of Web pages. You cannot view a report for a single Web page.

To view a report about your Web pages, follow these steps:

1. **Click on the Reports icon in the Views Bar.**

   If the Views Bar is not visible, then choose <u>V</u>iew⇨<u>V</u>iews Bar. FrontPage shows a site summary report along with a Reporting toolbar, as shown in Figure 21-1.

2. **Click on the Report list box in the Reporting toolbar and then choose the type of report that you want to view, such as Recently Added Files or Broken Hyperlinks.**

   FrontPage cheerfully displays your chosen report, as shown in Figure 21-2.

3. **Double-click on a Web page to view and correct any errors.**

From the Site Summary report, you can double-click on an item, such as External hyperlinks or Slow pages to view that report without having to use the Reporting toolbar.

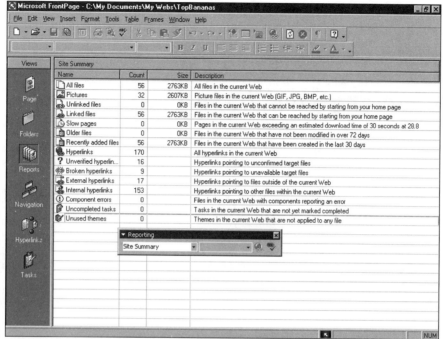

Figure 21-1:
A Site Summary report, listing information about your Web site.

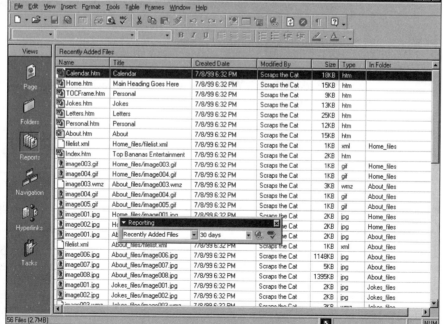

Figure 21-2:
A Recently Added Files report helps you determine who added a Web page and when it was added.

If you click on a gray column heading, such as Name, then you can sort your report in ascending or descending order.

Checking Your Hyperlinks

Almost every Web page has at least one hyperlink that points either to another one of your own Web pages (called an internal hyperlink) or to a Web site run by another person or company (called external hyperlinks).

After designing your Web pages and making hyperlinks, you may want to see a visual representation of where each Web page hyperlink points. That way you can better organize your hyperlinks so that one Web page is loaded with hyperlinks while another Web page has only one or two hyperlinks.

Before viewing your hyperlinks, checking first for any broken hyperlinks by viewing the Broken Hyperlinks report is a good idea.

To view your hyperlinks, follow these steps:

1. **Click on the Hyperlinks icon in the Views Bar.**

   If the Views Bar is not visible, then choose <u>V</u>iew⇨<u>V</u>iews Bar.

2. **Click on the Web page in the Folder List that you want to check.**

   If the Folder List is not visible, then choose <u>V</u>iew⇨Folder List. FrontPage happily displays all the hyperlinks pointing to and pointing away from your chosen Web page, as shown in Figure 21-3.

If you double-click on a Web page icon, then FrontPage displays that Web page for you to view or edit.

Defining Tasks

Whether you're designing an entire Web site on your own or with the help of other people, you may want to leave notes to yourself or others about what tasks need to be done next.

For example, you may specialize in adding graphics to a Web page, but your coworkers need to add the actual text and a video file on the Web page, as well. Rather than write a paper note and risk losing the paper, you can jot down a note (as a task) directly into the Web site itself. Then the next time that your coworkers open the Web site, they can view the tasks they need to do.

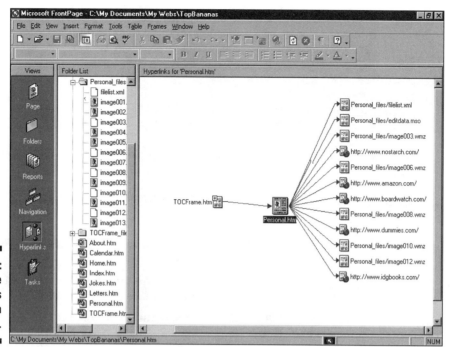

Figure 21-3:
Viewing the
hyperlinks
to and from
a Web page.

Tasks are only visible if everyone uses FrontPage 2000. If you use FrontPage 2000 to create and edit Web pages but your coworkers use a different Web page editing tool, then they won't see your tasks (which may not be such a bad thing after all, from your coworkers' points of view).

Making a task

Any time that you want, you can add a task for you (or preferably someone else) to do. To make a task, follow these steps:

1. **Click on a Web page in the Folder List (optional).**

   If the Folder List is not visible, then choose View➪Folder List. You need to choose Step 1 only if you want to define a task for a specific Web page.

2. **Choose Edit➪Task➪Add Task.**

   A New Task dialog box appears, as shown in Figure 21-4.

3. **Click on the Task Name text box and then type a short descriptive name for your task.**

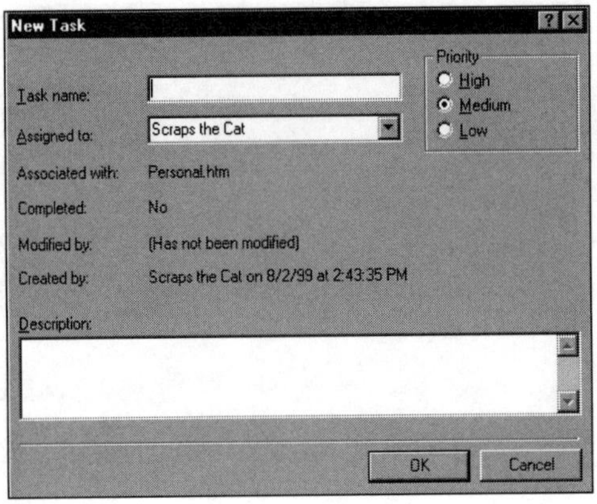

Figure 21-4:
The New
Task dialog
box for
writing
down a
task.

4. **Click on an option button in the Priority group, such as High, Medium, or Low.**

5. **Click on the Assigned to text box and then type the name of the person responsible for completing this task.**

6. **Click on the Description text box and then type the complete task that needs to be done.**

7. **Click on OK.**

Starting a task

When you first add a task, Microsoft FrontPage 2000 stores the task in the Tasks view and marks the task as Not Started, as shown in Figure 21-5.

Ideally, anyone working on your Web site will view the Tasks view first to see which tasks need to be done. After they see a task they want to start, they can follow these steps:

1. **Click on the Tasks icon in the Views Bar.**

   If the Views Bar is not visible, then choose View⇨Views Bar.

2. **Right-click on the task that you want to start and then click on Start Task.**

   FrontPage loads the page associated with your chosen task so that you can start working on your task right away.

Not all tasks need to be associated with a specific Web page. If a task is not associated with a Web page, the above steps will not work.

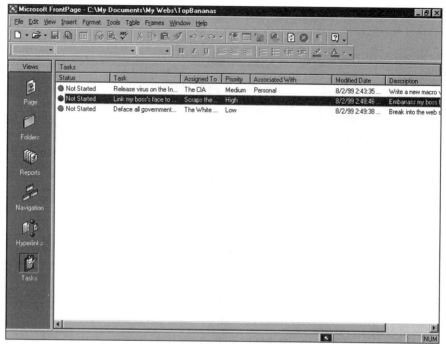

Figure 21-5:
The Tasks
view lists all
your tasks
and their
current
status.

Editing a task

After creating a task, you may want to edit it later. That way you can assign
the task to someone else or change the description of the task. To edit a task,
follow these steps:

1. **Click on the Tasks icon in the Views Bar.**

   If the Views Bar is not visible, then choose View⇨Views Bar.

2. **Right-click on the task that you want to edit and then click on Edit
   Task.**

   A Task Details dialog box appears, as shown in Figure 21-6.

3. **Make any changes that you want to the task name, description, priority, or the person assigned to the task and then click on OK.**

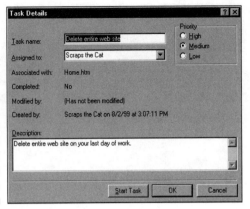

Figure 21-6:
The Task
Details
dialog box
for editing
an existing
task.

Completing a task

After you've finished a task (or at least want to lie about finishing the task),
you may want to mark the task as complete so nobody will ask you about it
again. To mark a task as complete, follow these steps:

1. **Click on the Tasks icon in the Views Bar.**

   If the Views Bar is not visible, then choose View⇨Views Bar.

2. **Right-click on the task that you want to mark as complete and then
   click on Mark as Completed.**

   FrontPage displays a green dot and the word Completed in the Status
   column.

Deleting a task

When you complete a task, you can leave the task on display for everyone to
see. But you eventually may want to delete old tasks (whether you completed
them or not). To delete a task, follow these steps:

1. **Click on the Tasks icon in the Views Bar.**

   If the Views Bar is not visible, then choose View⇨Views Bar.

2. **Right-click on the task that you want to delete and then click on Delete.**

   A dialog box appears, asking if you really want to delete your chosen task.

3. **Click on Yes or No.**

When you delete a task, the task is gone for good; you can't "undo" a deleted
task, so make sure that you really want to delete the task.

Chapter 22

Creating Web Graphics in Microsoft PhotoDraw 2000

. . . .

In This Chapter

▶ Understanding graphic file formats

▶ Making a Web graphic image

▶ Saving a Web graphic image

. . . .

Microsoft PhotoDraw 2000 is a full-blown graphics program that allows you to express yourself as an artist. But if your artistic abilities are limited to drawing stick figures, then don't despair. You can still draw stick figures, but with the help of PhotoDraw, they can be the best-looking stick figures that anyone has ever seen.

Although you can use Microsoft PhotoDraw 2000 for creating any type of graphic images, PhotoDraw can be especially handy for creating graphics for Web pages, such as those created using FrontPage 2000. (See how all the Office 2000 programs work together?)

Understanding Graphic File Formats

Microsoft PhotoDraw 2000 can save your graphic images in a variety of file formats, but the two most important file formats for Web pages are

   ✔ **GIF** (Graphics Interchange Format)

   ✔ **JPEG** (Joint Photographic Expert Group)

A third and newer graphics file format standard is PNG (Portable Network Graphics), but many older browsers don't support PNG yet, which essentially makes it pretty useless as a Web graphics standard for now.

So when should you save a picture as a GIF file and when should you save it as a JPEG file? Generally, you should save images in the GIF file format if they match one or more of the following criteria:

- ✔ Contain 256 colors or less
- ✔ Have transparent areas
- ✔ Need to create the smallest possible file size without losing any image resolution
- ✔ Are line drawings
- ✔ Do not contain gradients (a gradual progression of colors) or texture fills
- ✔ Use custom color palettes

You should save images in the JPEG file format if they match one or more of the following criteria:

- ✔ Contain more than 256 colors
- ✔ Contain many gradients (a gradual progression of colors)
- ✔ Need to create the smallest possible file size at the sacrifice of image resolution
- ✔ Are photographs or scanned images

 Don't worry too much about either GIF or JPEG file formats. For most pictures, either file format works just fine.

Making a Web Graphic Image

To make creating graphics for your Web pages easy, Microsoft PhotoDraw 2000 comes with plenty of templates, shown in Figure 22-1, that you can modify for your own use. Some of the different templates include

- ✔ **Banners:** For displaying headings or ads
- ✔ **Circular Buttons:** For displaying one or more hyperlink buttons
- ✔ **Connecting Buttons:** For creating two or more buttons that attach to each other like pieces in a jigsaw puzzle
- ✔ **Festive Buttons:** For creating buttons with a different shape, such as a star
- ✔ **Rectangular Buttons:** For creating buttons that resemble bars or squares

Drawing a Web graphic image

Microsoft PhotoDraw 2000 is smart enough to realize that most people can't draw, but most people can modify an existing drawing. So when you draw a new Web graphic image, PhotoDraw 2000 tries to guide you, step-by-step, into creating your chosen graphic. To draw a new graphic image, follow these steps:

1. **Click on the Templates button on the Visual Menu.**

   If the Visual Menu does not appear, then choose View⇨Visual Menu. A menu appears.

2. **Click on Web Graphics.**

   A Templates dialog box appears along with samples of the different Web graphics that you can make, as shown in Figure 22-1.

3. **Click on the type of Web graphic that you want to create (such as Banners or Festive Buttons).**

   PhotoDraw 2000 displays your available choices.

4. **Click on the choice that you want to use and then click on Next.**

   PhotoDraw 2000 displays a larger version of your chosen Web graphic, as shown in Figure 22-2.

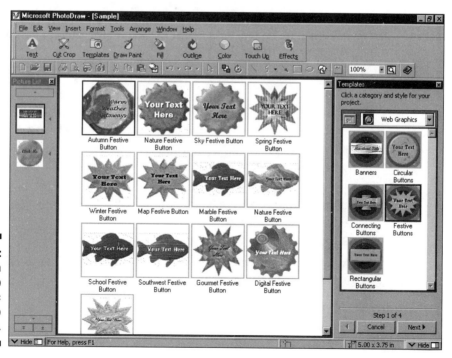

Figure 22-1: Picking a Web graphic image to use.

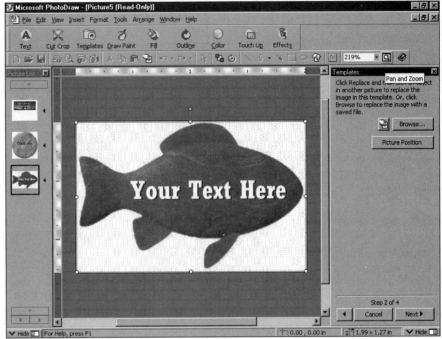

Figure 22-2:
A closer
look at your
chosen Web
graphic
image.

5. **Click on the Picture Position button, move the mouse pointer over the Web graphic image, hold down the left mouse button, and then move the image to where you want it.**

6. **Click Finish in the Position toolbar when you're happy with its location.**

7. **Click on Next.**

   PhotoDraw 2000 displays a dialog box where you can type any text you want to appear on your graphic image, as shown in Figure 22-3.

8. **Type the text that you want. (You can also change the font, type size, or style of your text at this time as well.)**

   If you need to adjust the text box on your graphic image, move the mouse pointer over the text box, hold down the left mouse button, and then drag the mouse.

9. **Click on Next and then click on Finish.**

   At this point you can either save your picture in a GIF or JPEG file format, or edit your picture some more.

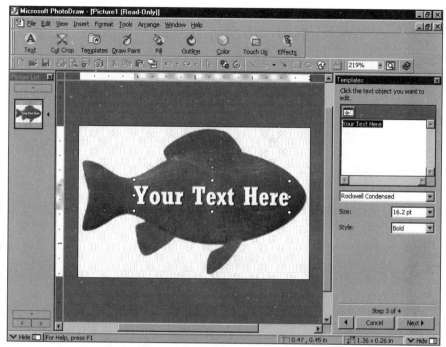

Figure 22-3:
Typing text
on to your
Web
graphic.

Saving a Web graphic

You should save your Web graphics in two separate files: First in the native PhotoDraw file format and then in a GIF or JPEG file. You need the GIF or JPEG version for posting on a Web page, but you need the native PhotoDraw file format if you want to edit the graphic image later.

Any Web graphic image saved in the PhotoDraw file format consists of separate objects, such as text box objects (for storing text) and graphic objects. If you try to edit the same graphic image saved as a GIF or JPEG file, you won't be able to edit the separate objects (such as text) easily.

If you only save a Web graphic image as a GIF or JPEG file, you can still edit it later, but PhotoDraw 2000 won't allow you to edit different parts of your graphic image (such as text) easily.

To save your Web graphic image, follow these steps:

1. **Choose File⇨Save, or press Ctrl+S.**

   A dialog box appears, asking you for a file name.

2. **Type a file name for your picture and then click on <u>S</u>ave.**

   Make sure the Save as type list box displays PhotoDraw. You may also want to store your picture in a different directory.

3. **Choose <u>F</u>ile⇨Save <u>f</u>or Use In.**

   A Save for Use in Wizard dialog box appears, as shown in Figure 22-4.

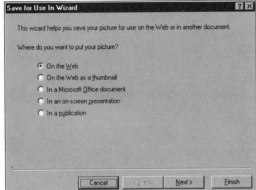

Figure 22-4: Choosing how to save your graphic image in a different file format.

4. **Click on the On the <u>W</u>eb option button and then click on <u>N</u>ext.**

   Another Save for Use in Wizard dialog box appears, asking how you want to display transparent parts of your image, as shown in Figure 22-5.

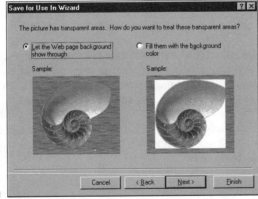

Figure 22-5: Choosing whether to use a transparent background or not.

5. **Click on an option button to choose an option (such as Let the Web page background show through) and then click on Next.**

Depending on which option you choose, still another Save for Use in Wizard dialog box appears, giving you options for making sure your Web graphic blends in with your Web pages, as shown in Figure 22-6.

Note: If you choose the Fill them with the background color option button, PhotoDraw 2000 displays two dialog boxes that are different than the one shown in Figure 22-6. The first dialog box asks for a color to fill in your graphic image's background. The second dialog box asks if you want to save the graphic image as a GIF or a JPEG file.

Figure 22-6:
Making sure your Web graphic image seamlessly blends into your Web page if you let the background show through.

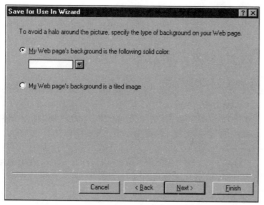

6. **Click on an option button to choose an option and then click on Next.**

One more Save for Use in Wizard dialog box appears, giving you details about your graphic file, as shown in Figure 22-7.

7. **Click on Save.**

A Save for Use In dialog box appears.

8. **Type a name for your file and then click on Save.**

Rather than go through the above steps, you can simply choose File➪ Save As and pick the GIF or JPEG file format instead. However, this method won't optimize your graphic image or give you the option to create a transparent background the way the Save for Use In Wizard does.

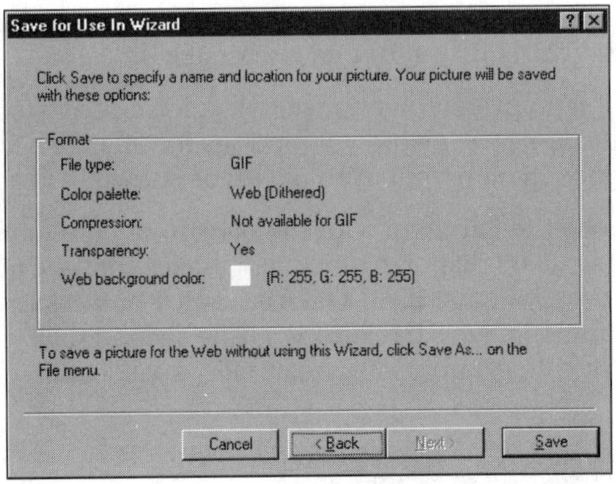

Figure 22-7:
PhotoDraw
automatically
chooses
the optimum
file format
for you.

Editing a Web graphic

In case you need to edit your Web graphic at a later time, edit the version
stored in the PhotoDraw file format. The PhotoDraw version of your Web
graphic divides your picture into separate objects, such as text boxes (for
displaying text) and graphic objects (for the different parts of your picture).

After you finish editing the PhotoDraw version of your Web graphic, you can
save your Web graphic as a GIF or JPEG file.

To edit a Web graphic, follow these steps:

1. **Choose File⇨Visual Open, or press Ctrl+Shift+O.**

   A Visual Open dialog box appears.

2. **Click on the Files of type list box and then choose PhotoDraw.**

   By choosing this command, PhotoDraw won't let you open a GIF or JPEG
   file by mistake.

3. **Click on the picture that you want to edit and then click on Open.**

   Your chosen picture appears. Notice that when you click on an object
   (such as a text box) in your picture, PhotoDraw displays white handles
   around that object, allowing you to move, resize, or edit the data inside,
   as shown in Figure 22-8.

4. **Make any changes to your picture.**

5. **Follow the steps in the previous "Saving a Web graphic" to save your
   modified version of the Web graphic as a GIF or JPEG file.**

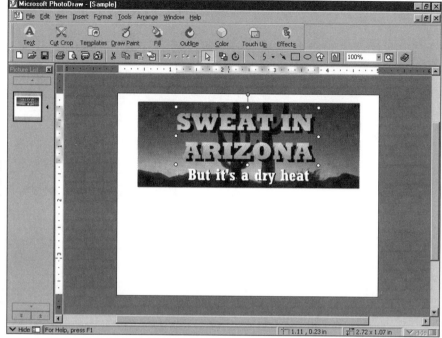

Figure 22-8:
PhotoDraw
displays
white
handles
around
objects
stored in the
PhotoDraw
file format.

Chapter 23

Drawing Pictures in Microsoft PhotoDraw 2000

In This Chapter

▶ Drawing lines and objects

▶ Changing the appearance of lines and objects

▶ Adding special visual effects

*W*hether you have artistic skills or not, you can use Microsoft PhotoDraw 2000 to create pictures from scratch. Although PhotoDraw can't turn you into an artist overnight, PhotoDraw can provide you with the tools that you need to create decent-looking pictures without much effort.

Drawing Lines and Objects

Pictures can be created two ways. The hard way is to paint a picture by dabbing blobs of colors on a background until you have a coherent picture. The easier way is to draw a picture using objects.

For example, one object may be a circle, another a wavy line, and still another can be a square. By placing these objects next to or on top of one another, you can create a decent-looking picture, much like drawing a stick figure. (Fortunately, PhotoDraw can help you draw something more interesting than stick figures.)

Making a straight line

The simplest part of any drawing is a line. Because drawing with the mouse can tax even the most experienced artist, Microsoft PhotoDraw 2000 provides some guidance in drawing straight edges and symmetrically shaped objects.

To draw a straight line, follow these steps:

1. **Click on the Draw Paint button on the Visual Menu.**

   If the Visual Menu does not appear, then choose View⇨Visual Menu. A menu appears.

2. **Click on Draw.**

   An AutoShapes toolbar appears, as shown in Figure 23-1.

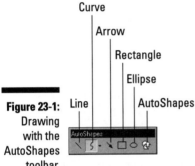

Figure 23-1: Drawing with the AutoShapes toolbar.

Curve
Arrow
Rectangle
Ellipse
Line
AutoShapes

3. **Click on the Line icon in the AutoShapes toolbar.**

4. **Move the mouse pointer where you want to draw your line, hold down the left mouse button, and then drag the mouse to draw your line.**

5. **Release the left mouse button when you're happy with your drawn line.**

   PhotoDraw displays a straight line. At this point you can edit your line by changing its color or brush style.

If you need to draw a straight line with an arrow on one end, click on the Arrow icon in the AutoShapes toolbar.

Making a curved line

Curved lines are a bit tougher to draw than straight lines (as anyone with an Etch-A-Sketch can tell you), but with Microsoft PhotoDraw 2000's help, you can actually draw a curved line that indeed looks curved.

To draw a curved line, follow these steps:

1. **Click on the Draw Paint button on the Visual Menu.**

If the Visual Menu does not appear, then choose View➪Visual Menu. A menu appears.

2. **Click on Draw.**

   An AutoShapes toolbar appears (refer to Figure 23-1).

3. **Click on the downward-pointing arrow next to the Curve icon in the AutoShapes toolbar.**

   A menu appears, as shown in Figure 23-2.

Figure 23-2:
Choosing the method you want to use for drawing a curved line.

Scribble

Freeform

Curve

4. **Click on the Curve icon.**

   The mouse pointer turns into a crosshair icon.

5. **Move the mouse pointer where you want to start drawing your curved line, click the left mouse button, and then drag the mouse.**

   PhotoDraw 2000 draws a line.

6. **Click the left mouse button where you want to draw a curve.**

7. **Repeat Steps 5 and 6 until you're finished drawing your curved line.**

8. **Click on the left mouse button and then press Esc when you're finished drawing your curved line.**

   PhotoDraw 2000 displays your curved line, ready for you to move, resize, or edit it any way you see fit.

Drawing a geometrically shaped object

Sometimes you may need to draw an object consisting of straight lines (such as a trapezoid, parallelogram, or an equally obscure object that you probably forgot about from your geometry class in high school).

To draw a geometrically shaped object, follow these steps:

1. **Click on the Draw Paint button on the Visual Menu.**

   If the Visual Menu does not appear, then choose View⇨Visual Menu. A menu appears.

2. **Click on Draw.**

   An AutoShapes toolbar appears (refer to Figure 23-1).

3. **Click on the downward-pointing arrow next to the Curve icon in the AutoShapes toolbar.**

   A menu appears (refer to Figure 23-2).

4. **Click on the Freeform icon.**

   The mouse pointer turns into a crosshair icon.

5. **Move the mouse pointer where you want to start drawing your line, click the left mouse button, and then drag the mouse.**

   PhotoDraw 2000 draws a straight line.

6. **Click on the left mouse button where you want to stop drawing your straight line.**

7. **Move the mouse to a new location.**

   PhotoDraw 2000 draws another straight line, attached to the last line you drew.

8. **Repeat Steps 6 and 7.**

9. **Click on the left mouse button and then press Esc when you're done.**

   PhotoDraw 2000 displays your complete object, ready for you to move, resize, or edit it any way you see fit.

If you need to draw rectangles or ellipses, you can click on the Rectangle or Ellipse icon on the AutoShapes toolbar.

Scribbling a line

Drawing geometrically shaped objects or curved lines may be nice, but sometimes you may want to just scribble so that the movement of the mouse corresponds with the drawing on your screen.

Fortunately, Microsoft PhotoDraw 2000 offers a special scribble feature that you can use by following these steps:

1. **Click on the Draw Paint button on the Visual Menu.**

   If the Visual Menu does not appear, then choose View⇨Visual Menu. A menu appears.

2. **Click on <u>D</u>raw.**

   An AutoShapes toolbar appears (refer to Figure 23-1).

3. **Click on the downward-pointing arrow next to the Curve icon in the AutoShapes toolbar.**

   A menu appears (refer to Figure 23-2).

4. **Click on the Scribble icon.**

   The mouse pointer turns into a crosshair icon.

5. **Move the mouse pointer where you want to start drawing your line.**

6. **Hold down the left mouse button and then move the mouse.**

   Notice that wherever you move the mouse, PhotoDraw 2000 obediently draws your line.

7. **Release the left mouse button when you're done drawing your line.**

Changing the Appearance of Lines and Objects

Don't worry about drawing your lines perfectly the first time. After you've drawn a line or an object, you can always move, rotate, or resize the line or object so that it looks just the way you want.

Feel free to experiment with changes to lines and objects because you can always press Ctrl+Z to reverse the last change you made to your drawing.

Rotating a line or an object

When you move a line or an object, you essentially slide the line or object to a new spot on the screen. If you want to get more sophisticated, you can rotate a line or an object as well. Rotating lets you spin your line or object clockwise or counterclockwise to create more visually interesting effects.

To rotate a line or an object, follow these steps:

1. **Click on the line or object that you want to rotate.**

   White handles appear around your chosen line or object. A single green handle appears at the top of your line or object, as shown in Figure 23-3, except that the handle's black in our figure.

Green handle

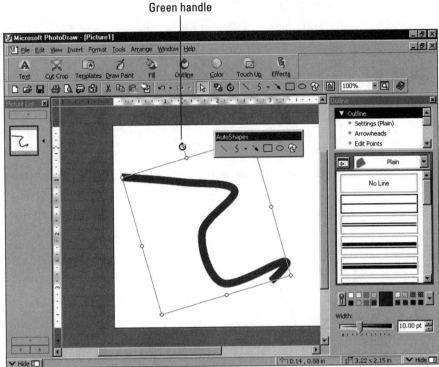

Figure 23-3:
To rotate a
line or an
object, use
the green
handle.

2. **Move the mouse pointer over the green handle.**

   The mouse pointer turns into a circular shaped arrow.

3. **Hold down the left mouse button and then drag the mouse left or right.**

   PhotoDraw 2000 rotates your chosen line or object so that you can see how it looks.

4. **Release the left mouse button when you're happy with the new position of your line or object.**

Changing the brush style

When you draw a line, the line is typically one solid color. For most purposes, a solid-color line may be okay, but for artistic types, such a line can look too plain. So that's why Microsoft PhotoDraw 2000 provides different brush styles for altering your line's (or your object's) appearance.

To change the style of a line or object, follow these steps:

1. **Click on the line or object that you want to modify.**

   White handles appear around your chosen line or object.

2. **Click on the Outline button on the Visual Menu.**

   If the Visual Menu does not appear, then choose View⇨Visual Menu. A menu appears.

3. **Click on Artistic Brushes.**

   An Outline window appears, as shown in Figure 23-4.

4. **Click on the brush style that you want.**

   PhotoDraw 2000 applies your chosen brush style to your line or object.

If you click on Photo Brushes in Step 3, then you can make a graphic image appear within your lines, as shown in Figure 23-5.

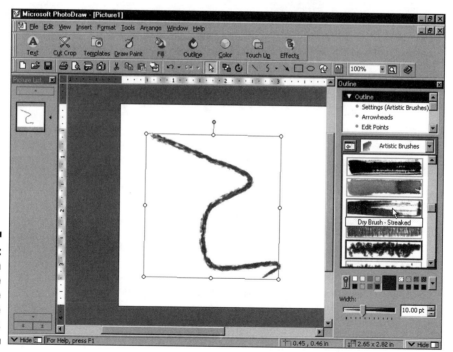

Figure 23-4: Choosing a brush style from the Outline window.

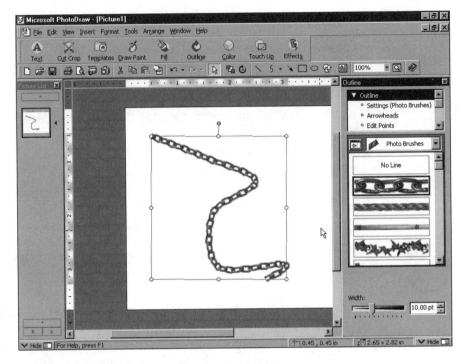

Figure 23-5:
Displaying
a graphic
image as
a line.

Softening the edges of a line

For another way to modify the appearance of your lines, try softening the edges by blurring the line slightly. Then the line appears to blend into the background.

Softening the edges of a line works best with solid lines.

To soften the edges of a line or an object, follow these steps:

1. **Click on the line or object that you want to modify.**

   White handles appear around your chosen line or object.

2. **Click on the Outline button on the Visual Menu.**

   If the Visual Menu does not appear, then choose View➪Visual Menu. A menu appears.

3. **Click on Soft Edges.**

   A Soft Edges window appears, as shown in Figure 23-6.

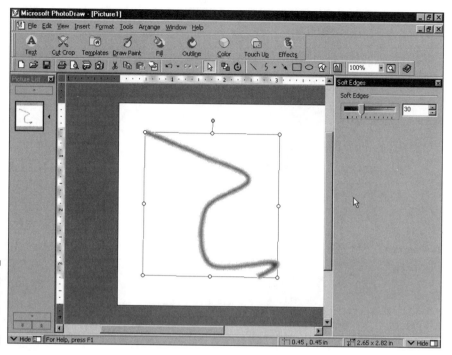

Figure 23-6:
Modifying
the edges
of a line.

4. **Type a value from 0 (no soft edge) to 100 (the line practically disappears).**

   PhotoDraw 2000 softens the edge of your chosen line or object.

Changing the color of a line or an object

Colors can make your lines look pretty or really ugly (depending on the colors that you choose). To define a color for a line or object, follow these steps:

1. **Click on the line or object that you want to modify.**

   White handles appear around your chosen line or object.

2. **Click on the Outline button on the Visual Menu.**

   If the Visual Menu does not appear, then choose View⇨Visual Menu. A menu appears.

3. **Click on Plain.**

   An Outline window appears, as shown in Figure 23-7.

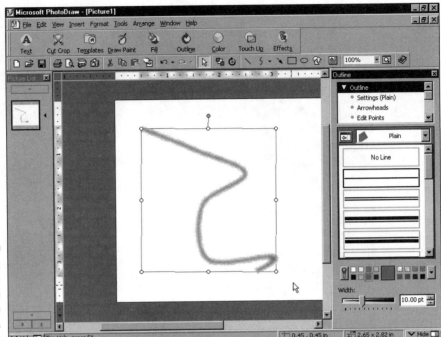

Figure 23-7:
Choosing a
color from
the Outline
window.

4. **Click on a color (displayed near the bottom of the Outline window)
   that you want to use.**

   PhotoDraw 2000 changes the color of your chosen line or object.

You can also change the width of your line by sliding the Width slider tab (at
the bottom of the Outline window) or click on the up/down arrows of the box
to choose a point size, such as 10.00 point.

Adding Special Visual Effects

To give you a few more options for making your drawings look nice, weird, or
artistic, try using some of Microsoft PhotoDraw 2000's visual effects. By spicing up your drawings with visual effects, you can make people forget that
your drawings may not be worth looking at in the first place.

Adding shadows

Shadows can emphasize your lines as if a light source were shining on them from a certain angle and casting a shadow behind your lines. To create a shadow for a line or an object, follow these steps:

1. **Click on the line or object that you want to modify.**

   White handles appear around your chosen line or object.

2. **Click on the Effects button on the Visual Menu.**

   If the Visual Menu does not appear, then choose View➪Visual Menu. A menu appears.

3. **Click on Shadow.**

   A Shadow window appears, as shown in Figure 23-8.

4. **Click on the Shadow style that you want.**

   PhotoDraw 2000 displays your line or object with a shadow.

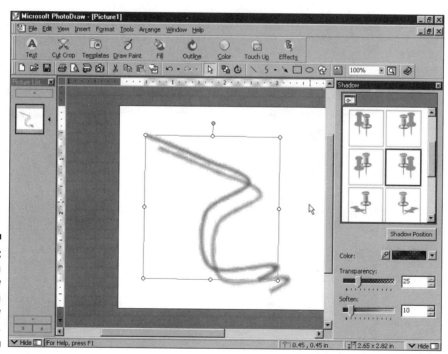

Figure 23-8: Picking a shadow style from the Shadow window.

Fading out a line

For another bizarre visual effect, try fading out your line, which makes one part of your line or object appear faint, as if it's slowly fading from view. To fade out a line or an object, follow these steps:

1. **Click on the line or object that you want to modify.**

   White handles appear around your chosen line or object.

2. **Click on the Effects button on the Visual Menu.**

   If the Visual Menu does not appear, then choose View⇨Visual Menu. A menu appears.

3. **Click on Fade Out.**

   The Transparency window appears, as shown in Figure 23-9.

4. **Click on the Start and End slider tabs and then slide the tab to the left (makes the line appear bolder) or to the right (makes the line appear fainter).**

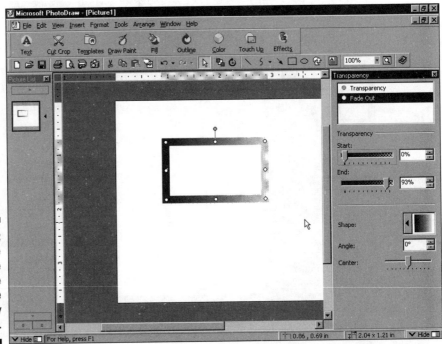

Figure 23-9: Defining the appearance of a line with the Transparency window.

Adding 3-D effects

Another way to alter the appearance of your lines and objects is to use 3-D effects.

When you apply a 3-D effect to a line or an object, Microsoft PhotoDraw 2000 may alter the basic shape of your line or object, such as making a rectangle appear with one end larger than the other (as if the larger end is sticking out of the screen).

To add a 3-D effect for a line or an object, follow these steps:

1. **Click on the line or object that you want to modify.**

   White handles appear around your chosen line or object.

2. **Click on the Effects button on the Visual Menu.**

   If the Visual Menu does not appear, then choose View⊅Visual Menu. A menu appears.

3. **Click on 3-D.**

   A 3-D window appears, showing you the different 3-D effects you can choose from, as shown in Figure 23-10.

4. **Click on the 3-D effect that you want to use.**

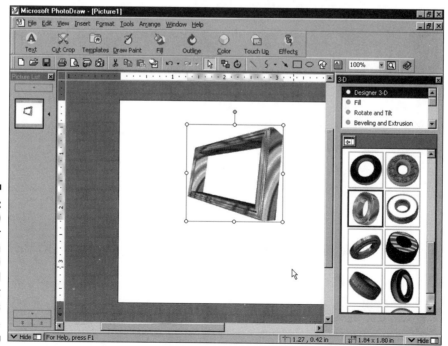

Figure 23-10: The 3-D window for picking a neat 3-D special effect for your lines and objects.

Part VIII

Using Microsoft Office 2000's Small Business Tools

The 5th Wave   By Rich Tennant

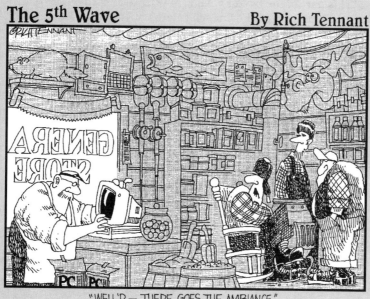

"WELL'P — THERE GOES THE AMBIANCE."

In this part . . .

Starting a business isn't easy and keeping a business from going bankrupt isn't easy either. But with the help of Microsoft Office 2000's Small Business Tools, you can plan a new business and nurture your plan from a simple idea to an actual business plan.

This part of the book explains how to keep in touch with customers, track the financial status of your business, and dig into information to help you learn as much as possible about running any type of business before you invest (or lose) a single penny.

By using the Small Business Tools, you may be able to create a software company that can one day compete against Microsoft (but only for those who like the idea of taking a really big risk with their money).

Chapter 24

Getting Started with the Business Planner

. . . .

In This Chapter

▶ Starting the Business Planner

▶ Navigating through the Business Planner

▶ Getting general business help

. . . .

*B*ecause many people fantasize about quitting their jobs, Microsoft decided to bundle some special business tools to help people use Microsoft Office 2000 to create and plan their own small businesses (which means that you can use Microsoft's products to help you develop a business to compete with Microsoft).

One of the most important tools for starting a business is the Business Planner. The Business Planner provides information and short explanations about the different aspects of running a variety of different businesses. That way you can determine what types of business options are available, what type of business you think you'd like to run, and some of the specific details involved in running different kinds of businesses.

The Standard edition of Microsoft Office 2000 does not include the Small Business Tools.

Starting the Business Planner

Think of the Business Planner as a reference that you can refer to again and again. The Business Planner can help you define the following for your current or potentially new business:

✔ **Planning:** Provides information about various ways to structure your business as a sole proprietorship, partnership, or corporation.

- ✔ **Operations:** Explains the details about running a business — everything from hiring employees to negotiating a favorable lease.

- ✔ **Legal:** Describes legal issues that your business may face, such as acquiring permits and licenses, in addition to explaining business contracts.

- ✔ **Finance:** Discusses accounting methods, tax benefits, and insurance.

- ✔ **Marketing:** Offers helpful hints for advertising, marketing, and promoting your business.

To start the Business Planner, follow these steps:

1. **Click on the Start button on the Windows taskbar.**

2. **Choose <u>P</u>rograms➪Microsoft Office Small Business Tools➪ Microsoft Business Planner.**

   A Personal Interviewer window appears, asking for information about your business to help determine what resources you may need. *Note:* If you have already answered the questions in the Personal Interviewer, then the Personal Interviewer window doesn't appear.

3. **Answer the questions in the Personal Interviewer.**

   When you're done answering the questions, the Business Planner appears, as shown in Figure 24-1.

Figure 24-1: The Business Planner, ready to give you the information that you need.

Navigating through the Business Planner

Because most people are familiar with the way the World Wide Web works, Microsoft deliberately designed the Business Planner to mimic a Web page. So if you want to navigate your way around the Business Planner, you have three choices:

- ✔ Click on a hyperlink (text or graphic).
- ✔ Click on the Back or Forward arrows at the top of the window.
- ✔ Click on the Go pull-down menus and choose an option.

 The Business Planner includes a special Find box where you type a word (such as "publishing") and the Business Planner displays all information related to your word (such as newspaper publishing, book publishing, and so on). Think of the Find box as a miniature search engine just for use in the Business Planner.

 Any time you want to return to the main Business Planner window (refer to Figure 24-1), click on Home on the menu bar.

From the main Business Planner window (refer to Figure 24-1), you can choose from three different options:

- ✔ **General business help** (Planning, Operations, Legal, Finance, and Marketing): Displays general information about starting and running any type of a business.
- ✔ **Wizards** (Business Plan and Marketing wizards): Provides specific information for creating a business plan or a marketing campaign.
- ✔ **Resource Center:** Displays links to third-party business resources, including phone numbers and addresses.

 Rather than read the information displayed on the screen, you can always choose File⇨Print to make a hard copy of the information so that you can read it at your leisure when away from your computer.

Getting general business help

If you're curious what type of permits a dance club may need or how to raise money to get a business going in the first place, browse through the Business Planner's general business help sections. To get general business help, follow these steps:

1. **Choose <u>G</u>o and then click on an option, such as <u>P</u>lanning or <u>M</u>arketing.**

   A list of topics appears, as shown in Figure 24-2. (If you're in the main Business Planner window, you can click on the graphic icon representing the type of help that you want, such as Planning, Legal, or Marketing.)

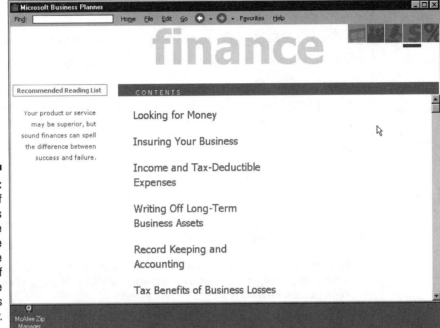

Figure 24-2:
A list of topics available within the Finance section of the Business Planner.

2. **Click on a topic that you want to read.**

To jump to a different general business help section, click on one of the business help icons displayed in the upper right-hand corner of the topic list (refer to Figure 24-2).

Using a wizard

Unlike the general business help sections that list information and then expect you to browse through them in any order that you find interesting, the Wizard provides more hands-on guidance.

Microsoft Office 2000 provides two wizards, a Business Plan Wizard and a Marketing Wizard. To choose a wizard, follow these steps:

1. **First choose <u>G</u>o and then click on an option, such as <u>B</u>usiness Plan Wizard or <u>M</u>arketing Wizard.**

   A menu appears, as shown in Figure 24-3.

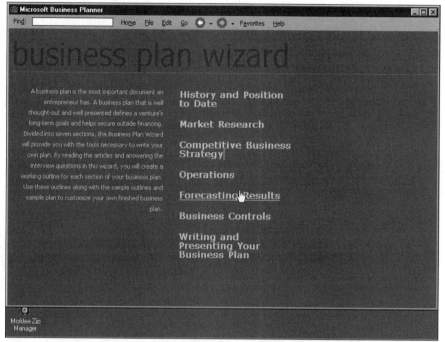

Figure 24-3:
The
Business
Plan Wizard
window.

2. **Click on a topic that you want more information about.**

   Depending on the options that you choose, the wizard may ask you a series of questions or display additional information for you to read.

Both the Business Plan and the Marketing Wizards can help you create a rough draft of a business or a marketing plan. However, after the Business Plan Wizard or the Marketing Wizard creates your business or marketing plan, you have to switch to Microsoft Word to edit and print your business or marketing plan.

Using the resource center

Even Microsoft knows it can never keep up with the latest news and information about running a business, so that's why it provides the resource center, which links to various organizations and groups that may be able to provide additional help for you and your fledging business.

Some of the resources listed in the resource center are Web sites that require an Internet account to access them.

By browsing through the resource center, you can get the latest information about running a business from sources other than Microsoft. To browse through the resource center, follow these steps:

1. **First choose <u>G</u>o and then click on an option, such as <u>R</u>eference Directory, <u>F</u>ederal Resources, or <u>L</u>isting by Business Type.**

2. **Click on the topic that you want to read about.**

   Figure 24-4 shows the type of information that you can find in the resource center. In this case, you're looking at an exciting listing of trade periodicals for butcher shops.

Starting and running a business can be fun and profitable, but make sure you run a business that you really enjoy. If you try to start a business that you don't like, chances are good that you'll be just as miserable as if you're working in a job you don't care about either.

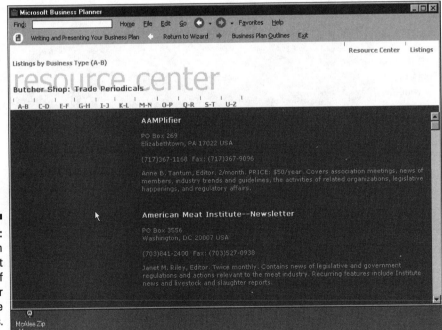

Figure 24-4:
An important listing of butcher shop trade publications.

Using the magical Find command

Rather than wade through different hyperlinks, menus, and wizards, you may find using the Find command much easier instead. To use the Find command, follow these steps:

1. **Click on the Find text box that appears in the upper left-hand corner.**

2. **Type a topic that you want to read about.**

   A list of topics appears in a window on the left-hand side of the screen, as shown in Figure 24-5.

3. **Click on the plus sign that appears to the left of the topic that you want to read about.**

   A list of additional topics appears.

4. **Click on the topic that you want to read about.**

   The Business Planner cheerfully displays your selected information (refer to Figure 24-5).

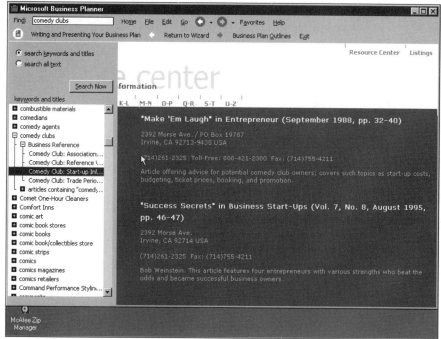

Figure 24-5: Using the Find command to quickly locate information for specific businesses.

Quitting the Business Planner

No matter how useful you may find the Business Planner, you'll eventually want to exit from it. To exit the Business Planner, choose one of the following:

- Choose File⇨Exit.
- Click on the close box of the Business Planner window.

Chapter 25

Advertising by Mail with the Direct Mail Manager

· ·

In This Chapter

▶ Starting a mailing list

▶ Adding documents to your mailing list

· ·

*O*ne of the most popular ways to advertise any business is through direct mail (known to its recipients as junk mail). The main advantage of direct mail advertising is that you get to target your market by sending ads directly to potential customers. The drawback is that you may wind up spending money for postage if you mail ads to people who don't have any intention of spending money on your business anyway.

To help you create a direct mail marketing campaign, the Small Business Tools include a Direct Mail Manager. Essentially, the Direct Mail Manager takes a list of names and addresses and verifies that zip codes are correct, spellings are right, and duplicates are eliminated. Then the Direct Mail Manager prints out your list on envelopes, on mailing labels, or on postcards.

Before using the Direct Mail Manager, you may want to use the Customer Manager (explained in Chapter 26) to narrow the list of people who you want to receive your advertising.

The Standard edition of Microsoft Office 2000 does not include the Direct Mail Manager.

Starting the Direct Mail Manager

To help you save money on unnecessary postage, the Direct Mail Manager can clean up an existing list of names and addresses to prevent misspellings or duplicate addresses. After the Direct Mail Manager finishes doing its work, you just have to pray that your advertisement pays for the cost of postage.

Before you use the Direct Mail Manager, you must first have a list of names and addresses stored in a database file, such as in Microsoft Access 2000 or Microsoft Outlook 2000.

To start the Direct Mail Manager, follow these steps:

1. **Click on the Start button on the Windows taskbar.**

2. **Choose Programs⇨Microsoft Office Small Business Tools⇨Microsoft Direct Mail Manager.**

   The Direct Mail Manager appears, as shown in Figure 25-1.

Figure 25-1: The Direct Mail Manager, ready to examine your Access database of names and addresses.

3. **Click on Next.**

   The Locate List window appears, asking for a database file to use, as shown in Figure 25-2.

4. **Click on an option button (such as File or Outlook Folder).**

   If you click on the File option button, you have to click on the Browse button to choose the database file containing your names and addresses. If you click on the Outlook Folder option button, you can choose your Outlook Contacts list.

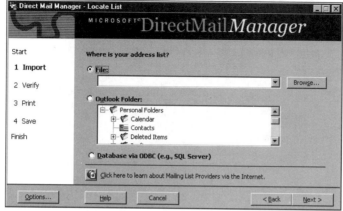

Figure 25-2:
The Locate List window asks for the database file containing your names and addresses.

5. **Click on Next after choosing the database file that you want to use.**

   If you choose the File option button, a Select a Table dialog box appears, as shown in Figure 25-3.

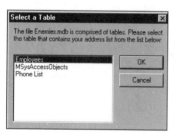

Figure 25-3:
The Select a Table dialog box for picking a table from within an Access database.

6. **Click on the table that you want to use and then click on OK.**

   The Direct Mail Manager dialog box displays a sample address so that you can make sure everything is formatted correctly, as shown in Figure 25-4.

7. **Click on an option button, such as Yes or No, and then click on Next.**

   If you clicked on the No option button, then the next dialog box displays the database tables, showing you the fields you can include to make sure your addresses are complete. Otherwise, another dialog box appears, asking if you want to import all names and addresses or just some of them.

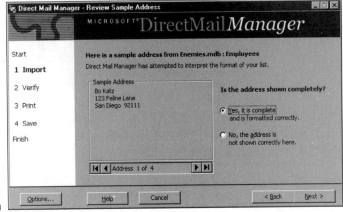

Figure 25-4:
Making sure
your
addresses
are
complete
and
formatted
correctly.

8. **Click on an option button, such as Yes, import the whole list, or No, import only this part of the list, and then click on Next.**

   If you clicked on the No option button, you have to create a filter to screen out names and addresses that you don't want to print. A dialog box appears, telling you that your address list has been imported, as shown in Figure 25-5.

Figure 25-5:
The Direct
Mail
Manager
making sure
your
address list
is imported
correctly.

9. **Click on an option button to import another list, such as Yes, import another list, or No, this is it, and then click on Next.**

   If you choose to import another list, you can combine names and addresses stored in a second or third database file. Then you have to follow Steps 3 through 9 all over again. If you click on the No option

button, then an Address Verification dialog box appears, telling you that
Direct Mail Manager will check your addresses using the Internet,
as shown in Figure 25-6. If your addresses are accurate or if you skip
Address Verification, the dialog box displays your recipients' names
and addresses, as shown in Figure 25-7.

If you don't want to run Address Verification or if you don't have an
Internet account, click on Cancel, then click on the Options button, then
click on the Run Address Verification check box to clear it, and then
click on OK.

10. **Make any changes to your list and then click on Next.**

    A dialog box appears, asking how you want to send your mailing, as
    shown in Figure 25-8.

11. **Click on a radio button and then click on Next.**

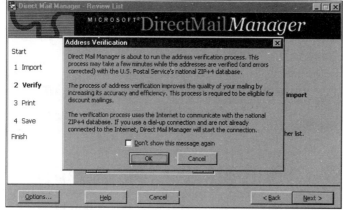

Figure 25-6:
The Address
Verification
dialog box
for checking
that your zip
codes are
accurate.

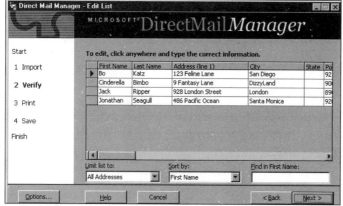

Figure 25-7:
A listing of
your names
and
addresses
in case you
need to
edit them.

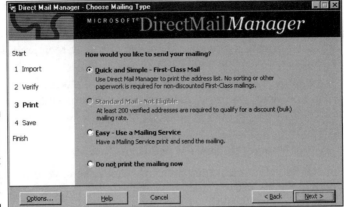

Figure 25-8:
Choosing a
way to print
your mailing
list.

A dialog box appears, showing you the design of your mailing, as shown in Figure 25-9.

12. **If you want to change the design, then click on the Design button to type in a return address or to change the fonts.**

Figure 25-9:
Designing
your
mailing.

13. **Click on Next.**

   A dialog box appears, showing you print settings for your mailing.

14. **Make any changes for printing (such as choosing a printer) and then click on OK.**

   The Direct Mail Manager uses Microsoft Word 2000 to print your mailing list.

   A dialog box appears, asking if you want to save your mailing list in a new file or in the original file (or no file at all).

15. **Click on an option button and then click on Next.**

    If you choose to save your file under a new file name, then you have to type the new file name in a Save dialog box that pops up.

Using Other Documents with Your Direct Mailings

After you have printed and saved your newly created mailing list, you may want to add a form letter (such as one created in Microsoft Word 2000) or an advertisement (such as a flyer created in Microsoft Publisher 2000) to the list. Luckily for you, Direct Mail Manager is one step ahead of you. Before you can exit Direct Mail Manager, a dialog box pops up, asking if you want to print a form letter to go along with your mailing list.

Now you can create form letters using either Microsoft Word 2000 or Microsoft Publisher 2000.

Making form letters with Microsoft Word 2000

To create simple form letters that don't require any fancy graphics, Microsoft Word 2000 is fast and easy to use (compared to using Microsoft Publisher 2000). To make a form letter with Microsoft Word 2000, follow these steps:

1. **Click on an option button to choose Word and then click on Next.**

   A dialog box appears, shown in Figure 25-10, asking if you want to use an existing document or create a new one.

2. **Click on Browse to use an existing document or click on Create to make a new form letter.**

   A dialog box appears, asking if you need help in creating a mail-merge document.

3. **Click on Yes or No.**

   A Select Mail Merge Template dialog box appears.

4. **Click on the Simple Form Letter Wizard icon and then click on Open.**

   Word displays a form letter, as shown in Figure 25-11. All you have to do is type the specific text that you want.

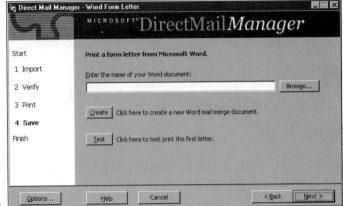

Figure 25-10:
Creating a
form letter
with your
mailing list.

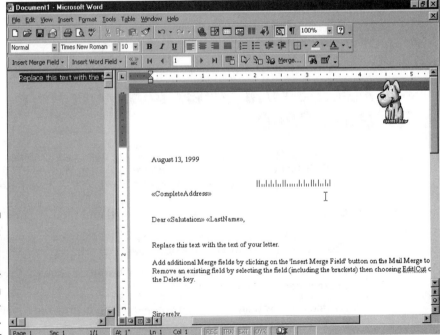

Figure 25-11:
Word
writing a
form letter
for you
automat-
ically.

5. **Choose Tools⇨Mail Merge.**

A dialog box appears.

6. Click on Merge.

A Merge dialog box appears, asking if you want to start printing or if you want to save your merged data in a separate file.

7. Click on Merge when you're ready to merge your data into your form letter.

At this point you can save your form letter or you can print it.

8. Choose File⇨Exit to exit from Word.

If you haven't saved your form letter, a dialog box pops up asking if you want to save it. After you finally exit from Word, the Direct Mail Manager appears again.

9. Click on Finish.

The Direct Mail Manager simply guides you step-by-step into creating a mailing list and form letters. You can accomplish these same tasks manually by using Access and Word as explained in Chapter 21 in the original *Microsoft Office 2000 For Windows For Dummies* (published by IDG Books Worldwide, Inc.). You'll recognize one of the authors' names, and the other author is Roger C. Parker.

Making form letters with Microsoft Publisher 2000

Microsoft Publisher 2000 can create fancy publications (such as brochures or flyers) with a potential customer's name printed on the publications. Think how excited people get when they receive a personalized certificate from the Publisher's Clearinghouse Sweepstakes stating that "Mr. John Doe may have already won $5,000,000!" By using Microsoft Publisher 2000, you can create mail advertisements that rival the Publisher's Clearinghouse Sweepstakes in appearance.

To use mail-merge features with Microsoft Publisher 2000, you may have to install this feature from your Microsoft Office 2000 CD.

To use Microsoft Publisher 2000 to create a form letter (or other type of publication), follow these steps:

1. Click on an option button to choose Publisher and then click on Next.

Another dialog box appears, asking if you want to use an existing document or create a new one.

2. **Click on Browse to use an existing document (skip to Step 14) or click on Create to make a new form publication.**

   If you click on Create, then a dialog box appears, asking if you need help with creating a mail-merge document using Publisher 2000. Click on Yes or No. Publisher 2000 loads and displays a Catalog dialog box so that you can choose the type of publication that you want to use (such as a postcard or greeting card).

3. **Click on the type of publication that you want to create (such as a postcard).**

   Publisher 2000 displays a list of different types of publications that you can choose to create. For example, if you choose to create a Greeting Card, then Publisher 2000 displays a list of different greeting cards, such as thank you, birthday, or get-well cards.

4. **Click on the type of publication that you want to create (such as a Get Well card), click on the publication design that you want to use, and then click on Start Wizard.**

   Publisher 2000 creates your chosen publication. You may need to click on the Next button in the Wizard dialog box (on the left side of the screen) before you can actually edit your publication.

5. **Draw a text box for your publication (or click on an existing text box).**

6. **Choose Mail-Merge⇨Open Data Source.**

   An Open Data Source dialog box appears, as shown in Figure 25-12.

Figure 25-12:
The Open
Data Source
dialog box
helps
Publisher
2000 find
names and
addresses
to insert in
your
publication.

Figure 25-12:
The Open Data Source dialog box helps Publisher 2000 find names and addresses to insert in your publication.

7. **Click on Merge from an Outlook contact list or Merge information from another type of file.**

   If you choose Merge information from another type of file, then an Open Data Source dialog box appears. You have to choose the file you want to use (such as an Access database) and click on Open. Then click on a specific table that you want to use. An Insert Fields dialog box appears, as shown in Figure 25-13.

8. **Click on the field that you want to display (such as FirstName) and then click on Insert. Repeat this step for each additional field that you want to include in your publication.**

   Each time you choose a field, Publisher 2000 displays that field within brackets, such as <<FirstName>>. You may need to add spaces or any other punctuation marks to separate the fields.

9. **Choose Mail-Merge➪Merge.**

   A Preview Data dialog box appears, and Publisher 2000 displays your data in your publication. You can click on the First Record, Previous Record, Next Record, or Last Record buttons on the Preview Data dialog box to view how each record appears in your publication.

10. **Click on Close.**

11. **Choose File➪Exit.**

    A dialog box appears, asking if you want to save your file.

12. **Click on Yes.**

    A Save As dialog box appears, asking for a file name.

13. **Type a file name and then click on Save.**

    The Direct Mail Manager dialog box appears again.

14. **Click on Browse.**

    A Select Mail-Merge Document dialog box appears.

15. **Click on the file name that you typed in Step 14 and then click on Open.**

16. **Click on Next.**

    A Printer Settings for Mail Merge dialog box appears.

17. **Click on OK.**

    Another dialog box appears, asking if you want your database file (the one you chose in Step 7) added to your publication.

18. **Click on Yes.**

    Publisher 2000 cheerfully prints out your publication using mail-merge.

19. **Click on Finish.**

    The Direct Mail Manager dialog box goes away.

Chapter 26

Tracking Your Business with the Customer Manager

● ●

In This Chapter
▶ Starting the Customer Manager
▶ Sorting your data
▶ Printing stuff

● ●

*I*f you're lucky enough to have the Small Business Tools with your copy of Microsoft Office 2000, you can use the Customer Manager to help you monitor the health (or gradual demise) of your business.

The Customer Manager can help you track customer and sales information so that you can quickly find out who your best (and worst) customers are, what products are selling the fastest (or slowest), or which sales region is the most (or least) profitable.

To work properly, the Customer Manager uses both your Microsoft Outlook 2000 customer list and your business data, stored using 12-period accounting. (If you don't know what 12-period accounting is, you may not want to fiddle around with the Customer Manager.) Your accounting data can be stored in programs, such as Microsoft Money, QuickBooks, or Simply Accounting.

The Standard edition of Microsoft Office 2000 does not include the Customer Manager.

Starting the Customer Manager

The Customer Manager works with Microsoft Access 2000, so if you didn't install Microsoft Access 2000 for some reason, you won't be able to use the Customer Manager.

To start the Customer Manager, follow these steps:

1. **Click on the Start button on the Windows taskbar.**

2. **Choose Programs➪Microsoft Office Small Business Tools➪ Microsoft Small Business Customer Manager.**

   A Microsoft Customer Manager dialog box appears, asking if you want to create a new database or open an existing one.

3. **Click on the New Database Wizard or Open an existing database option button.**

   If you need to create a new database, then click on the New Database Wizard option button, which enlists the New Database Wizard to help you import your Outlook and accounting data into an Access database. If you just want to see how the Customer Manager works, then click on the Open an existing database option button and choose the Northwind Traders Sample Company database.

4. **Click on OK.**

   If you choose to open an existing database, the Customer Manager appears, as shown in Figure 26-1. If you choose to create a new database, then the New Database Wizard dialog box appears, which helps you create a new database where you can type in your business information.

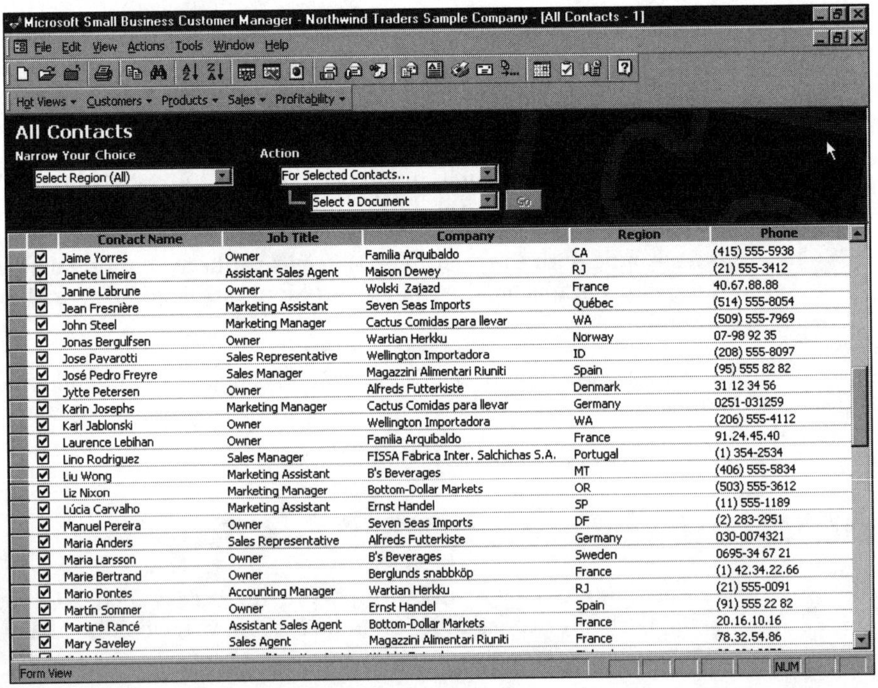

Figure 26-1:
The Customer Manager displaying data from the Northwind Traders Sample Company database.

Sorting through Your Data

After you have loaded a database through the Customer Manager, you can sort through your data to help you understand how well (or poorly) your business may be doing.

Some of the different ways the Customer Manager can sort your data include

- By the top 10 percent of salespeople
- By customers ordering the largest volume of products
- By product
- By the greatest profitability per salesperson

The Customer Manager sorts your data into categories, which appear on the Views toolbar. If the Views toolbar is not visible, then choose View⇨Toolbars⇨Views to make sure that a check mark appears in front of Views.

To sort data with the Customer Manager, follow these steps:

1. **Click on a view in the Views toolbar, such as Profitability.**

   A pull-down menu appears.

2. **Click on the criterion for viewing your data, such as sorting data by profitability by product.**

   The Customer Manager rearranges your data according to your chosen criterion, as shown in Figure 26-2.

You can also click on the list boxes under the Narrow Your Choice heading in the left-hand corner of the Customer Manager window, shown in Figure 26-3, to tighten your criteria.

Putting Stuff on Paper

Sorting your data can help you see which aspects of your business are doing well and which areas could possibly drag you into bankruptcy. But rather than stare at your sorted data on the screen, you may as well print it so that you can view the data on paper.

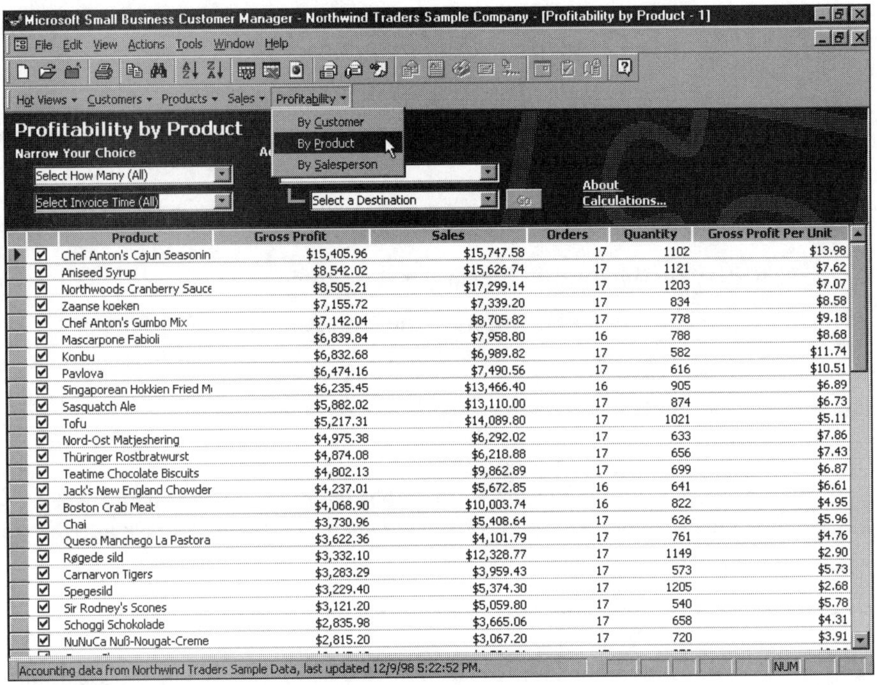

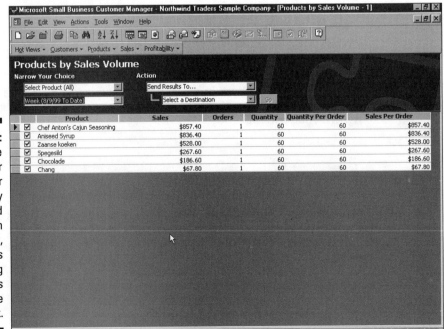

Figure 26-2:
The Customer Manager sorting product data by gross profit for the Northwind Traders Sample Company.

Figure 26-3:
The Customer Manager can display data based on certain criteria, such as displaying all products sold in the past week.

To print data displayed by the Customer Manager, follow these steps:

1. **Choose Actions⇨Send Results To.**

   A pull-down menu appears, listing all the different locations to send your data, such as:

   - **Microsoft Word:** Displays your data as a table in a Word document, as shown in Figure 26-4.

   - **Microsoft Excel:** Displays your data in a worksheet.

   - **Web Browser:** Displays your data as a table in an HTML file.

   - **Mail Recipient:** Displays your data as a table in an e-mail message.

   - **Mail Recipient** (as an Attachment): Stores your data as an attached HTML file.

2. **Choose File⇨Print (or click on Send if you're sending the data to someone over e-mail).**

You may want to edit and save your file before printing. If you need to perform any calculations with your data, such as adding the profits of all products, store your data as an Excel worksheet.

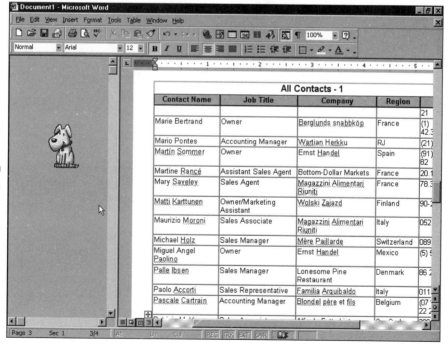

Figure 26-4:
Displaying
data in
another
program
where you
can edit,
save, and
print the
data.

	All Contacts - 1		
Contact Name	**Job Title**	**Company**	**Region**
			21
Marie Bertrand	Owner	Berglunds snabbköp	France (1) 42.3
Mario Pontes	Accounting Manager	Wartian Herkku	RJ (21)
Martín Sommer	Owner	Ernst Handel	Spain (91) 82
Martine Rancé	Assistant Sales Agent	Bottom-Dollar Markets	France 20.1
Mary Saveley	Sales Agent	Magazzini Alimentari Riuniti	France 78.3
Matti Karttunen	Owner/Marketing Assistant	Wolski Zajazd	Finland 90-
Maurizio Moroni	Sales Associate	Magazzini Alimentari Riuniti	Italy 052
Michael Holz	Sales Manager	Mère Paillarde	Switzerland 089
Miguel Angel Paolino	Owner	Ernst Handel	Mexico (5) 5
Palle Ibsen	Sales Manager	Lonesome Pine Restaurant	Denmark 86 2
Paolo Accorti	Sales Representative	Familia Arquibaldo	Italy 011
Pascale Cartrain	Accounting Manager	Blondel père et fils	Belgium (07 22 2

Page 3   Sec 1   3/4   At   Ln   Col   REC TRK EXT OVR

Chapter 27

Letting Your Financial Manager Watch Your Money

• •

In This Chapter

▶ Starting the Financial Manager
▶ Using the analysis tool
▶ Reporting on your business
▶ Charting your money

• •

*L*ike the Customer Manager, the Financial Manager works with your accounting data and your Microsoft Outlook 2000 contact data. By using the Financial Manager, you can quickly plot charts to see your cash flow or determine whether you should buy or lease your business property.

The Financial Manager is nothing more than an Excel workbook loaded with macros to automate various business-related tasks. You can perform these same tasks by yourself using Excel, but the Financial Manager simply provides these features for you.

The Standard edition of Microsoft Office 2000 does not include the Financial Manager.

Starting the Financial Manager

The Financial Manager provides six different options:

  ✔ **Import:** Displays a New Database Wizard dialog box to help you import your accounting and Outlook data into an Access database file.

  ✔ **Update:** Makes sure that any new, updated data in your accounting files get stored in the Financial Manager database file for accuracy.

- ✔ **Analyze:** Allows you to compare your business with other types of businesses to determine whether you should buy or lease and provides other comparisons to help you determine whether your business is growing, stagnating, or ready to disappear completely.

- ✔ **Report:** Creates a written report that lists actual numbers, such as profits, losses, or quantity of products sold.

- ✔ **Visit Office Update:** Accesses Microsoft's Web site so that you can download the latest files for importing data from the latest versions of various accounting programs, such as QuickBooks and Simply Accounting.

- ✔ **Chart:** Creates a chart that graphically displays the financial health (or gradual demise) of your small business.

The Financial Manager works with Microsoft Excel 2000, so if you didn't install Microsoft Excel 2000, you won't be able to use the Financial Manager.

The Financial Manager uses macros, which means that you should run an antivirus program to make sure that your computer is free of any macro viruses. If a macro virus has infected the Financial Manager and you run Financial Manager, then you can spread the virus further on your computer.

To start the Financial Manager, follow these steps:

1. **Click on the Start button on the Windows taskbar.**

2. **Choose Programs➪Microsoft Office Small Business Tools➪ Microsoft Small Business Financial Manager.**

   A Microsoft Excel dialog box appears, asking if you want to disable or enable macros.

3. **Click on the Enable macros button.**

   The Small Business Financial Manager appears, as shown in Figure 27-1.

To use the Financial Manager, click on the Import button and then load your own business accounting data to use with the Financial Manager.

In case you lose sight of the Small Business Financial Manager start-up screen, you can always find it again by either clicking on the Startup Screen tab or choosing Window➪Report Workbook1 (assuming you haven't saved the Report Workbook1 file under a different name).

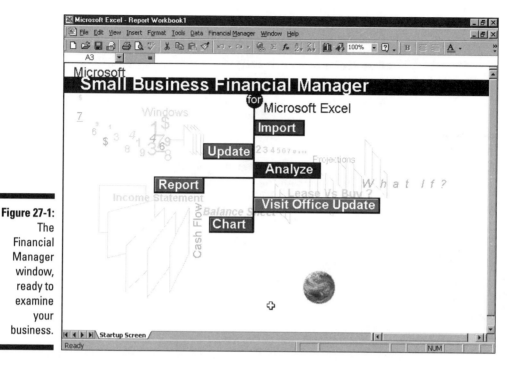

Figure 27-1:
The
Financial
Manager
window,
ready to
examine
your
business.

Using the Analysis Tool

The Analysis Tool offers five different options for analyzing your business:

- **Business Comparison:** Compares your business with other types of businesses so that you can see who's making more money.

- **Buy Vs. Lease:** Shows the different financial implications of paying in cash, leasing, or taking out a loan.

- **Create Project Wizard:** Runs a wizard to help you create your own projects for your business, such as determining how much longer your business can lose money and still not go bankrupt.

- **Projection Reports:** Creates a report so that you can see what the future may bring for your business's cash flow, balance sheet, or income statement.

- **What-If Analysis:** Lets you change different numbers around and store them in separate worksheets.

To use the Analysis Tool of the Financial Manager, follow these steps:

1. **Click on the Analyze button in the Small Business Financial Manager window (refer to Figure 27-1).**

   A Select a Financial Manager Analysis Tool dialog box appears, as shown in Figure 27-2.

Figure 27-2:
The Select a Financial Manager Analysis Tool dialog box for picking a way to examine your data.

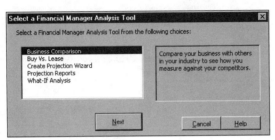

2. **Click on a tool that you want to use (such as Buy Vs. Lease) and then click on Next.**

   Depending on the tool you choose, a different dialog box pops up, guiding you step-by-step through what you do next, eventually producing a report that you can examine with your own eyes, as shown in Figure 27-3.

The Financial Manager displays your information in a separate workbook (file) that you can save, edit, or print at your convenience.

Reporting on Your Business

Another way the Financial Manager can help you is by creating a report, such as a balance sheet, cash flow, or income statement. By studying the various reports that the Financial Manager can create for your business, you can see whether you're making money or losing money with no hope of paying back your bank loan, just like a Third World country.

To create a report with the Financial Manager, follow these steps:

1. **Click on the Report button in the Small Business Financial Manager window (refer to Figure 27-1).**

   A Create a Financial Report dialog box appears, as shown in Figure 27-4.

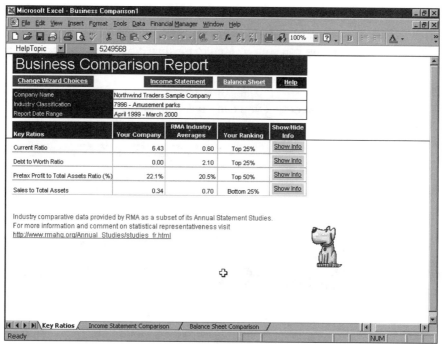

Figure 27-3:
Comparing a trading company with an amusement park to see which can lose the most money the fastest.

2. **Click on a report that you want to see (such as Income Statement).**

3. **Click on the Browse button.**

   A Select dialog box appears.

4. **Click on the Access database file that you want to use and then click on Open.**

   The Create a Financial Report dialog box reappears.

Figure 27-4:
The Create a Financial Report dialog box for picking a way to examine your business.

5. **Click on Next.**

   Depending on the report you choose, a different dialog box pops up, guiding you step-by-step to produce your chosen report, as shown in Figure 27-5.

When the Financial Manager creates a report, it stores the report on a separate worksheet that you can save, edit, or print at your convenience.

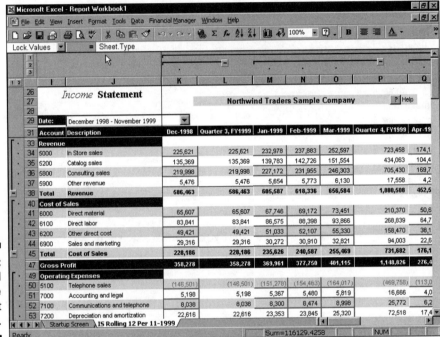

Figure 27-5:
A typical
Income
Statement
report.

Charting Your Money

The reports that the Financial Manager can create can overwhelm you with columns of numbers that may make no sense whatsoever. To help make your numbers more understandable, the Financial Manager can turn them into eye-pleasing charts.

To create a chart with the Financial Manager, follow these steps:

1. **Click on the Chart button in the Small Business Financial Manager window (refer to Figure 27-1).**

   A Create a Financial Chart dialog box appears, as shown in Figure 27-6.

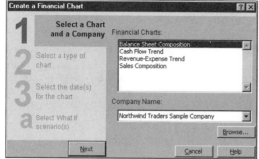

Figure 27-6:
The Create
a Financial
Chart dialog
box for pick-
ing a chart
to display
your data.

2. **Click on a chart that you want to use (such as Cash Flow Trend) and then click on Next.**

   Depending on the chart you choose, a different dialog box pops up, guiding you step-by-step to creating your chart, as shown in Figure 27-7.

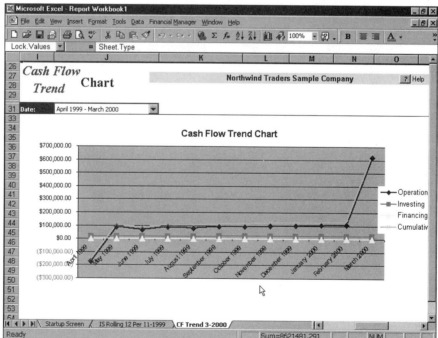

Figure 27-7:
A typical
Cash Flow
Trend Chart
for a
fictitious
company
that is
making an
equally
fictitious
profit.

The Financial Manager displays your chart on a separate worksheet that you can save, edit, or print at your convenience.

Index

• Q •

• R •

Notes

Discover Dummies Online!

The Dummies Web Site is your fun and friendly online resource for the latest information about *...For Dummies®* books and your favorite topics. The Web site is the place to communicate with us, exchange ideas with other *...For Dummies* readers, chat with authors, and have fun!

Ten Fun and Useful Things You Can Do at www.dummies.com

1. Win free *...For Dummies* books and more!
2. Register your book and be entered in a prize drawing.
3. Meet your favorite authors through the IDG Books Author Chat Series.
4. Exchange helpful information with other *...For Dummies* readers.
5. Discover other great *...For Dummies* books you must have!
6. Purchase Dummieswear™ exclusively from our Web site.
7. Buy *...For Dummies* books online.
8. Talk to us. Make comments, ask questions, get answers!
9. Download free software.
10. Find additional useful resources from authors.

Link directly to these ten fun and useful things at
http://www.dummies.com/10useful

For other technology titles from IDG Books Worldwide, go to
www.idgbooks.com

Not on the Web yet? It's easy to get started with *Dummies 101®: The Internet For Windows®98* or *The Internet For Dummies®, 6th Edition*, at local retailers everywhere.

Find other *...For Dummies* books on these topics:

Business • Career • Databases • Food & Beverage • Games • Gardening • Graphics • Hardware
Health & Fitness • Internet and the World Wide Web • Networking • Office Suites
Operating Systems • Personal Finance • Pets • Programming • Recreation • Sports
Spreadsheets • Teacher Resources • Test Prep • Word Processing

IDG BOOKS WORLDWIDE BOOK REGISTRATION

We want to hear from you!

Visit **http://my2cents.dummies.com** to register this book and tell us how you liked it!

- Get entered in our monthly prize giveaway.

- Give us feedback about this book — tell us what you like best, what you like least, or maybe what you'd like to ask the author and us to change!

- Let us know any other ...*For Dummies*® topics that interest you.

Your feedback helps us determine what books to publish, tells us what coverage to add as we revise our books, and lets us know whether we're meeting your needs as a ...*For Dummies* reader. You're our most valuable resource, and what you have to say is important to us!

Not on the Web yet? It's easy to get started with *Dummies 101*®: *The Internet For Windows*® *98* or *The Internet For Dummies*®, 6th Edition, at local retailers everywhere.

Or let us know what you think by sending us a letter at the following address:

...*For Dummies* Book Registration
Dummies Press
7260 Shadeland Station, Suite 100
Indianapolis, IN 46256-3917
Fax 317-596-5498

BESTSELLING BOOK SERIES